Process Improvement

and Quality Management in the Retail Industry

Process Improvement

and Quality Management in the Retail Industry

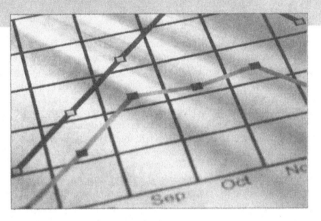

STEPHEN GEORGE

CHRIS THOMAS

ARNOLD WEIMERSKIRCH

WILEY

JOHN WILEY & SONS, INC.

Library of Congress Cataloging-in-Publication Data:

ISBN-13: 978-0-471-72323-3
ISBN-10: 0-471-72323-1

10 9 8 7 6 5 4 3 2 1

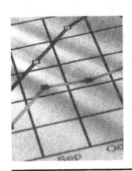

Contents

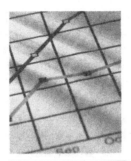

Preface

In this book, most of the companies cited as examples of successful quality management efforts have been winners of the Malcolm Baldrige National Quality Award. We believe the Baldrige criteria define a management model because they provide one of the most comprehensive guides to understanding, assessing, controlling, and improving an organization—no matter what the type of business or industry.

No other model has gained such widespread global acceptance. As evidence, consider these facts:

- Since the Baldrige program was introduced in 1988, more than 1,000 companies have applied for the awards. The National Institute of Standards and Technology (NIST) has distributed millions of copies of the criteria, and continues to improve them every year.
- Companies also get the criteria from state award programs. There are 49 active state and local quality award programs in 41 states based on the Baldrige criteria.
- The national Baldrige Awards are now open to education, health care, and nonprofit companies. Many state programs have also broadened their awards eligibility to include these fields as well as government agencies.
- Studies have shown that 70 percent of the companies that use the criteria use them as a source of information on how to achieve excellence.
- More than 20 countries, including Australia, Brazil, Canada, India, Japan, and Sweden, have implemented quality award programs based on the Baldrige criteria.

- The criteria for the European Quality Award, first presented in 1992, are patterned after the Baldrige criteria.
- Companies such as AT&T, Carrier, Eastman Kodak, Honeywell, IBM, and Intel have adopted the Baldrige criteria as their internal assessment tool and adapted the rules to create their own in-house corporate quality awards. Many other large companies are asking suppliers to assess their organizations by using the Baldrige criteria.

In our experience, people who examine their organizations from a Baldrige perspective acquire a discipline for seeing wholes, for seeing interrelationships rather than things, and for seeing patterns of change. They become "systems thinkers," a term you will note throughout this book.

In *Process Improvement and Quality Management in the Retail Industry*, we begin in Chapter 1 with a brief history of the search for quality, mostly in the manufacturing industries of the nineteenth and twentieth centuries. Chapter 2 continues with a look at what makes today's corporate executives into quality champions, who know how to strategize for the long-term, set "stretch" goals, and motivate their people to strive for them.

Chapters 3 and 7 discuss customer relationships, outlining a total of eight companies' experiences in researching who their customers are and what they expect, compiling and using data to create products and services that satisfy the expectations, and managing day-to-day customer contact to keep communication open and feedback timely.

Successful companies treat their workers as a customer group as well, determining their needs and expectations and tailoring work teams, training, pay, and benefits to meet them. Chapters 5 and 6 focus on the importance of creative, satisfied employees who are well trained and empowered to use their brains and skills to suggest and spearhead process improvements.

Effective management of work teams, with clearly communicated goals and plans, is discussed in Chapter 4, but it is also a topic within several chapters. Suppliers come into play in Chapters 8 and 9, and the companies profiled here have learned to treat their vendors as equals and partners in the quest for quality. These companies don't just buy from the lowest-priced vendors; they expect quality commitments from their suppliers and check up on them regularly to ensure it is being provided. Some work side by side on product design teams with suppliers; in other cases, suppliers' representatives actually work on-site at the company.

In Chapter 10 are model companies that take the lead in publicly important areas—from environmental concerns and social activism, to educational and artistic philanthropy, to volunteer programs for employees. These efforts serve their communities as well as contribute to higher morale and their own public relations. At times, the ultimate benefits to bottom-line profits may be difficult to quantify, but increasingly, the connection can be made.

Chapters 11 and 12 wrap up all the work of various departments and teams with the practical reality of winning any type of award—in order to see where you're going, you'd better be able to measure how far you've come. Data collection and a variety of quality-related measurements are explained. Benchmarking and full system assessments, which are both major undertakings for any business, are also covered, including the importance of senior management's commitment to intensive study of processes and competitors to get ideas for improvements.

In short, companies today know that quality attainment itself is a cyclical, never-ending process that involves multiple steps and hard work. The Baldrige system was created to promote an understanding of the requirements for world-class performance. That the system also defines a new management model surprises no one who has been active in the implementation of Total Quality Management (TQM). Since the 1980s, TQM has long been misunderstood as some kind of limited add-on program that may help improve quality but does not really affect the rest of the organization. Our benchmarks and other quality leaders demonstrate that, in fact, quality *is* the system.

Although all of its companies profiled here are leaders in their industries (and many are Baldrige Award winners), the book does not ignore many of the business-related problems of modern times. Financial scandals, controversial social activism, morale in changing times (or with changing ownership), and the impact of outsourcing to other countries are all discussed.

A side benefit of being involved in a quality improvement program is that most workers—from sales associates to senior executives—find that it makes their jobs more challenging and interesting. Perhaps this is the ultimate benefit of Total Quality Management for the people involved. When a company involves everyone in continuous improvement, makes customer satisfaction the top priority, values people for who they are, and sees its systems as treasure chests filled with endless opportunities, these companies have the most joyful, outgoing, and well-rewarded people we know. Their enthusiasm is infectious; their commitment is inspiring. They invariably seem more alive and fulfilled and challenged than the millions who just go through the motions day after day.

In this book, you will learn how to join them.

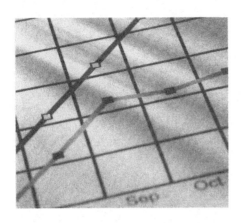

Total Quality— An Overview

As long as there have been merchants, there have been rules for the workplace and standards of quality in various industries. From the makers of knights' armor in the Middle Ages to the blacksmiths' shops of the 1820s to the mega-factories of today's largest manufacturers, people in business continually learn new and better ways to satisfy customers and increase profits by improving their (and their employees') performance.

Today, companies around the world are putting systems into place to better their products and services and their relationships with employees, customers, and suppliers. These systems go by a variety of names, but they are all based on a few common principles. This chapter includes the following introductory information about such systems:

Malcolm Baldrige. (Photo
courtesy of National Institute
of Standards and Technology)

- Basic definitions of quality improvement processes
- A look at the Baldrige Award criteria
- A brief history of business process improvements and breakthroughs
- Some current popular management theories and methods of quality control and continuous improvement

It would be easy to dismiss the moniker "Total Quality Management" as passé—a business fad from the 1980s that has long since outlived its usefulness. In fact, nothing could be further from the truth. Thousands of companies that began with TQM continue to use it in some form, even if the catchphrase itself has changed over the years. In this textbook, most of the companies used as examples of TQM principles in action are winners of the prestigious Malcolm Baldrige National Quality Award—or at least, they have used the Baldrige (or similar) criteria to make the progress outlined in these chapters.

The Baldrige Awards are given annually by the U.S. Department of Commerce and are named for former Commerce Secretary Malcolm Baldrige. He was a fascinating and colorful man, a Nebraska ranch hand who grew up to be a Yale University graduate, an Army captain in World War II, and an iron company president. He became known for managerial excellence in what some would say is the most unlikely of all places—the United States government.

In the 1980s, President Ronald Reagan asked Baldrige to chair a Cabinet-level Trade Strike Force, searching out unfair trade practices and working to reform the U.S. antitrust laws. But Baldrige's most impressive credential was his use of corporate TQM principles to reform his portion of the federal bureaucracy. Within the Commerce Department, he instituted improvements that cut the administrative workforce by 25 percent, and the agency's budget by more than 30 percent.

Malcolm Baldrige took some adventurous chances in life as well as at work. He never forgot his ranching heritage and continued to be an award-winning team roper on the professional rodeo circuit even as a Cabinet-level executive. He died in a rodeo accident in California in 1987.[1]

Today, the companies that apply for Baldrige Awards undergo an exhaustive process that includes at least 300 hours of review by quality experts and business consultants. Depending on their size and for-profit or nonprofit status, they pay an application fee of between $500 and $5,000—a price that at least one trade journal has called "arguably the best bargain in consulting in America."

DEFINITIONS AND PARAMETERS

As mentioned, process improvement and quality management have come to be known by different names in different companies and government agencies. However, they generally fall into three broad categories:

- A **performance-based model** or system uses a set of award criteria to measure how well a company does in certain predetermined areas of business. The Baldrige Award criteria are perhaps the best known of these. There is also a European Quality Award (EQA).
- A **process improvement system** emphasizes delivering a product or service more efficiently, quickly, and/or effectively by breaking it down to a series of processes and managing each one by measuring, analyzing, and improving it. It may be referred to as continuous improvement, **Continuous Quality Improvement (CQI)**, or Total Quality and Productivity (TQP), to name a few. To varying degrees, examples of this concept in action are Lean Enterprise, Six Sigma, and Total Quality Management.
- A **management system** focuses on producing products that meet certain minimum quality standards, usually because either a law or a customer

requires compliance. When a company claims to be ISO 9000-compliant, or that it meets the U.S. Code of Federal Regulations' (CFR) Good Manufacturing Practices (GMPs), this means its products are designed and manufactured to meet these published quality standards.

Overall, no matter what name or system is used, the ideas behind continuous quality improvement include the following:

- A philosophy that just about anything can be done better if people put their minds to it and are committed to making improvements
- A set of clearly defined rules and guiding principles that ensure an organization's managers and employees are working toward continuous improvement of every system within the organization
- The application of management techniques, technical tools, and quantitative methods to achieve and measure progress and make corrections if necessary

The definition of quality is among the keys to beginning any quality improvement program. Merriam Webster's Collegiate Dictionary, Tenth Edition (1994) defines *quality* as "an inherent feature; a degree of excellence; and superiority in kind"—a few of the word's many uses. In business, however, a more specific definition is required. *Quality* has been widely defined in the corporate world as "meeting or exceeding customer expectations," but even that is too broad-based. We like this summary, from NASA's Office of Safety and Mission Assurance in Washington, D.C., which incorporates the ISO 9000:2000 quality definition in its first sentence (the portion in quotation marks):

> Quality is "the totality of characteristics of an entity that bear on its ability to satisfy stated and implied needs." A quality system should address these five facets of quality:
>
> - Quality due to definition of needs
> - Quality due to manufacturing
> - Quality due to product design
> - Quality due to conformance
> - Quality due to product support throughout its lifetime[2]

NASA has a Quality Leadership Forum where participants discuss quality issues and concerns in the U.S. Space Program.

But how does a company "get to" total quality? Is it even possible? The Baldrige Award criteria break total quality into a set of interrelated principles, which the Baldrige program refers to as Core Values and Concepts. For 2005, they were as follows:

- Visionary leadership
- Customer-driven excellence

- Organizational and personal learning
- Valuing employees and partners
- Agility
- Focus on the future
- Managing for innovation
- Management by fact
- Social responsibility
- Focus on results and creating value
- Systems perspective[3]

This book focuses on the achievement of these concepts, by companies of all types and sizes. TQM efforts that succeed do so, at least in part, because of the interrelatedness of these 11 factors. A business learns exactly who its customers are and what they truly want and need. The business then provides a quality product or service to these customers. The business's competitive position in the marketplace improves as sales increase, which in turn, increases productivity and lowers costs to the customers. The customers become loyal, remaining in the loop not only because they are satisfied, but also because they provide feedback for future improvements and product introductions.

It all sounds pretty simple. In fact, it is not. TQM processes and practices can be tripped up at almost any point in the life cycle of either a product or the company that offers it. An unwillingness to commit to the sometimes frustrating process of changing the corporate culture, a lack of continuous training, a lack of encouragement or commitment by senior management, the lack of specific and measurable goals; ineffective techniques for research or incorrect analysis of the data, the absence of teamwork—all of these problems cost companies millions of dollars and result in the loss of many of their best employees who cease to feel valued in a system that seems to chew them up rather than listen to their suggestions.

A (VERY) BRIEF HISTORY OF QUALITY AND PROCESS IMPROVEMENT

As early as the 1700s, the owners of various manufacturing businesses were observing and documenting how long and how well their employees could work; but it was not until the 1800s that worker fatigue and overall working conditions were studied as two factors that could adversely impact productivity and quality. The man who made these then-controversial findings was Robert Owen, a Welshman whose introduction to the trades came at the tender age of nine when he was hired out by his family to make draperies.

ROBERT OWEN: WORKPLACE PIONEER

It was a childhood accident—swallowing a mouthful of scalding-hot porridge—that Robert Owen later credited with giving him "the habits of close observation and continual reflection." He loved to read, and borrowed books from the educated people of Newtown, the small Welsh community where he lived in the 1770s. By age nine, his family hired him out as a draper's apprentice; at age 11, he moved to London, working 18-hour days in the drapery trade, six days a week. The conditions were so dismal that Owen asked friends to be on the lookout for other opportunities for him.

His drapery work ended when a supplier encouraged him to go into business for himself, manufacturing the "new and curious machines" that spun cotton. By age 20, Owen was able to sell the modestly successful business and began managing a textile mill that employed 500 workers; he was part-owner of a second mill. But it was not until Owen became a member of the Manchester Board of Health that he saw firsthand the deplorable working conditions in the factories, especially for children as young as ages five and six.

When Owen met Anne Caroline Dale, he was smitten. The daughter of a wealthy cotton manufacturer, he negotiated to buy the Dale textile mills in New Lanark—and soon after, he married Miss Dale. The New Lanark mills had been run in more humanitarian fashion than the norm, and Robert Owen continued the trend. He refused to hire children under age 10, provided some schooling for young workers, and lengthened meal breaks. For adult workers, he improved workflow processes and quietly discouraged on-the-job pilfering and drunkenness. In the town, he paved streets and improved housing conditions. He opened a company store and used the profits to start a school for the workers' children.

In nearby Scotland, University of Glasgow professor Adam Smith advocated dividing the labor required to make a product into simple, repetitive tasks in order to develop workers' skills, save time, and use specialized tools. He also asserted that the value of goods should be measured by the labor used to produce them.

Across the Atlantic, Americans were also studying ways to make work processes more efficient. In the 1800s, Eli Whitney, perhaps best known for his invention of the cotton gin, also owned gun-manufacturing shops, where he proposed manufacturing different types of muskets (guns) with interchangeable parts, creating the tooling process for production. Clockmaker Seth Thomas standardized his factory's manufacturing processes, also with interchangeable parts.

While the production line was being picked apart and analyzed, so was the way the factories were managed. Mechanical engineer Frederick Winslow Taylor became known for his scientific research—accomplishments like designing different types of coal shovels to allow fewer workers to do the

New Lanark gained international fame when the mills showed increased profits and productivity, but Owen's business partners over the years were not always supportive of his charitable efforts, which they saw as "social experiments" that ultimately drained profit. Eventually, he was bought out but stayed on as manager. He was defeated, but just barely, in an attempt to gain a seat in the British Parliament in the early 1800s.

In 1824, the family moved to the United States. The now-famous Owens settled on 20,000 acres near Harmony, Indiana, and attempted unsuccessfully to found a communal village called "New Harmony." Owen's four sons all became American citizens—but his utopian community did not succeed. In five short years, he had lost most of his fortune and returned to England, where the failure of New Harmony gave his critics a stronger voice. He was branded revolutionary, eccentric, naïve, and more.

Still, he never gave up his Socialist ideals. The last two decades of Owen's life were spent helping to form the first British trade unions and creating various business cooperatives. He passionately believed that people could, and should, work together for the good of the whole.

He died in 1858 during a visit to his hometown of Newtown, Wales, where he is buried.

Source: Adapted from Brian J. Hayes, "*Robert Owen Biography,*" www.age-of-the-sage.org, October 2002.

shoveling at Pennsylvania's Bethlehem Steel Works—but also for his then-radical belief that scientific standards should be applied equitably to managers as well as workers. Taylor called his model "Scientific Management," and his framework for a well-run organization included these components:

- Task specialization
- A clear chain of command
- Personal responsibility
- The separation of planning and operations functions
- Incentives for workers

It was the "separation of planning and operations" that prompted criticism of the system. The better-educated engineers did the planning and gave the orders; the poor immigrants were the manual laborers who carried them out. The foreman was responsible for the finished product—the laborers, only for their specific task. Taylor was blunt in his belief that most workers would do as little as possible to get their jobs done, but also that they would work

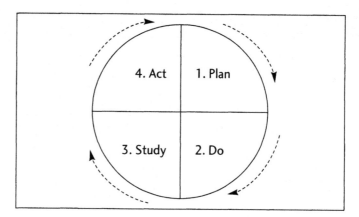

Figure 1-1 Shewhart Cycle.

harder for more pay—that is, if they were paid by the piece or by the pound and, conversely, docked pay for substandard work. His theories were criticized for dehumanizing workers, timing their output with stopwatches and designing compensation structures with money as the sole motivator.

Not long afterward, Frank and Lillian Gilbreth introduced another concept to the workplace: **motion economy**. Working in construction, Frank Gilbreth studied bricklayers and noticed how differently each individual completed the same task. By honing in on the optimum methods and movements, Gilbreth came up with a standardized process to raise a single bricklayer's daily output from 1,000 to 2,700 bricks. His wife Lillian added the component of photography, filming the work process in order to study it more precisely. They believed the way a task is performed is as important as the time it takes to do it. Together, their research made a strong case for allowing regular rest periods for workers to maximize productivity.

While corporate leaders like Henry Ford were improving production methods and seeking higher quality from their manufacturing facilities in the early 1900s—Ford introduced the first continuous-motion assembly line in 1913 to make Model T cars—the idea of organizing and controlling manufacturing processes and predicting their outcomes began to take on scientific significance in the 1920s at two American companies, Western Electric and Bell Telephone Laboratories. They must have been exciting places to work back then—at least, for people who loved science and math!

Walter Shewhart was a physics PhD who worked at both companies. He developed the first statistical control chart, assigning controls (such as specific limits and random variations) and studying how these influenced the results of a manufacturing process. Shewhart was masterful at applying theory in real-world work environments. One of many common-sense processes he imparted to students and coworkers is still known as the *Shewhart Cycle*—plan, do, study, act. The Shewhart Cycle is shown in Figure 1-1 and today is often simply referred to as "PDSA."

Shewhart focused on understanding what customers want and designing products to satisfy them. He believed that beyond a certain point, "trying harder" often makes things worse and that there are simple statistical ways to determine whether that point has been reached. When used correctly, he proved that statistical controls can balance losses from these common corporate mistakes:

- Overreaction to small variations in a process
- Missing valuable clues for improvement[4]

A few years later, Shewhart's Bell coworkers H. F. Dodge and H. G. Romig began using the concept of sampling products as a quality control measure—of measuring "lot quality" instead of "unit quality." This was fairly radical in an industry in which workers spent much time inspecting each and every item on a production line. Their theory was that products in a factory, for example, would be made to **acceptable quality levels** (AQLs) that were decided in advance. Then, each group (or lot) of finished products could either be inspected or not. If the AQLs are high enough, there may be an occasional defect in a lot that was not inspected, but it still makes more economic sense *not* to inspect each and every product individually. The Dodge-Romig method is known as **Statistical Quality Control**, or **SQC**. (In the 1970s, it was reborn as **Statistical Process Control**, or **SPC**.)

Also during the 1930s, the Western Electric Hawthorne Works in Chicago was the site of some interesting work experiments. The workers surely didn't know it at the time, but volunteering for this duty, they would help change the future of personnel management.

The manufacturing plant had been trying to determine whether the light levels in a person's work environment impacted productivity, but their findings weren't panning out. They asked for the assistance of Professor Elton Mayo of the Harvard Business School, who soon discovered light didn't have as much to do with workers' output as the camaraderie of the work group members and their supervisor. They simply liked working together, were treated well by the supervisor, and were happier on the job than other workers who didn't receive the personal attention of this select group.

The result? The human element must be factored into any work-related equation. Today, it is still known as the **Hawthorne Effect**.

Quality across the Pacific

When Walter Shewhart was asked to come to Japan to lecture about his quality control findings, he was ill and suggested another man who had studied under him go in his place. Today, W. Edwards Deming is arguably the world's most famous quality control expert because he has written so extensively about the topic and published many scholarly studies. Deming was a great admirer of Shewhart. As a physicist, he took Shewhart's ideas and applied them to new types of situations in his government jobs at the U.S. Department of Agriculture, the Census Department, and the War Standards Board. Deming became one of the catalysts for Japan's economic renaissance after World War II. His "14 Points" were first presented in his book *Out of the Crisis*. They include the following:

- Create and communicate to all employees a statement of the company's aims and purposes.
- Adapt to the new philosophy of the day, because industries and economics are always changing.
- Institute on-the-job training.
- Drive out fear and create trust.
- Teach and institute leadership to improve all job functions.

Another Shewhart admirer, Joseph M. Juran also worked at Western Electric in the 1920s and 1930s. In the 1950s, Juran traveled to Japan to teach his own theories—that hands-on management was necessary at all levels of a corporation to ensure quality control, and that problems are opportunities to make improvements. His approach is still known today as the **Juran Trilogy:** planning, control, and improvement. In a nutshell, the three components break down as follows:

- *Planning* includes identifying both external and internal customers, determining their needs, and deciding what type of product or service best meets those needs. In Juran's model, planning also includes developing the processes to create the product or service—everything from where it is produced, to what kinds of training are required, to how the manufacturing or service facilities are operated and maintained.
- *Control* (sometimes called Statistical Process Control, or SPC) is the term for measuring all of the other processes. It includes deciding exactly what is going to be measured and how to measure it; setting goals for the measurement; and when measurement is complete, comparing the actual performance to the goals, interpreting the results, and deciding what (if anything) to do about them.
- *Improvement* involves setting up an internal structure (that is, within a company) to identify projects or processes that can be modified or improved to attain higher performance levels, and to assign people and resources to these tasks. Dr. Juran is neither the first nor the last of the process improvement experts to suggest that improvement must be ongoing—that there is always something more to be done as new goals are set, new products are introduced, and new lessons are learned.

Another of Juran's famous observations is that in the scheme of any organization, only a few problems are truly monumental, and most of a company's losses can be traced to these "vital few," as he termed them. For the most part, problems are small (in Juran's words, the "useful many") that companies can learn from, and that can be fixed by good on-the-job team-work. The theory as a whole is known as the *Pareto Principle*, named after an Italian economist at the turn of the previous century. We'll talk more about it in Chapter 11, with the introduction of Pareto charts.

In 1960, Japan's Emperor Hirohito presented W. Edwards Deming and Joseph Juran with the Second Order of the Sacred Treasure, an award for helping to rebuild the Japanese economy that had been left in postwar shambles. They had been invited by the Japanese Union of Scientists and Engineers to teach their principles of statistical process control and quality management to senior managers of Japanese corporations, who learned their lessons well.

In Japan, the following individuals took seeds from this training and went on to develop their own major contributions to what is now Total Quality Management and/or one of its equally famous "continuous improvement" counterparts:

- Kaoru Ishikawa headed the Japanese Union of Scientists and Engineers, whose members expanded the concepts of quality management and quality assurance out of factories and into all aspects of business management. A PhD who studied under both Deming and Juran, he developed a **cause-and-effect diagram** that is still widely used and is also known as an **Ishikawa diagram** or a **fishbone diagram**.
- Taichi Ohno, known as "the father of Just-in-Time production," was a cocreator of the **Toyota Production System (TPS)** in the late 1970s and early 1980s. He helped catapult the Japanese automaker to technological supremacy by combining a number of proven techniques to eliminate waste in the manufacturing process and therefore reduce costs. One of Ohno's most famous concepts is **waste identification**, or learning to pinpoint the wasted time and materials in any production process in order to correct them.
- Shigeo Shingo worked with Ohno on the TPS process and developed some of its most popular concepts, including **poka-yoke** (which means "mistake-proof" in Japanese and refers to taking human judgment out of some types of production, thereby minimizing human error), and the **Single Minute Exchange of Dies**, or SMED (the goal of reducing all factory setup times to one minute). Shingo also believed that "constructive dissatisfaction" is required for most companies to prompt improvements in their quality control efforts.[5]
- Genichi Taguchi is a PhD in mechanical engineering who was the first to equate the quality of a product with its cost. He combined cost, target, and variation into a single metric known as a **loss function concept**, a mathematical equation that quantifies the decline in a customer's perceived value of a product as its quality declines. In the 1980s, Taguchi also found a way to determine the effects of uncontrollable variables

(commonly referred to as **noise factors**) on a system or process to make the expected outcome more "robust." **Robustness** is Taguchi's term for a more realistic outcome.

Communicating the TQM Message

No one knows for sure who first coined the term "Total Quality Management," but it was probably Armand V. Feigenbaum, who worked for General Electric Company and authored its internal manual called *Total Quality Control* in the 1950s.

As one of the world's largest and most diverse manufacturing companies, General Electric had undertaken a massive decentralization process in the 1950s and 1960s that was designed to give greater autonomy to the operating managers of its various business units. These managers had to meet or exceed certain production and profit goals, and Feigenbaum's Quality Control Services was an internal department that "sold" the individual managers on trying new methods and ideas to improve their results. In each department, for example, he suggested a permanent design review board for new product development.

Feigenbaum insisted that quality could not be consistently attained without genuine commitment and involvement of managers and employees at all levels—that it took a "total" effort to "manage" it. After his retirement from General Electric, he went on to become a quality control consultant and lecturer, to spread the word about TQM.[6]

In 1979, Philip Crosby's book *Quality Is Free* took the business world by storm. It proposed the common-sense idea that doing things right the first time is far more cost-effective than detecting and correcting problems after the fact. He followed in 1984 with *Quality without Tears*, which laid out a four-point quality management philosophy that remains in wide use:

- "Quality" means conforming to a set of specific requirements.
- A company's objective should be to prevent nonconformance, and the system for "causing" quality is prevention, not appraisal.
- A standard for performance must be nothing less than "zero defects"—not "that's close enough"—and that zero defects is a realistic and attainable goal.
- The cost of nonconformance is the ultimate measurement of quality.

Crosby crafted his theories on the job as a corporate executive in manufacturing firms. His strength was in his ability to communicate them. Unlike his contemporaries' scientific equations, Crosby boiled things down to terminology that could be easily understood by nontechnical people. The consulting company that still bears his name puts his theories to work in many different types of organizations.

Today, many of the quality control concepts of past centuries seem like common sense to us, but at the time they were first introduced, at least some were considered unrealistic and/or downright controversial. And recent years have continued to produce new management concepts and their gurus—from Peter Drucker's *The Effective Executive*, to Stephen Covey's *The 7 Habits of Highly Effective People*, to Ken Blanchard's *The One-Minute Manager* (and more recently, *The One-Minute Apology*). Religion has even entered the management field, with best sellers like *The Purpose-Driven Life* by minister and "spiritual entrepreneur" Dr. Rick Warren, and *God Is My CEO* by management consultant Larry S. Julian. Each book, and plenty of others, makes salient points about effective leadership, ethics, productivity, personal responsibility, morale, and so on. All of them include advice on how to deal with the only apparent constant in the business world: change.

A NEW MANAGEMENT MODEL

What is really happening here? Responding to intense competition in a rapidly changing world, today's business leaders and managers have been forced to seek ways to become more competitive. Many choose the quickest route, if not the easiest—they lay people off, sell off divisions or whole businesses, and demand more from those who remain. Eventually, these sources run dry. At this point, leaders and managers turn their full attention to their companies, and to the systems they lead and manage. Many notice the signs and symptoms of inefficiencies, errors, dissatisfaction, high costs, slow responses, and defecting customers, but it is difficult to detect the sources of these problems.

When it comes to understanding the systems they lead and manage, most executives *know* their companies could do significantly better if they could only focus everybody's attention on what is important; but what *is* important? Where do we look first? How do we make sense of this complex, confusing system we call our company? How do we attack something we cannot see?

Employees face similar frustrations with resignation rather than renewed commitment. A problem that should have been solved reappears. A supplied component repeatedly fails. A time-consuming effort gets tossed aside when priorities suddenly change—or worse, when jobs are eliminated, suddenly and with minimal explanation.

Internal systems have always had problems—and they always will. What has changed is that companies are finding it harder and harder to survive their problems. What has changed is *change*. When American companies could capture markets by the sheer volume of their production, when they could compete just by working hard, and when they could sustain growth with a stream of innovative products, they could afford to follow a business theory built on capital, driven by profits, and organized as a hierarchy. Change was slow and predictable, and the theory worked—for a while.

However, global competition has made the old management model obsolete. One of America's leading management experts, Peter Drucker, described the transition in an article in the *Wall Street Journal*. Inspired by the major turnarounds then underway at General Motors, IBM, Westinghouse, and American Express, he wrote:

> To start this turnaround thus requires a willingness to rethink and to reexamine the company's business theory. It requires stopping saying "we know" and instead saying "let's ask." And there are two sets of questions that need to be asked. First: Who are the customers and who are the non-customers? What is value to them? What do they pay for? Second: What do the [successful companies] do that we do not do? What do they not do that we *know* is essential? What do they assume that we *know* to be wrong?

Unlike the old model, the new management model is *customer-driven*. As Drucker suggests, the focus of the new model is not on how much a company is making, but on how well it is meeting its customers' requirements. The benchmark companies in this book make understanding and satisfying customer requirements a top priority. They have learned from experience that customer satisfaction determines financial success.

However, American businesses—especially retailers—continue to define themselves primarily in terms of dollars. When *Fortune* magazine announces its latest list of 500, it places the successes and the failures into three categories: (1) biggest moneymakers and losers, (2) biggest sales increases and decreases, and (3) best and worst investments. Almost every article about company performance in business newspapers and magazines uses a financial yardstick, whether the article is about product innovation, quality improvement, customer service, or any other of the myriad issues companies address. This system of financial measures has become the common language we use to assess and compare performance, but it shows only one part of performance—perhaps not even the most important one.

Leaders who rely on dollar figures alone to evaluate their companies' performance will never understand what will eventually hit them. By contrast, the themes of *customer orientation, consensus thinking, integration,* and *teamwork* point to a solution. To take advantage of this approach, leaders and managers must have a very good grasp of the system in which they work.

A company cannot take a haphazard approach to knowing its customers, turning the organization on its side, integrating functions, and working through teams. Those that have tried have failed. Studies by accountants and consultants at Ernst & Young have suggested that some companies have wasted millions of dollars on such quality initiatives as team building, benchmarking, and reengineering.

Some of the companies in this book have saved millions of dollars through similar initiatives. The primary difference is that the losers, without understanding their own systems first, adopted programs they had seen work for others in hopes of a quick fix to a persistent problem. The winners become "systems thinkers" who integrate these initiatives into a broader process of continuous improvement. Systems perspective is discussed further in Chapter 12.

QUALITY AND PROFIT

For leaders who are reluctant to take their eyes off the bottom line, the Baldrige winners have proven over the years that the pursuit of quality excellence does not come at the expense of financial excellence. For them, financial results are one more tool with which to measure the effectiveness of the system. The difference is that the goal of the new model is not profits; it is customer satisfaction, with the understanding that profits will improve as quality improves.

Figure 1-2 shows how delivering greater perceived value while continually refining processes improves profitability and delights shareholders. In particular, the model shows:

- Delighting customers, reducing waste, and increasing productivity are natural by-products of a systematic process of continuous improvement.
- Products and services that exceed customer requirements are of greater value to customers than competitors' products and services. More customers are likely to purchase higher quality, which in turn improves market share and grows revenues.
- Less waste and greater productivity result in lower costs, which in turn improve margins, asset utilization, and competitive position.
- Higher revenues and more favorable margins, asset utilization, and competitive position improve the bottom line, which delights shareholders.

Of course, in the real world, the connections between improving quality and improving profitability are not always this evident. We have all read

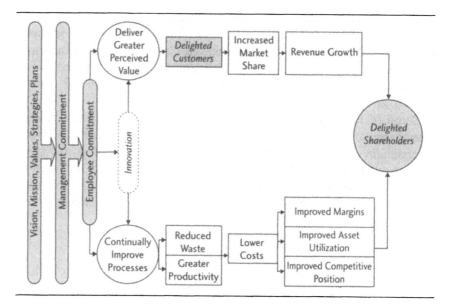

Figure 1-2 Value creation model.

about quality leaders who have stumbled financially. The business media are quick to hold these companies up as proof that the quality movement is a "passing fad" with limited value, which is like saying a baseball team finished a season in last place because it had a poor spring training. A company's financial success depends on many different factors, not the least of which is the company's leadership. *The new management model gives leaders the ability to control and improve their entire company, but it does not make the decisions for them.* Even the best management models are subject to the skill of the people who use them.

Skilled leaders have embraced this model because it makes them more effective. Financial performance depends on how well a company does in three areas, and the new model strengthens a company's position in all three:

1. **Strategy development.** By contributing to more efficient strategies and better business decisions, it improves the development of strategies and helps companies respond to a changing environment.
2. **Market performance.** It increases customer retention, market share, and revenues, which improves performance in the marketplace.
3. **Internal performance.** It improves asset utilization and productivity and lowers operating costs, which improves performance throughout the organization.

The new management model accomplishes all this by focusing the entire company on the customer, then identifying and improving the processes that lead to customer satisfaction.

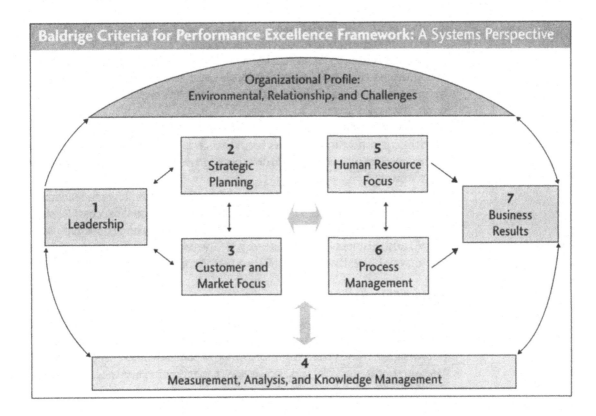

Baldrige Criteria for Performance Excellence Framework: A Systems Perspective

Organizational Profile:
Environmental, Relationship, and Challenges

2 Strategic Planning

5 Human Resource Focus

1 Leadership

7 Business Results

3 Customer and Market Focus

6 Process Management

4 Measurement, Analysis, and Knowledge Management

The Baldrige Model

The Baldrige framework for performance excellence divides the Core Values and Concepts into seven Categories. The way these Categories interact with each other is shown in Figure 1-3. The paragraphs that follow are how the Baldrige organization explains the framework.

Organizational Profile

Your Organizational Profile [top of figure] sets the context for the way your organization operates. Your environment, key working relationships, and strategic challenges serve as an overarching guide for your organizational performance management system.

System Operations

The system operations are composed of the six Baldrige Categories in the center of the figure that define your operations and the results you achieve. Leadership (Category 1), Strategic Planning (Category 2), and Customer and Market Focus (Category 3) represent the leadership triad. These Categories are placed together to emphasize the importance of a leadership focus on

Figure 1-3 Baldrige criteria for performance excellence framework: a systems perspective.

strategy and customers. Senior leaders set your organizational direction and seek future opportunities for your organization.

Human Resource Focus (Category 5), Process Management (Category 6), and Business Results (Category 7) represent the results triad. Your organization's employees and key processes accomplish the work of the organization that yields your business results.

All actions point toward Business Results—a composite of product and service, customer and market, financial, and internal operational performance results, including human resource, governance, and social responsibility results.

The horizontal arrow in the center of the framework links the leadership triad to the results triad, a linkage critical to organizational success. Furthermore, the arrow indicates the central relationship between Leadership (Category 1) and Business Results (Category 7). The two-headed arrows indicate the importance of feedback in an effective performance management system.

System Foundation

Measurement, Analysis, and Knowledge Management (Category 4) are critical to the effective management of your organization and to a fact-based, knowledge-driven system for improving performance and competitiveness. Measurement, analysis, and knowledge management serve as a foundation for the performance management system.[7]

MANY PATHS TO ONE GOAL

Many of the processes, theories, methods, and breakthroughs in quality improvement have overlapped over the years. The timeline in Table 1-1 places them roughly in chronological order, which should help you keep them straight. Note that many of these are still in use in some form today.

In this section, we'll attempt to briefly explain at least a few of the major quality concepts of the last 20 years, although it is impossible to do any of them justice in a few paragraphs. Each has been the subject of entire books about how to utilize it successfully in a corporate environment; here, they are listed alphabetically.

Balanced Scorecard. This method is based on a popular management book of the same name that was published in 1996. Its authors, Robert Kaplan and David Norton, suggest that a business's executive team measure progress in four areas that are equally important—customer knowledge, financial performance, internal business processes, and learning/growth—and

Table 1-1 Continuous Improvement Methods and Concepts from the Twentieth Century	
1900s	Scientific Management, Motion Economy
1920s	Acceptance Sampling, Control Charts
1930s	Statistical Quality Control, Hawthorne Effect
1950s	Juran Trilogy
1960s	Total Quality Control
1970s	Just-In-Time, Kaizen, Quality Circles, Statistical Process Control, Toyota Production System, Zero Defects
1980s	Baldrige Awards, ISO 9000 Standards, Lean Enterprise
1990s	Balanced Scorecard, Six Sigma

use the knowledge to focus the entire organization and its various programs on "balancing" the scorecard. A similar strategy in Japanese companies is called *hoshin kanri*, or Hoshin Planning.

ISO Standards. The International Standardization Organization (ISO) is headquartered in Switzerland. More than 100 nations are "members" that define, agree on, and abide by a wide range of product and process safety and quality standards. The first standards for quality management systems (QMSs) were published in 1987.

The idea behind ISO certification is that products made in different nations be compatible for use in others. This allows manufacturers, for instance, to buy parts from suppliers in other countries. The QMS standards are known as the "ISO 9000" family of standards, the environmental management systems are "ISO 14000," and so on. (See Table 1-2.)

Table 1-2 The ISO 9000 Standards for Quality Management Systems (QMS)		
Identifying Number	*Type of Standard*	*Description of Contents*
ISO 9000:2000	Vocabulary and basic concepts	Outlines the concepts and terminology used in the other 9000 Series standards
ISO 9001:2000	Requirements for registration	How to show that a company or process conforms to these QMS standards
ISO 9004:2000	Guidelines for performance improvement	How to establish a QMS with continuous improvement as a priority

Some industries, especially in high-tech fields, have added their own subsets of quality standards for their specific industries. For example, the automotive industry's standard is known as ISO/TS 16949.

If there is a problem with ISO standards, it's that the certification process (for a company to say publicly that it is "ISO 9000-certified," for instance) is rigorous and expensive. It involves a specialized audit to show that the company meets at least 20 standards, and periodic re-audits after that. The initial audit can cost a small company from $10,000 to $30,000. Some decide it's not worth the investment, embarking on their own quality improvement programs and stating that they are "ISO 9000-compliant" instead of "ISO 9000-certified."[8]

Just-In-Time. This is a manufacturing theory of producing just enough product to fill current orders as they are due. The system strips a manufacturing process down to its essence—only enough workers and raw materials to get the job done, eliminating the extra expense associated with buying extra materials and storing inventory—thereby eliminating waste. Successful JIT production is a finely tuned system that also requires suppliers of the materials to deliver smaller quantities "just in time" for them to be used. While some companies adopted the system with less-than-stellar results since the 1970s, Toyota made JIT a cornerstone of its Toyota Production System, with great success.

In recent years, companies have taken JIT a step further. "JIT II," which you'll learn more about in Chapter 9 of this book, brings the supplier-customer relationship even closer in manufacturing environments, by having suppliers' representatives work directly in the customer's facility, so they can be more proactive about what must be ordered when.

Kaizen. This is the Japanese term for "unending improvement," which comes from a Buddhist phrase, "Renew the heart and make it good"—in this case, the heart of a company. Kaizen represents a system in which management encourages and implements small, incremental improvements, involving employees as team members and creating a culture of workers who are all striving to do better. It focuses on simplifying complex processes, and training employees to measurably improve them. Kaizen also includes work-life balance, with the theory that human resources are the most important assets of a company.

Companies that adopt a Kaizen management system combine a number of famous production techniques (some of which were explained earlier in this chapter), including motion study, Just-In-Time principles, the "Five S's" of workplace organization (Japanese words for proper arrangement of tools and parts, orderliness, cleanup, and so on), *poka-yoke* (error detection and prevention), teamwork, and more.

Lean Enterprise. The Toyota Production System combined the principles of Kaizen but sped them up for its automotive plant output. Also known as "**Lean Manufacturing**," or simply "Lean," the system is another amalgam of improvement-centered tools and methods, most of which have handy three-letter acronyms—from JIT to Total Quality Control (TQC) to Visual Control Systems (VCS, the idea that showing progress on video screens as work is accomplished keeps everyone up to speed). There's even a four-letter acronym, mentioned earlier in the chapter: SMED, for Single Minute Exchange of Dies, Shigeo Shingo's method of reducing factory setup times to one minute or less.

Ford Motor Company has its own lean system, known as the Ford Production System (FPS) and modeled after the Toyota Production System.

Quality Circles. This team effort was most popular in the late 1970s and early 1980s. It is based on a Japanese method of grouping people together in "**Quality Control**" (**QC**) **circles**, meetings where they shared their expertise and worked to solve a problem or improve a process. QCs have had limited success in most American companies. They're useful for solving small or localized problems, but not really designed for visionary or "big-picture" quality management.

Six Sigma®. The latest quality management concept continues to race like wildfire through the ranks of companies large and small. Created by Motorola in the 1980s, Six Sigma® is the cornerstone of a huge international consulting business at Motorola University.

The name refers to a scientific way of describing quality based on variations that occur in any process—plus or minus three "sigmas." (Sigma is the Greek letter that signifies the standard deviation in a mathematical formula.) The "sigma level" quantifies defects per million opportunities (DPMO). A metric of six sigma, then, equates to 3.4 DPMO.

There is much more to Six Sigma® than these few paragraphs, but its problem-solving framework for improving business processes is fairly simple. It is referred to as **DMAIC**, which stands for

- **Define** the opportunity. (What needs to improve?)
- **Measure** performance (the current state versus the desired outcome).
- **Analyze** the opportunity. (Determine the root cause of the gap.)
- **Improve** the performance. (Brainstorm, select, and implement the solution.)
- **Control** the performance. (Devise a way to monitor it, make someone accountable for it in the future, and so on.)

Much of the praise for this system lies in its rigorous system of personal instruction. "Green Belts" have been trained in the methodology and tools and can work on Six Sigma® process improvement teams; "Black Belts" have completed enough training to lead such teams; "Master Black Belts" are experts who can serve as coaches and teachers.[9]

Total Quality Management. This theory, mentioned earlier in the discussion of Armand V. Feigenbaum, is that quality (including the qualities of products or services) is managed by the total effort of an organization, and that each department or phase of production is responsible for making its part of the product or service as flawless as possible before passing it on to the next user or phase. Employees in all functions are trained and empowered to problem-solve and identify and eliminate waste. A good TQM system is dependent on planning and goal setting; those that haven't worked as well have generally been missing these components.

CHAPTER SUMMARY

It is one thing for a company to say it is focused on quality. It is quite another to embark on a continuous quality improvement program. If Total Quality Management and its many loosely related cousins seem more like common sense than a whole new way of doing business, it is because the concepts behind them have been evolving for decades and, in some cases, centuries! Today, many of them have become "business as usual." This chapter covered the long and interesting history of quality control very briefly, highlighting the achievements of a dozen management gurus in the United States, Europe, and Japan.

While American business has a history of intense competition, it also has become known for being more concerned about "the bottom line" (shareholders' returns, stock prices) than any other component of measurement. Indeed, most business news is generally reported in terms of profits and losses. However, in a global business environment, today's management experts agree a more intelligent benchmark is to focus on satisfying customers' needs—and if this is done well, with continuous improvement built into the system, the profit will follow.

The chapter introduces the most recent Baldrige Award criteria, as well as describing how they are grouped into Categories and how the Categories interrelate. It offers the Baldrige model as a way to alleviate the frustrations of a typical company's executives and employees—who may be willing to change the way things are done but are uncertain about where to start or what to do. Of course, there are plenty of other successful management tools, a few of which are also discussed briefly.

DISCUSSION QUESTIONS

1. Do you think that making production lines (or other mundane, repetitive types of work) more efficient automatically makes them less humane or, in other ways, "worse" for the workers?
2. Do you agree with F. W. Taylor's early assertion that most workers would do as little as possible on the job, and that money is their primary motivator? Why or why not?
3. Why would "overreaction to small variations in a process" be a mistake, as cited in the work of Walter Shewhart? Could it indicate real concern for correcting a problem?
4. Explain the role of mathematics in quality improvement concepts. If you had to assign a percentage, how much of it would you say is math or statistics—and how much is psychology? Explain your answer.
5. Why do some assert that the various quality control methodologies are fads, which come and go with the latest best-selling management books? What do *you* think? Of the systems described in this chapter, which make the most sense to you, and why?

ENDNOTES

1. *"Malcolm Baldrige, 26th Secretary of Commerce,"* Baldrige National Quality Program, National Institute of Standards and Technology, U.S. Department of Commerce, Gaithersburg, Maryland.
2. Recommended Practices for Survey/Audit and Assessment/Evaluation, NASA Office of Safety and Mission Assurance, Washington, D.C.
3. *2005 Criteria for Performance Excellence*, Baldrige National Quality Program, National Institute of Standards and Technology, U.S. Department of Commerce, Gaithersburg, Maryland.
4. Beth Blankenship and Peter B. Petersen, "W. Edwards Deming's mentor and others who made a significant impact on his views during the 1920s and 1930s," *Journal of Management History* (Volume 5, Number 8, 1999), MCB University Press, Bradford, West Yorkshire, England.
5. Bruce E. Hamilton and Preston G. Smith, CMC, "Implementing TQM on a Shoestring," *Journal of Management Consulting* (Volume 7, Number 4, Fall 1993), Institute of Management Consultants USA, Washington, D.C.
6. Lawrence P. Huggins, "Total quality management and the contributions of A. V. Feigenbaum," *Journal of Management History* (Volume 4, Number 1, 1998), MCB University Press, Bradford, West Yorkshire, England.

7. *2005 Criteria for Performance Excellence*, Baldrige National Quality Program, National Institute of Standards and Technology, U.S. Department of Commerce, Gaithersburg, Maryland.
8. See endnote 5.
9. *Six Sigma Dictionary*, Motorola University, Motorola.com ©1999–2004. Motorola, Inc. All rights reserved.

Additional Notes

- MCB University Press has been renamed Emerald and can be found on the World Wide Web at www.titania.emeraldinsight.com.
- *The Journal of Management Consulting* has been renamed C2M, Consulting to Management, and can be found on the World Wide Web at www.c2m.com.
- The author also gratefully acknowledges the following sources for biographical information about the lives and discoveries of various TQM researchers and participants through the centuries:

  ◇ **Accel-Team.** Located in Cumbria, U.K., British management consultant Cliff F. Grimes's business includes a very thorough and well-researched Web site, www.accel-team.com.
  ◇ **SkyMark Corporation.** The developers of PathMaker software include extensive historical and background research about management topics on their Web site, www.SkyMark.com.

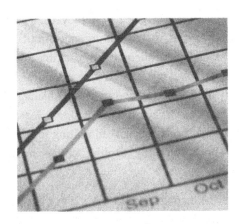

CHAPTER 7

Leadership

It is not uncommon these days to see television news footage of corporate executives on their way to jail after huge accounting scandals or charges of pension fund mismanagement. And yet, 70 percent of employees still believe their company's leadership is either "extremely trustworthy" or "moderately trustworthy," according to a 2004 poll of almost 800 employees and human resources (HR) executives. The same percentage described themselves as "extremely loyal" or "moderately loyal" to their employers.

However, the poll found ethics to be an area in which some corporate leaders are lacking. Less than half (45 percent) of the HR executives and 27 percent of the employees surveyed "strongly agreed" that their company leaders are ethical.[1] The inference is that the rest . . . don't think so.

If a leader does not have the trust of his or her employees, a clear vision about company goals and priorities, a sense of urgency about their importance, and the ability to communicate them, the remarkable thing is that progress is still made in most companies. But it is made more slowly and less efficiently. Efforts may be duplicated and down-line managers, frustrated with the lack of guidance or the cutting of budgets, learn to come up with their own ideas and methods rather than waiting for direction. When those ideas and methods clash, the resulting ripples impact the whole company.

In this chapter, we examine the management philosophies of senior executives at three world-class companies, and the impact of their attitudes on their businesses—attitudes that members of the Baldrige Board of Examiners consider "visionary." Topics include

- What makes clear and consistent leadership
- Four steps required of leaders in any quality improvement program
- How good leaders interact with employees
- How company values are expressed
- How company values are communicated

Although much of the chapter will focus on the highest-ranking company officials, their methods of leadership are shared by the senior executives who report to them. The corporate examples we will focus on in this chapter include the following.

Corning Incorporated. Established in 1851, Corning is best known for its invention of fiber-optic cable in the 1980s and is still the top manufacturer of that indispensable commodity today. Corning also makes semiconductor materials, specialty glass for television, computer and liquid crystal display (LCD) screens, and advanced materials for the scientific, environmental, and consumer marketplaces. Headquartered in Corning, New York, the company has more than 20,000 employees worldwide. In 2003, the company sold its photonic components business to Avanex in exchange for a 17 percent ownership share in that company. Corning's Telecommunications Products Division—which accounts for a little less than half of its total revenue—won the Baldrige Award in 1995.

FedEx Corporation. Federal Express was founded in 1971 as the "big idea" of charter airplane pilot Fred Smith. It launched its overnight air express business in 1973, and just 10 years later, it was the first U.S. company to top $1 billion in revenues in its first decade. Today, FedEx (its nickname, "FedEx," officially became the company name in 2000) is the world's largest express transportation company—almost 196,000 employees move more than 3 million items to more than 200 countries each business day, up from 110,000 workers and 2 million packages just five years ago! In 1990, FedEx became the first service company to win the Baldrige Award. Since then, the company has expanded its ground delivery business by purchasing both Parcel Direct (formerly a division of Quad/Graphics, now renamed FedEx SmartPost) and more than 1,100 Kinko's locations (now FedEx Kinko's Office and Print Centers) in 2004.

Marlow Industries. Marlow manufactures customized thermoelectric coolers—small, solid-state electronic devices that heat, cool, or stabilize the temperature of electronic equipment—for commercial and defense applications. Located in Dallas, Texas, Marlow employs more than 250 people. Marlow Industries won the Baldrige Award in 1991 and was named by *Industry Week* magazine as one of "America's 10 Best Plants" (1993) and "Top 25 Growing Manufacturing Companies" (1999). CEO and president Raymond Marlow founded the company in 1973 and initiated a systematic quality improvement process in 1987, even though Marlow's market share was more than 50 percent at the time. Its market share in its major markets is still greater than 70 percent. The company's record for process improvement prompted the creation of the Quality Texas Foundation, a nonprofit business association that bestows annual "Texas Quality Awards" based on the Baldrige Award criteria. Mr. Marlow is its founding chairman.

QUALITY BEGINS AT THE TOP

How does a company get its leaders involved in the quality improvement process? People ask this question in organizations where quality improvement has not been a priority—because senior management has not *made* it a priority. Rank-and-file employees and middle managers become tired of fixing pieces of the system, only to have apathy and resistance to change swallow up their efforts. They recognize that the company's leaders have the power to change the entire system by making quality improvement part of the corporate culture. But how does this happen? And what in the world does it take to prompt this mind-set in people who have risen to leadership positions but don't seem to have it?

Leadership holds the key to the door of continuous improvement. If the key stays in leadership's pocket, the organization has no chance of becoming a quality leader. The company may implement scattered improvements through the diligence of a quality champion. It may train everyone in the fundamentals of quality and urge their involvement. It may achieve ISO certification for the documentation of its processes. It may even win an award from a customer. But without clear and consistent leadership, the company will never be a *quality leader*. Its management system will never be sound and efficient, and its improvement efforts will eventually be replaced by an intriguing new management fad.

In contrast, look at the Baldrige Award winners—companies that are driven by their senior executives' zeal for quality. When Ray Marlow dons a cape and plumed hat for a corporate video appearance as "Captain TQM," he proves (among other things) that there is truth in humor! Good leaders meet with employees frequently, to inspire and recognize their best efforts. They visit with customers regularly, to find out what they need and expect. They track quality improvements religiously, take and teach quality courses, demand excellence (100 percent customer satisfaction, 100 percent of the time), and preach "quality" to every audience that will listen—and that includes civic groups, schools, government agencies, foreign companies, and trade associations, among others. They lead the quality improvement process because they are responsible for making the company more competitive and profitable, and the only way to do that consistently and for the long term is through continuous improvement of the entire system. That's not a one-speech, quick-fix kind of commitment. It is a relentless, all-consuming desire to make the company the best it can be.

"There is no greater source of individual power and commitment than loving what you do, or what you want to do," says Frederick W. Smith, the founder of FedEx. "You have to be, at least, a zealot in your commitment to the quality improvement process to be effective. You've got to speak it and reinforce it at every opportunity."

So how do you make a *company leader* into a *quality leader*? Perhaps the most frustrating realization is—you can't. You can no more make a CEO walk the quality path than you can make him or her convert to a new faith. In fact, the analogy to a religious conversion often surfaces in the way leaders talk about instituting quality measurements and improvements in their companies. Many describe it as a "leap of faith." J. M. Juran likes to say that quality leaders have "the faith of the true believers," a faith they got by "witnessing the miracles."

Like those who experience a religious awakening, these leaders are eager to spread the gospel of quality. "When you get into quality, you become intolerant of the lack of quality in business, education, government, and other organizations," explains James B. Houghton, board chairman and chief executive officer of Corning Incorporated. Houghton is the leader who initiated Corning's "Total Quality" strategy in 1983. "I made a lot of outside speeches because I think quality is in a spillover phase in our society," he said.

Houghton did more than give speeches. Six months after he took the reins at Corning in 1983 (he retired in 1996, but returned in 2002), Houghton announced that the company would spend $5 million to set up a Quality Institute, which is, today, the Quality Texas Foundation. The Texas governor presents these highly coveted annual awards.

"We were barely breaking even at the time," Houghton remembers, "and the cynics thought this was my new toy. Today there are very few cynics, for two reasons: we've never stopped promoting quality, and people now realize that quality means survival."

The survival issue is prominent in the minds of quality leaders. FedEx's Fred Smith compares the awakening to quality to "a near-death experience. A lot of times it's brought on by trauma." Leaders often embrace Total Quality Management because they see no alternative: improve or die. Whatever inspires them—the fear of failure, the promise of success, the achievement of other companies, the belief that there must be a better way to manage a company—triggers the leap of faith. Once they are on the quality path, the cultural changes they see all around them frequently breed a missionary zeal about the need for, and the benefits of, the quality improvement process.

FOUR STEPS TO QUALITY LEADERSHIP

In the course of becoming quality leaders, our role models sought to identify the words and actions that would bring everyone into the fold:

- What can we do as senior executives to personally lead the quality improvement process?
- What are our company's quality values and goals?
- How can we communicate those values and goals to our customers, employees, suppliers, and other groups?
- How can we improve as quality leaders?

There are four basic steps involved in answering these questions and leading the transition from quality as a good idea, to quality as a commitment to better overall systems management.

Step One: Commit to Quality

The first step for any company president, chairman, or CEO is committing himself or herself, as well as the company, to the process. Jamie Houghton took this step in 1983, shortly after he became Corning's chairman. Fred Smith and his top executives founded FedEx on the idea of providing the highest quality of service, then participated in quality training in the first year of the company's existence. Ray Marlow initiated a systematic approach to quality improvement at Marlow Industries in 1987. All did it thoughtfully and deliberately, knowing that such a commitment would redefine their roles for as long as they remained leaders.

As Houghton put it, "When you start things as a leader, you've got to make up your mind—then you've got to do it, even though you may not have one clue how effective it's going to be." In his 2004 biographical statement on the company's Web site, he described his leadership philosophy thusly:

> Leadership is about personal integrity, and instinctively knowing and doing 'the right thing.' It is about having enough modesty to constantly doubt, be open, and listen. It is about performance over time, not charisma. It is about responsibility, not privilege. It is a deep-seated belief in the organization's values and goals, and the ability to live them, articulate them, and push them forward with constancy over time. It is the willingness to change everything except those basic values and goals.

Another company we'll learn more about in Chapter 4 is Engelhard, an international manufacturing firm. But we mention them here because their Corporate Governance Guidelines document lists core personality and character traits that are required not just of Engelhard's day-to-day leaders, but of its board of directors. The criteria for board selection literally includes independence, wisdom, and integrity, as well as an inquiring mind, a willingness to speak one's mind, and the ability to challenge and stimulate management.[2] Engelhard believes a leader cannot possibly be truly "committed to the cause" without these attributes.

Step Two: Know the Company's Systems and Values

But what *are* the values and goals? Have they been stated? Have others "bought into" them? Being a leader automatically makes a person vulnerable to questions of substance about any "new" management system— sensible questions like, "What are we doing now? What do you intend to change, and why?" So the second step in leading a transition is for the leaders to know their way around the system, because they will be looked to as the leaders of the quality improvements as well.

Fred Smith, Ray Marlow, Jamie Houghton, and their executive staffs created their companies' visions, missions, policies, and values. To do that, they looked at other companies' visions, studied their customers and their competition, assessed their own companies' strengths, and pinned down exactly what their companies stood for and aspired to achieve. Their values are presented later in this chapter. Each of the leaders has had to explain these values again and again, in myriad ways, to make sure the message sticks.

The explanations are often one-on-one. Fred Smith visits FedEx facilities and employees weekly; he invites their questions about any topic. After Ray Marlow introduced his company's quality policy, he went over it a phrase at a time at six straight monthly all-employee meetings. Years later, he still reviews the policy and talks about the company's quality pledge and quality tools. "You've got to keep it in front of people," he says.

At the end of one meeting, during which he had been stressing the understanding and use of Marlow's eight quality tools, an hourly employee asked Marlow—in front of the whole group—if he, Marlow, could name the tools. "I got 'em," Marlow said proudly. In so doing, Marlow showed his people that he could "walk the talk."

That is what quality leaders are asked to do every day. As the embodiment of their company's values, they are under constant surveillance to see whether they will break stride. If they do, people become cynical about the value of the quality improvement process, and that cynicism poisons the process. We have all had leaders who say one thing and do another, and we are smart enough to know that what they do is what is really important. Leaders who talk about quality and actively participate in the quality improvement process leave no doubt about where their company's priorities lie.

After years of headlines about major corporate financial scandals—capped with senior management making off with profits, getting caught, and being prosecuted, but not before padding their own nests substantially—most workers are understandably wary. Today's leaders would also be wise to spearhead development of a corporate ethics policy, a written document that outlines a company's guidelines about potentially sticky on-the-job situations like accepting gifts from clients, calculation and disbursement of bonuses, how sensitive information is disclosed to the public and/or the news media, and so on. Leaders create and encourage an atmosphere of trust by making sure everyone knows the rules, and by living by them as well.

Step Three: Participate in the Quality Process

Active participation, the third step in leading the transition, can take many forms. At FedEx, Fred Smith has been directly involved in the development of every quality process and system the company has implemented. He founded the company on a belief that customers would value a time-definite express delivery service, then used on-time delivery as the company's primary measure of performance. In the late 1980s, he helped develop a more comprehensive, proactive, customer-oriented measure of customer satisfaction and service quality: the Service Quality Index (SQI).

Table 2-1 FedEx's Service Quality Indicators	
Indicator	**Weight**
1. Damaged packages	10
2. Lost packages	10
3. Missed pickups	10
4. Complaints reopened	5
5. Overgoods (lost and found)	5
6. Wrong-day late deliveries	5
7. Abandoned calls	1
8. International	1
9. Invoice adjustments requested	1
10. Missing proofs of delivery	1
11. Right-day late deliveries	1
12. Traces	1

The SQI measures 12 indicators that FedEx has determined are most important for customer satisfaction and service quality (see Table 2-1). As Smith said, "We believe that service quality must be mathematically measured." The company tracks these 12 indicators daily, individually and in total, across its entire system. Each indicator is weighted: the greater the weight, the greater the impact on customer satisfaction.

One of FedEx's service goals is to reduce the totals of the SQI every year. Service is one of the company's three overall corporate objectives: *People-Service-Profit*. Every manager at FedEx, including Fred Smith and the senior executive staff, has annual benchmarks for each of these three corporate objectives. Smith sets his own personal objectives with input from the board of directors, and the process cascades through the organization from there. Managers are evaluated on how well they achieve their objectives.

To develop and implement such broad measures and objectives, Smith and his staff had to understand the company's quality objectives, its customers' needs, and the potential effectiveness of SQI as a measure and motivator. Many other service companies are still trying to figure out what to measure. Smith led the development of a measure that tells all FedEx employees, every day, exactly how they are doing on customer satisfaction and service quality. Active participation in the quality improvement process doesn't get any better than that.

Good leaders know that having a customer focus is critical. At FedEx, each officer is assigned responsibility for the major customers in a sales district. Smith and his staff talk to customers continuously at the executive level to make sure their needs are being met.

Quality leaders reinforce a customer focus by investing their own time in improving customer relationships. Marlow Industries has a standing rule: Every customer (which means anybody from a customer's company) who visits Marlow meets with either Ray Marlow or Barry Nickerson, the president and chief operating officer.

"We're not like Xerox," Marlow says. "We don't have something we sell to thousands of customers. Our products are customized for a select group, and we develop relationships with those customers. As we enter the commercial market and our customer base expands, that's much more difficult. You stay on the road a lot."

Leaders like Marlow, Smith, and Houghton spend a great deal of their time discussing customer requirements and quality with employees, customers, suppliers, distributors, and other groups that affect, and are affected by, their companies. Later in the chapter, we look at how they do this.

Step Four: Integrate Quality into the Management Model

Once a leader is committed to management by quality, understands its basics, and physically participates in the transition, the fourth step is to institutionalize systems management as the company's business management model.

An example was reported by the International Human Resource Group in Westport, Connecticut, which surveyed many of the Baldrige Award winners in the early 1990s to see what roles the HR departments played in these companies. A common thread is that human resources functions not as a single, monolithic organization, but in partnership with other departments, serving all the departments as if they are customers. In some winning firms, there is at least one HR representative assigned to every department or business unit. In this way, communication is integrated directly into the system. Training programs are introduced, benefits programs are adapted, and quality standards are consistently reinforced—all based on what is actually happening in the departments, not strictly on a board of directors' theories or projections. The company president can't be everywhere at once; but HR can carry the flag, working with department heads to focus on the goals, determine how well progress is being made, and also bring feedback to the executive board from employees. The result is greater ability to respond to changes, while keeping quality top of mind.

This is critical for a company like FedEx. About half of its employees are frontline, with direct customer contact, so they must all understand and deliver the same quality standards—no matter what the weather, the size of the package, or the logistical hassles involved in getting it from Point A to Point B. FedEx senior executives created an integrated system that made customer satisfaction and service delivery into corporate strengths.

Marlow Industries hails integration as a breakthrough for the company. "We made the mistake of having two structures—business and quality—when we started to pursue quality," said the company's former chief operating officer Chris Witzke. "We kept moving quality into the business area until we collapsed business and quality into one structure." To reflect this broader scope, Marlow changed the name of its "Total Quality Management Council" to the "Total Quality Culture Council."

EXPRESSING COMPANY VALUES

FedEx, Corning, Marlow Industries, and other quality leaders build quality improvement processes on clear and precise quality values. These are not idealistic wish lists to be framed and displayed in every corporate conference room, but the values that can guide a company's quality efforts in tangible, measurable ways.

FedEx has three corporate goals: *People–Service–Profit*. As Smith summarizes, "when people are placed first, they will provide the highest possible service, and profits will follow." The three corporate goals are translated into measurable objectives throughout the corporation. Progress on the people goal is determined by the Leadership Index, a statistical measurement of subordinates' opinions of management's performance. Service is based on the Service Quality Indicators described earlier. The profit goal is a percentage of pretax margin, determined by the previous year's financial results. Success in meeting the objectives for each area determines the annual bonuses for management and professionals. (The bonuses can account for up to 40 percent of these employees' total compensation.)

FedEx has two primary corporate quality goals:

- 100 percent customer satisfaction after every interaction and transaction
- 100 percent service performance on every package handled

Of course, many people doubt the ability to achieve 100 percent of anything. "We acknowledge that 100 percent is impossible," says Smith, "but that doesn't keep us from striving to achieve it. We have to be wary of being satisfied with 99 percent performance because the law of large numbers catches up with us. When you're handling millions of packages a day, a 1 percent failure rate is totally unacceptable. We believe the road toward 100 percent is worth the effort."

The business philosophy of Marlow Industries is expressed in its quality policy:

For every product or service we provide, we will meet or exceed the customers' expectations, without exception. Our standard of performance is: Do It Right Today, Better Tomorrow.

Marlow even has a pledge that states each employee's personal commitment to quality:

I pledge to make a constant, conscious effort to do my job right today, better tomorrow, recognizing that my individual contribution is critical to the success of Marlow Industries.

The policy and pledge are further defined by Marlow's quality values:

- Senior executives must be the leaders.
- Employees have the authority to make decisions and take actions on their own.
- Honesty with customers, employees, and suppliers.
- Meeting the customers' requirements.
- Quality comes from prevention.
- Anticipate problems and take appropriate action before the problem happens.
- Do it right the first time.
- Continuous improvements toward customer satisfaction.

Notice that there is nothing radical or earth-shaking on the list. In fact, many companies espouse similar values. The difference is that Marlow Industries actually lives by them. The company's leaders will allow nothing less.

When Corning started its quality initiative in 1983, one of its first tasks was to identify the principles, actions, and strategies on which its system would be built. It introduced the foundations of its system in January 1984 and has been improving them ever since.

Corning's purpose is stated thusly:

To deliver superior, long-range economic benefits to our customers, our shareholders, our employees, and the communities in which we operate. We accomplish this while living our values in an operating environment that enables corporate and personal growth to flourish.

The company has seven values that encompass its moral and ethical standards:

1. Quality
2. Integrity
3. Performance

4. Leadership
5. Innovation
6. Independence
7. The Individual

To help employees understand how to act on these succinct value concepts, Corning has also identified eight operating environment dimensions. The first five describe how to do business; the last three depict how to work together:

1. Customer-focused
2. Results-oriented
3. Forward-looking
4. Entrepreneurial
5. Rigorous
6. Open
7. Engaging
8. Enabling

COMMUNICATING COMPANY VALUES

All three of the role models excel at communication. As mentioned, Ray Marlow and his senior staff members use monthly all-employee meetings to reinforce the company's customer focus and values. During these meetings, Marlow hands out the Employee of the Month Award; there are also training awards. Senior managers frequently talk to employees in the manufacturing area, go to lunch with different employees, and act as mentors for employee effectiveness teams. They are involved in quality training, either as instructors or as students. All employees are required to take a certain number of hours of training; all officers are required to take the training as well as to teach some of the courses.

Marlow's leaders discuss quality regularly with their customers and suppliers, and they have been strong quality advocates outside the company. Ray Marlow helped found the Texas Quality Consortium, a group of small companies that meets to discuss W. Edwards Deming's 14 principles of management. Marlow and his staff made 25 presentations on quality the year before the company won the Baldrige Award; they have made many more since then. In 1993, Ray Marlow helped to organize and incorporate Quality Texas as a not-for-profit state quality award presented by the Governor of Texas.

Unlike Ray Marlow, Fred Smith does not have the luxury of communicating his quality values to a few hundred people in one building. To provide what Smith calls "timely communication of the company's quality goals to our far-flung workforce," FedEx invested $8 million in FXT, a television network that connects 1,200 downlink sites in the United States and Canada and six facilities in Europe. Each weekday morning, a five- to seven-minute morning news program is broadcast from FedEx's Memphis headquarters. The program includes features on company products and services, stock prices, package volume and service performance, forecasts of the day's volume, and frequent segments on company quality goals and initiatives.

"Open, two-way communication is absolutely essential to achieving our quality goals," says Smith. In the company's early days, Smith and his senior executive staff held regular meetings at a local hotel. Any employee could attend these "family briefings." When FedEx outgrew such meetings, the television network became the vehicle for continuing two-way communication. Smith appears on the network live every six months or so, to discuss the state of the company and to field questions from employees throughout the FedEx network.

Employees are not afraid to ask tough questions; open communication is part of the company's culture. During Smith's weekly forays to FedEx facilities, he asks for input and questions from the employees he meets. He and his staff also reinforce the company's customer focus and values by establishing and monitoring measures tied directly to each. On a quarterly basis, representatives of about a dozen employee teams come to Memphis to share their "quarterly success stories." Smith frequently opens these meetings, then he and his staff remain to hear about the improvements being made—and to show by their presence that quality efforts at every level are important to FedEx.

Communication about quality extends to FedEx's customers and suppliers. "Fred Smith talks to customers continuously," says Tom Martin, managing director of public relations, "and he encourages his direct reports to do the same. Being assigned a sales district (which every senior executive is) certainly encourages communication with customers."

"I try to take a business trip to a different district every month," says Smith, "and to schedule one or two customer visits per trip."

The cumulative effect of this unrelenting communication about quality is the creation of a quality organization. Marlow describes it as "consistency of purpose," the leader's responsibility to nurture an environment where excellence is everyone's goal.

In an article in *Total Quality Management* magazine, Houghton described what leadership meant to him:

> In the end, quality is something that becomes deeply personal. It is a commitment to a way of life—to a way of interacting with others. Quality isn't just a little pool for wading. It is an ocean. If you

don't take the plunge, if you don't totally immerse yourself, you can't hope to coax a whole organization to jump in. That's why quality starts at the top, with the leaders of an organization.

IMPROVING AS A LEADER

According to the new business management model, the key to improving as a leader is to establish key indicators of performance, track those indicators, and develop actions to improve. Ray Marlow monitors how many customer contacts he has, studies customer service measurements to determine how well he is leading in that area, and regularly reviews charts and graphs posted throughout his facility to see whether the company is improving.

Quality leaders tend to apply what they say about quality to what they do. "I'm always trying to find ways to engineer out rework," says Fred Smith, "and to be more effective in dealing with my external and internal customers. Not a quarter goes by that we don't formally evaluate that." Smith believes the ultimate measures of his effectiveness as a leader are FedEx's measures of customer satisfaction and service quality. "The name of the game is driving the Customer Satisfaction Index up and the Service Quality Indicator score down."

In addition to working to improve their own leadership skills, the leaders at FedEx and Corning have helped develop a set of criteria or attributes that define leadership for their organizations.

In 1989, an internal FedEx task force implemented a Leadership Evaluation and Awareness Process (LEAP). An employee must complete this process before becoming a first-line manager. When FedEx implemented the process, its manager turnover rate dropped from 10.7 percent to 1.7 percent.

The LEAP identified three "transformational leadership behavioral dimensions" and six "leadership qualities" as the most important attributes a candidate for management must have in a people-first work environment. The dimensions are

1. **Charismatic leadership.** Charisma derives from an ability to see what is really important and to transmit a sense of mission to others. It is found in people throughout business organizations and is one of the elements that separate an ordinary manager from a true leader.
2. **Individual consideration.** Managers who practice the individualized consideration concept of transformational leadership treat each subordinate as an individual and serve as coaches and teachers through delegation and learning opportunities.

3. **Intellectual stimulation.** Leaders perceived as using intellectual stimulation successfully are those who encourage others to look at problems in new ways, rethink ideas, and use problem-solving techniques.

The leadership requirements are

1. **Courage.** A courageous leader stands up for unpopular ideas, does not avoid confrontations, gives negative feedback to subordinates and superiors when appropriate, has confidence in his or her own capability, desires to act independently, and does the right thing for the company or subordinates in spite of personal hardship or sacrifice.
2. **Dependability.** A dependable leader follows through, keeps commitments, meets deadlines, takes and accepts responsibility for actions, admits mistakes to superiors, works effectively with little or no contact with a supervisor, and keeps a supervisor informed on progress.
3. **Flexibility.** A flexible leader functions effectively in a changing environment, provides stability, remains objective when confronted with many responsibilities at once, handles several problems simultaneously, focuses on critical items, and changes course when required.
4. **Integrity.** A leader with integrity adheres to a code of business ethics and moral values, behaves in a manner that is consistent with the corporate climate and professional responsibility, does not abuse management privilege, gains trust/respect, and serves as a role model in support of corporate policies, professional ethics, and corporate culture.
5. **Judgment.** A leader with judgment uses logical and intellectual discernment to reach sound evaluations of alternative actions, bases decisions on logical and factual information and consideration of human factors, knows his or her own authority and is careful not to exceed it, uses past experiences and information to gain perspective on present decisions, and makes objective evaluations.
6. **Respect for others.** A leader with respect for others honors rather than belittles the opinions or work of others, regardless of their status or position in the organization, and demonstrates a belief in each individual's value regardless of each individual's background.

These dimensions and qualities define leadership at FedEx, and prove if nothing else that the senior executives have thought carefully about what a leader is.

At Corning, the criteria for leadership at any level are honesty, vision, caring, strength, and change. To be a leader within the Corning network, there are 10 key traits a person *must* have, and 10 more traits he or she *should* have.

To be a leader, one *must*

1. Believe in and live the corporate values.
2. Develop and communicate a rallying vision.

3. Be a strategic thinker.
4. Be a risk taker.
5. Have a proven track record.
6. Be a catalyst for change.
7. Earn the trust of the organization.
8. Be a listener and an enabler.
9. Develop good, strong subordinates for succession.
10. Be an optimist and have a sense of humor.

To be a leader, one *should*

1. Have different work experiences.
2. Have an international orientation.
3. Be financially adept.
4. Understand and know how to deploy technology.
5. Be able to deal with ambiguity.
6. Be skilled at alliance management.
7. Have a balanced, healthy lifestyle.
8. Contribute to the local community, both personally and financially.
9. Be active in at least one business activity outside Corning.
10. Be active in at least one nonbusiness, nonlocal activity.

This list, drawn from more than 140 leadership characteristics identified during research, reflects Corning's culture and the values of its leadership. Like FedEx's dimensions and qualities, Corning's criteria remove leadership from the realm of the mysterious and make it tangible and measurable. And what can be measured can be improved.

The list also redefines leadership for the new business management model. "The way I see it, leadership does not begin with power, but rather with a compelling vision or goal of excellence," says Fred Smith. "One becomes a leader when he or she is able to communicate that vision in such a way that others feel empowered to achieve success."

A SHIFT IN THINKING

A new business management model requires a dramatic shift in thinking among senior executives who must resist a "systems view" of their organizations. The model is not something that can be fit into the way a company already operates, nor is it something that can be done in addition to normal operations. It is a different way of leading and managing, and can change employees' views of the company, of their own "systems," and their roles in making improvements.

This is why leaders talk about taking a leap of faith when they embrace new principles. Despite evidence that the "TQM" model works, when leaders are confronted with the task of changing a corporate culture, they soon realize that many within the culture hate (or at least, resent) the change. This means the leaders must first accept *their* responsibilities in the new management model. They, in turn, "model" the model to others. We discuss many of those responsibilities here and in other chapters, but for now, put yourself in a leadership role at the company of your choice, and follow along with this summary that shows how you affect, and would be affected by, the introduction of a new management model:

- You lead the quality improvement process. No one else in the organization can lead it as effectively.
- You are a quality zealot. The leaders introduced throughout this text do not lead the improvement effort by spending all their time strictly on financial matters; they walk, talk, and think quality.
- You understand your customers' needs and expectations. Because quality is defined by the customers, you need to spend time with them and compare what you learn with what others in your company know about them and about your markets. Only then will you know whether your system is truly being driven by customers' needs and expectations.
- You empower everyone in the company to meet customers' needs and expectations. You get all employees involved in improving quality and customer satisfaction. You promote training so that they can achieve their objectives. You establish rewards and recognition that encourage employees to work together toward common goals. You create a culture in which every person is considered a valuable resource and employee satisfaction is seen as an indicator of customer satisfaction.
- You manage by studying facts. If you think of your business system as a car, you have within view all the gauges and indicators you need to assess the condition of the system and to decide what to do next.
- You promote process improvement. If you were to step back and observe any part of your company for any period of time, you would notice that work follows different processes. The better you manage the processes, the more productive people are and the higher their quality of work is. You can help the company focus on process improvement by studying the processes in which you are involved.
- You use a strategic planning process to keep the company focused. Quality leaders establish clear missions, goals, and objectives for their organizations, then use the planning process to translate corporate objectives into team and individual actions.
- You demand rapid, continuous improvement. A business exists to meet customer requirements and to achieve superior operational performance. By setting ambitious goals for each purpose, you challenge people to

change and improve, to channel their energy, knowledge, and determination toward a shared vision.

Leaders such as Ray Marlow, Jamie Houghton, and Fred Smith run their companies according to this paradigm. As the results of Marlow Industries, Corning, and FedEx demonstrate, such a systems approach to leadership results in profitable, successful organizations.

CHAPTER SUMMARY

This chapter "starts at the top" by focusing on what it takes to be a good leader. Of course, it helps to be the kind of person who enjoys being in the public eye, making speeches ("preaching" about quality), interacting with employees, and even having a little fun at company meetings. But can a leader be a leader without all the charisma? That depends largely on his or her innate ability to focus intently on the business, where it is headed and how it is going to get there profitably, as well as the ability to convince others of this vision.

As Jamie Houghton of Corning put it, it is about "performance over time, not charisma." Good leaders combine knowledge of what the customers need, what the organization is actually capable of doing, and what its competitors are doing, to craft the strategy and direction for the company. They communicate this information consistently, and their actions back up their verbiage—or as the saying goes, they "walk the talk." If these don't match up, building trust among their troops is difficult at best. The requirements for the modern company leader include establishment of and adherence to standards of corporate ethics as well as product-, quality-, and profit-related goals.

Many firms, including those profiled in the chapter, have written lists of the qualities and behaviors they expect from their leaders. While some of the characteristics are subjective—more like personality traits than conduct that can be learned in business school—they provide an overview of the type of person who can guide and inspire others. A successful leader possesses enough of these traits, whether inborn or gleaned from experience, to impart a vision and empower (instead of controlling) subordinates to carry it out.

Yes, business still gets done without a visionary leader. But not very well, and not for very long—and quality often suffers in the process.

DISCUSSION QUESTIONS

1. Do you agree or disagree with FedEx's 100 percent satisfaction goals as described in this chapter? Do you think they are realistic or not? Does realism *matter*, in terms of a company's public relations?

2. If you were to put the four "steps" listed in this chapter on a timeline, what would you feel would be realistic for a company of less than 300 employees to achieve each of them, in order?

3. You've read the philosophies of a couple of companies in this chapter. Select a company that's *not in this book*, and from what you know about them, draft your own version of their "corporate quality policy" or purpose statement, of no more than a paragraph. (Use your own words, not something you find on their Web site!)

4. Examine the leadership criteria at Corning. What do you think makes the difference between corporate "cheerleading" and meaningful commitment?

5. Of the eight points at the end of the chapter (about how leaders affect, and are affected by, a new management model), which one would be the most difficult for you to achieve as a leader, personally? Why?

ENDNOTES

1. Employee Trust and Organizational Loyalty poll, Society of Human Resource Management (Alexandria, Virginia) and CareerJournal.com (Princeton, New Jersey), July 27, 2004.
2. *Corporate Governance Guidelines 2004*, Engelhard Corporation, Iselin, New Jersey.

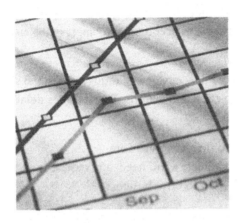

Customer Focus

The famous circus owner P. T. Barnum said, "Every crowd has a silver lining." In the corporate world, a business will never know just how much silver its "crowd" of customers can deliver unless it truly understands them.

Here's another quote you probably *have* read or heard: "The new business management model is customer-driven." Unfortunately, so many people say this so often that it rarely even registers anymore. And what does it really mean? Isn't every company customer-driven if it delivers products and services to customers?

The answer is no, not by a long shot. "Customer-Driven Excellence" is among the Baldrige Core Values. According to the criteria for 2005 award applicants, it is a strategic concept that goes beyond reducing defects and errors. It encompasses "making things right" when customers are dissatisfied, knowing their needs well enough to anticipate them, and differentiating products and services accordingly to impress the customers and gain their loyalty.

In this chapter, we explore how customers' requirements and satisfaction dictate a company's direction and actions. This includes details about how successful companies

- Determine exactly who their customers are
- Decide what these customers want, need, and require from them
- Use customer satisfaction to drive business

We will continue the discussion in Chapter 7, with a look at how companies use their customer focus data to manage individual customer contacts and build relationships.

There are several excellent reasons for having an intensive customer focus—or, as senior executives of Xerox Corporation aptly put it, "customer obsession":

1. **It improves financial returns.** This is how Xerox sees it: Putting the customer first leads to fully satisfied customers who exhibit superior customer loyalty, which improves market share, which improves financial returns. Xerox launched a Customer First initiative that included training for all employees in 1997.
2. **It fulfills certain needs of Xerox's people.** Employees have a basic human need to receive positive feedback from those whom they serve. Giving them permission to do what's right for customers enables them to provide a quality of service that their customers will value.
3. **It provides an integrating focus for empowerment.** Customer First is a unifying vision that guides everyone's efforts toward shared goals.
4. **It can be institutionalized to provide a sustainable competitive advantage.** When customers perceive that the entire organization is obsessed with satisfying their requirements, they become loyal, not because of the product's features and price, but because they know Xerox supports their business goals.

Xerox learned long ago what many companies still struggle with—that total customer satisfaction must be a system-wide goal in order to be achieved. This means that a company's most important job is to know what its customers expect and require. The end result is a happy crowd that delivers the "silver lining" with its repeat business.

The corporations whose policies are profiled in this chapter include Xerox, IBM Rochester, L.L.Bean, the Louisville Bats, and Staples.

Xerox. This Fortune 500 company is so well known that, like FedEx, its name has become a verb! ("Can you Xerox this for me, please?") The company's service-marked term for its specialty is "Smarter Document Management," with more than 250 types of document-processing equipment, including copiers and other duplicating equipment, electronic printers and typing equipment, networks, workstations, and software products. The U.S. Customer Operations Division featured in this chapter employs about 35,000 people and is the largest group within Xerox; the total company headcount is now more than 59,000. Xerox Business Products and Systems won the Baldrige Award in 1989.

IBM Rochester. This company develops and manufactures commercial computer server systems, a half-million of which have been installed worldwide. The Rochester, Minnesota, facility employs 5,000 people who are responsible for product development and manufacturing. IBM Rochester won the Baldrige Award in 1990.

L.L.Bean. This is the world's largest mail-order catalog company in the outdoor specialty field. It employs about 9,300 people during peak times. Headquartered in Freeport, Maine, the company distributes more than 100 million catalogs annually, in addition to an impressive e-commerce division that, in recent years, has grown more than twice as fast as its retail sales division. Total annual sales have topped $1.2 billion. Of the more than 19,000 items stocked for catalog sales, 90 percent carry the L.L.Bean label.

The Louisville Bats. In the world of sports (which is surely as competitive as any other type of retail) the Bats are a Triple-A (minor-league) baseball club. One of 28 Triple-A teams, the Bats play a rigorous 144-game schedule. The club has undergone several major changes in the past decade, including a name change (from the Louisville Redbirds to the Louisville River-Bats, which was shortened to "Bats" in 2001), and a change of team affiliation, from the St. Louis Cardinals to the Cincinnati Reds. However, smart marketing has given them the honor of being the first minor-league franchise to attract a million fans in one year, primarily by providing entertaining events for their customers. The Bats moved into a beautiful new stadium of their own (instead of sharing one with the University of Louisville) in April 2000.

Staples. This fast-growing, deep-discount office supply retailer operates office products superstores throughout the United States and in five European countries. Merchandise includes general office supplies, computers and software, electronics, office furniture, and business services such as photocopying, binding, and printing. In five years, the company grew from 650 to 1,600 locations and from 26,000 to 60,000 employees. Based in Westborough, Massachusetts, Staple's Contract and Commercial Division operates a mail-order delivery business as well as regional and national contract stationer operations.

IDENTIFYING AND SEGMENTING CUSTOMERS

Most companies assume they know who their customers are, and they are probably right. Most companies also measure or monitor customer satisfaction. But there are degrees of knowledge in each of these areas, based on the types (and depth) of research done and how it is used to satisfy customer requirements and spearhead continuous improvement.

As an example, let's go to the ballpark—a major-league-quality park, for a minor-league team that was doing well enough to justify moving to a classy new stadium of their own in 2000. The Louisville Bats maintain a database containing 90 percent of their customers' names, addresses, and phone numbers, which they use for target marketing and frequent direct mailings. The primary targets: children and their parents. "Kids, on the weekend, probably have 80 percent of the say in where the family goes," said Dale Owens, a former general manager of the team when it was still the Redbirds. "Parents want to do something with their children. Our goal is to entertain and to provide a sense of community." Owens began targeting the kids-and-parents group in the 1990s because of his own memories of going to Louisville Colonels games when he was a child. The focus has paid off handsomely: Attendance at Redbirds games has grown steadily since then, now topping 9,300 fans per game and leading the league in ticket sales for five years in a row (1999 to 2004).

Of course, few companies have the luxury of being able to relate so directly to their customers. Employees who are making, selling, or servicing computers, copiers, or office products have to work a little harder to put themselves in the customers' shoes. Some companies are making it easier by involving customers in such activities as strategic planning, product design and development, process management, and benchmarking. They are encouraging employees to participate in customers teams, interact with their peers at the customers' companies, and be aware of customer satisfaction measurements and results. They know what the Louisville Bats have acted on: *The better you understand your customers, the more likely you are to satisfy their requirements.*

Staples pursues a variety of marketing strategies to attract and retain target customers. This is known as **multichannel marketing**, making goods available in several different ways (in retail stores, online, by mail-order, and so on) to appeal to customers' need for convenience. Staples' marketing arsenal includes broad-based media advertising (radio, television, newspaper circulars, and print ads), as well as catalogs and a sophisticated direct-marketing system. In addition, the company markets to larger companies through a combination of direct-mail catalogs, customized catalogs, and a field sales force. Technology allows Staples to track the buying habits of many of its customers, measure the response rate to various catalog marketing and promotional efforts, and respond to changes in purchasing patterns and customer demands.

In 1995, Staples launched its first customer loyalty program, called Dividend$, which rewarded top store and catalog customers with rebates and a variety of other benefits. Staples introduced the program (1) to encourage its customers to buy more and become repeat customers and (2) to create a database of its "best" customers, to help the company understand them better.

In recent years, Dividend$ has been augmented by "Staples Business Rewards®," a frequent-buyer program that rewards customers who spend more than $200 per quarter with 2 percent rebates, and customers who spend more than $1,000 per quarter with "Gold" status and 5 percent rebates. The company has also partnered with U.S. Bancorp to offer a Staples-branded business credit card, the first to be offered by an office supply retailer—and one of the only cards without an annual fee. The target? Staples' Executive Vice President of Marketing Bob Moore says it was geared specifically to small and start-up business owners. The Staples Visa Business Card ties the cardholder to the same rebate programs as other frequent-buyer customers, and offers a lower interest rate for purchases over $1,000.

To improve its marketing, L.L.Bean reexamines the way it segments its customers. The company used to survey primarily about customer satisfaction, and group customers by the frequency, size, and timing of their purchases. Revolving-door buyers, big spenders, and recent customers attracted an overbalanced amount of the company's attention. The segmentation was based on L.L.Bean's financial goals, which the company soon realized provided little guidance when it came to predicting actual buying behavior and, especially, repeat purchase potential.

So the company shifted to customer-defined segmentation. It identified a half-dozen customer groups, based on what they generally purchase from L.L.Bean. For example, a customer who usually buys sporting goods will be placed in that segment. Perhaps more importantly, the company has aligned its customer satisfaction surveys and other monitoring systems to the new segments. This allows L.L.Bean to identify and track the specific requirements for each segment, and to better predict customers' buying behavior. All of this helps the company improve customer satisfaction.

Xerox segments customers according to their industry, environment, geography, and business need and then maps that information back to Xerox's core competencies. The process involves lengthy discussions with customer groups. Xerox listens to their requirements and checks to make sure it has heard them accurately. The process also involves market analysis, to understand the general field in which Xerox is competing, the problems people have in that field, and the ways in which Xerox can help solve them. Xerox has positioned itself as "The Document Company" to help customers better manage their documents and information.

One of Xerox's core competencies is understanding document technology: how it is formed, developed, used, revised, thrown away, collaborated on, and so forth. Another core competency is work flow. These core competencies, combined with the customers' need to improve their work processes, revealed the juncture at which Xerox could potentially excel—that is, helping customers improve their information flow for work processes that are document-intensive. "We're about helping people solve productivity problems or take advantage of marketplace opportunities, and our focus is on document-intensive work processes," says Sam Malone, director of quality services. "That gives us the shape of the market we are after."

Xerox's process for identifying its customers and market segments gives it great insight and flexibility. Rather than fall into the trap of assuming it knows who its customers are:

1. Xerox searches for specific needs that it is well suited to meet.
2. Xerox then verifies the validity of those needs and the promise of the market by talking to, and listening to, potential customers.

Getting close to customers, talking and listening, checking, verifying, testing—this type of dialogue is endless, and priceless.

DETERMINING CUSTOMER REQUIREMENTS

As L.L.Bean discovered, it is not enough to determine levels of customer satisfaction. That makes "customer satisfaction" useful as validation of a company's performance—*after* the service is performed or the product is shipped. It is equally important to do the research that impacts the service or product *before* it is delivered.

Let's use IBM Rochester as an example. The company routinely does the following:

• Surveys its customers monthly and quarterly. The surveys ask how customers feel about all 44 attributes that are regarded as customer satisfiers (described in the next section).

- Does product-specific surveys, talking to customers of a particular product after anywhere from 90 days to a year after purchase.
- Calls all of its U.S. customers within 90 to 120 days after installing a product. This customer contact is different from the product-specific surveys.
- Has a closed-loop process for responding to customer complaints, and the complaint information is fed into its customer management database.
- Conducts a win/loss analysis for every competitive bid.
- Has a "competitive analysis team" that buys, uses, and studies competitors' products.
- Forms councils and focus groups, bringing in present and potential customers to discuss their requirements. These meetings are held annually for worldwide customers and quarterly for regional focus groups.
- Validates all its customer information with independent surveys and double-blind surveys conducted by its marketing organization.
- Aggregates customer satisfaction and dissatisfaction from a host of sources, and determines pervasive deficiencies and requirements.

Like IBM Rochester, Xerox collects customer information from a variety of sources, including the following:

- Telephone surveys, using a sample of customers who contacted Xerox during the previous month
- Monthly customer surveys, to gauge satisfaction levels
- Competitive benchmark surveys of the marketplace
- Regular focus groups, in which Xerox is not identified as the sponsor
- Ongoing customer panels to share new product ideas and gather input
- Roundtables with salespeople, to determine problems and solutions
- Market research focused on potential product opportunities
- Collaborative development with customers, in which Xerox installs prototypes at a few customer locations to see how well they work and whether they meet the customers' needs
- Competitive product analysis
- Discussions with industry experts
- Conjoint analysis, with customers, of specific product and service features
- Problems and usage reported in real time by 30,000 copiers linked by phone lines to Xerox service offices
- Collaboration with co-suppliers (such as computer hardware and software developers)

The information from these different listening posts is compiled and used to evaluate and refine Xerox's market segments and to facilitate continuous improvement. Both IBM Rochester and Xerox spend considerable time collecting, comparing, and correlating information. This is partly because of the changeable nature of the high-tech industries in which they compete, but the primary reason is that their management models are built on customer satisfaction. They have set up their businesses to move in the direction their customers point them.

Using Information Databases

Staples uses its database of customer information to build evaluation techniques that help it identify sites for new superstores. It also uses analysis of the data to set up the new store locations, anticipating the buying trends and types of services that will appeal to potential customers in the area. In addition to the database, Staples gets customer information through a variety of market research methods, including focus groups, outbound telemarketing, and customer comment cards placed in stores.

One of the great advantages of pulling everything into a database is that it offers the ability to manipulate the information, to use it as IBM Rochester, Xerox, and Staples do: grouping their customers into major markets, then extracting the precise customer requirements for each. However, the database is not a prerequisite for collecting, organizing, and using information to understand customers. These functions can be performed by teams in the senior staff, or by a company's marketing department or customer service department. The company may decide to identify key measures of customer satisfaction for each requirement, then post results on these measures so that every employee knows how things are going. The critical factor is not the database itself, but the aggregation and use of all available customer information in a timely manner.

L.L.Bean can speak to the issue of timeliness. It used to do annual customer satisfaction surveys, but it now conducts them monthly. "As a direct result of our involvement with the quality movement, customer focus has taken on a more significant role in our overall management," said Greg Sweeney who, at the time of this interview, was vice president of customer loyalty. "For example, we used to contact several thousand customers by phone or mail. That number has grown with our monthly customer satisfaction surveys and specific surveys in stores and packages and by phone.

The information fuels a new focus on customer-defined segmentation. "In the past, we had limited information about what we wanted to do—and we hoped the customers would go along with us," Sweeney added. "Now we have a better profile of our customers that allows us to develop better strategies to meet their needs."

Companies intent on staying close to their customers make it a point to factor information about dissatisfaction into the equation. L.L.Bean compiles all customer complaints and distributes that information within the company. The company uses a Product Suggestion Report to note all comments, suggestions, and complaints, broken down by area. The report allows L.L. Bean to aggregate customer feedback from a variety of sources and get it to the people who can identify the root causes of any problems. The company also asks customers, through surveys and focus groups, to compare its performance to that of its competitors.

Staples closely monitors indicators of customer dissatisfaction through a number of methods. Here is a sampling:

- Purchase patterns are reported monthly from response rates to catalog and merchandise offerings.
- Customer service measures are systematically reported. Problem orders and presidential complaints are tracked daily and reported weekly through the company's call center data collection. In addition, mystery shops are conducted and reported monthly.
- Comprehensive customer behavior analysis is performed and shared with top management quarterly. The analysis includes database patterns such as new customer additions, retention, and sales per average account. It also covers merchandise sales patterns, customer feedback, and operational performance.

Reviewing the different types of customer information collected by these companies confirms that setting up such an information-gathering organization is hard work. Gone are the days when you can assume you know your customers' requirements. Xerox's Malone talks about the "science" of understanding customer requirements: "A lot of times they can't tell us what problems they have in specific terms, only vaguely, so we must listen carefully and use our knowledge of their work processes, any new technologies, and our core competencies to guide us."

The other caution about technology is that a database is only as good as its relevance to the company. If it is not adequately maintained—that is, it is full of outdated or thorough but irrelevant details—or if it is not used and interpreted in a timely fashion, the zeal for keeping it up will quickly fade and so will its usefulness in meeting customer satisfaction goals.

USING CUSTOMER SATISFACTION TO DRIVE BUSINESS

In 1991, when the Louisville RiverBats were still the Louisville Redbirds, team management spent $300,000 to rebuild their old stadium's concession stands. In fact, in the decade before moving into their new ballpark in spring 2000, they had spent $1 million fixing up the state-owned stadium they had shared with the University of Louisville football team. Even then, the team's administrators were in the business of customer satisfaction. They made the ice cream stand bigger (so the kids could get back to the game faster), and they added closed-circuit television (so the parents would not miss the action).

Parents and their children are the Bats' target customers, and their business is satisfying those customers. Vice President and General Manager Dale Owens and his staff circulate at every home game, talking to fans to find out what they like and dislike, then using that information to make each game fun, safe, and memorable.

As with most baseball teams, this one has had a mascot over the years. The old Redbirds first developed "Billy Bird" to appeal to their youngest customers—toddlers who come to the games with their parents but are quickly bored with the game itself. Before Owens came along, the mascot was a beady-eyed cardinal that scared small children—not the desired response—so Owens hired one of the sports scene's most popular mascots, the San Diego Chicken (Ted Giannoulas), to redesign Billy Bird. Then, when the team name changed in 2001, the mascot changed accordingly. "Buddy Bat" is a larger-than-life bat (but certainly not Halloween-scary) with wings and a huge grin. The children adore him.

The RiverBats also target parents. They hired a great rock-and-roll organist to play music that couples would like. Off-duty police officers are paid to provide excellent security. A doctor is on duty at the stadium for every game. Attendants check the restrooms three times a night to make sure they are clean and well stocked. This attention to details helps create a positive experience that brings customers back.

The Bats run a lot of contests to keep fans entertained during games. For example, if a Bats' player hits a grand-slam home run on a Friday night, some lucky ticket holder wins $10,000. The team also holds promotions for 50 to 60 of its 72 home games. (By comparison, the Minnesota Twins, a major league club, have only 20 promotions during their 81-game home schedule.) For example, the Bats have experimented with things like "Quarter Night," when everything except admission costs a quarter, and Bats' staff members tape quarters to 10,000 seats (which is as much work as it sounds). "I throw all of our promotions out every year, with a few exceptions," says Owens. "Typically, we determine next year's promotions, then match sponsors with them. There are thousands of companies you can approach about supporting these events."

The Bats' focus on satisfying their customer drives the team's business. According to Owens, the average minor-league team run in the traditional way—with a few promotions, basic concessions, and the game itself as the sole entertainment—can make money drawing 250,000 people. But this team has drawn nearly 650,000 fans per season since the early 1990s. "We run it as a community asset," Owens says. "We want to pass it on to the next generation of Louisville youth. And it also happens to be a way to make money."

Few companies have the luxury of focusing on customer satisfaction to the point where making money is almost an afterthought. Efforts to satisfy customers obviously cannot be allowed to wipe out a company's financial resources, but improving customer satisfaction can still be the company's driving force. The Louisville RiverBats are making money. They could also make money while doing far less for their customers, but they have chosen their course because they want *satisfied* customers. As a result, they have a shared vision of what they wish to be: a company with a much sounder customer base, a strong competitive position in their marketplace, and a clear understanding of their customers' requirements. And they're making 650,000 customers happy in the process.

Owens and his staff get feedback from these customers at least 72 times a year, when the Bats play at home. They learn from them what works, what does not, and what they would like to see added or changed. Owens uses that knowledge to improve. He understands that customers' requirements constantly change (usually becoming more demanding), which is one reason the ball club offers a fresh slate of promotions each season.

Larger companies recognize the same dynamics at work in their customer base. "We believe that managing to satisfy customer requirements is a little like the hierarchy of needs," says Xerox's Malone. "We look at the basics people expect to have, understanding that the line keeps going up." He gives an example. People expect Xerox to be easy to do business with. In 1990, the company began offering a customer satisfaction guarantee that basically said, "If you're not happy with a Xerox product, we'll replace it at your request with no hassle, period." Malone says, "At the time, the guarantee was an industry first and a differentiator, but now others are following and it's become an expected service."

As noted earlier, Xerox aggregates into a database all the customer information it gathers. The database is then used to generate customer satisfaction levels and trends. This information is updated weekly and reviewed during regular management meetings. Always one of the first topics on the agenda, customer satisfaction data is used to identify gaps and to develop action plans that will address them. The levels and trends are also communicated to employees. Control charts for overall customer satisfaction and the supporting internal process measures are prominently displayed on walls and in work areas throughout the organization—including the boardroom, where the top management of U.S. operations meets. The trends are easy to track in the charts:

- Xerox's overall customer satisfaction has improved more than 43 percent since 1985.
- In the category of low-volume copiers, Xerox improved 33 percent, compared to a 16 percent improvement for its competitors.

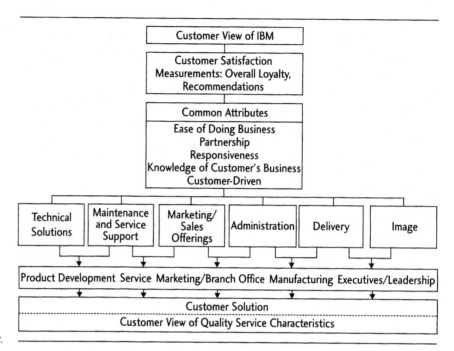

Figure 3-1 The customer view model of IBM Rochester.

- In the 1990s, when many U.S.-based manufacturers were steadily losing share to Japanese competitors, Xerox actually recaptured market share from them.
- In the category of both mid- and high-volume copiers, Xerox remains the leader.

Outside research companies confirm these trends and levels. At the same time, adverse indicators, such as sales returns and accommodation adjustments, have declined.

IBM Rochester tracks customer satisfaction in six general categories, using what it calls the customer view model, shown in Figure 3-1. Like Xerox, IBM Rochester recognizes that the items that satisfy customers are constantly changing. "Image" only recently made the list when IBM Rochester's information showed that its customers were factoring a company's image into their buying decisions. Other items, such as ease of doing business, have become attributes a company is expected to have.

IBM Rochester's goal is to be the undisputed leader in all six satisfiers: technical solutions, maintenance and service support, marketing/sales offerings, administration, delivery, and image. Under these general headings are 44 more specific satisfiers. Monthly customer surveys ask for input on all 44, except for those not valid for a particular customer. The executive team reviews the results monthly. If an area shows a potential problem, the executive in charge of the general satisfier establishes an action team to

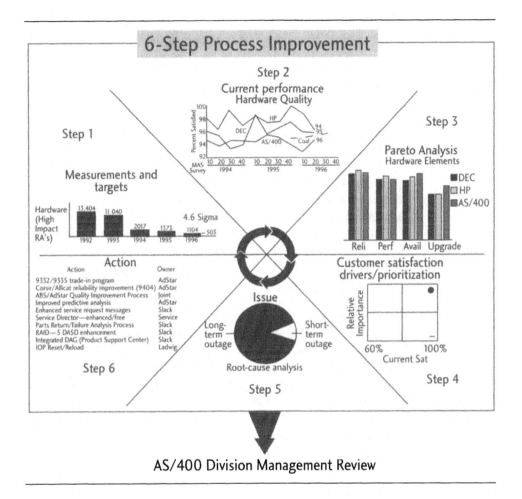

AS/400 Division Management Review

address it. Figure 3-2 shows how IBM Rochester uses customer satisfaction information to drive its business.

Figure 3-2 IBM Rochester's process for measuring customer satisfaction.

Hardware quality is a key quality indicator under the "technical solutions" satisfier identified in Figure 3-1, and the measurement of hardware quality is the first step in the closed-loop process shown in Figure 3-2. The six steps in the improvement process are

- **Step 1.** Measure and benchmark the key quality indicator.
- **Step 2.** Trend the results.
- **Step 3.** Prioritize the key elements that affect the indicator (Pareto analysis).
- **Step 4.** Use a leverage matrix to determine which elements to work on.
- **Step 5.** For each element chosen, perform a root-cause analysis to identify the drivers of dissatisfaction or the satisfaction inhibitors. Choose the key drivers that will be addressed.

- **Step 6.** Identify actions to reduce the driver defects. Assign owners to each action. Track the impact of the actions.

The process continues with measurement of the key quality indicator to gauge the effects of the improvement actions—the return to Step 1 that closes the loop.

By institutionalizing customer satisfaction, IBM Rochester steers an entire organization along a course charted by its customers. It analyzes and improves its processes in order to improve performance in its six primary satisfiers. It is not in the business of making computers or servicing computers or selling solutions; *it is in the business of satisfying customers better than anyone else.* That is what it means to use customer satisfaction to drive a business.

Often, companies that are accustomed to defining their activities by other criteria (such as departmental goals, financial targets, or quality measures) find that the shift in thinking to a total customer focus requires *deep-rooted cultural change.*

"We learned about the way customer satisfaction affects our entire system, including measuring, planning, processes, and results," said Steve Hoisington when he was senior manager of market-driven quality for IBM Rochester. "Winning the Baldrige Award in 1990 was a catalyst for expanding our use of customer satisfaction information even further. IBM Rochester has been able to determine a direct correlation between customer satisfaction and business results, including revenue, market share, and stock price."

Today, Hoisington is vice president of quality at Johnson Controls, and has been a Baldrige Award examiner for more than a decade, holding applicants to the same high standards of performance as he helped to introduce in the 1980s at IBM Rochester.

THE BOTTOM-LINE RESULTS OF CUSTOMER FOCUS

In addition to companies' internal feedback mechanisms, there are a number of external measurements that offer a look at what customers are thinking and doing. For example, at the University of Michigan's Stephen M. Ross School of Business, a model was created in 1994 to test overall customer satisfaction. Known as the American Customer Satisfaction Index (ACSI), faculty members track the ups and downs of consumers' attitudes by compiling performance data for 7 economic sectors, 39 industries, and more than 200 corporations and government agencies. Much of the data is gathered the (relatively) old-fashioned way—by telephoning more than 65,000 consumers per year and asking their opinions.

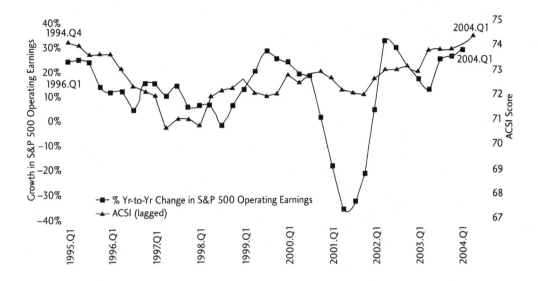

Figure 3-3 ACSI and annual percentage growth in S&P 500 earnings.

The premise of the ACSI is that satisfied customers are real (if intangible) economic assets to the companies with which they choose to do business. Interestingly, when compared to both earnings and shareholder value over the same time periods, the correlations are evident.

From the graphs, shown in Figures 3-3 and 3-4, we can deduce that when customers are dissatisfied, a snowball effect occurs that ultimately impacts a company's bottom line:

- Consumer spending trends decline—that is, a dissatisfied customer is less profitable than a satisfied customer. As seen in Figure 3-3, there is a lag of a few months, but the ACSI trends seem to predict corporate earnings.
- According to the ACSI data, satisfied customers are less sensitive to price increases. They're liable to buy again from a company they feel good about. If their experience was not good, they are reluctant to buy again unless the price is cut.
- When customer satisfaction is not a priority, businesses end up spending more on customer acquisition to make up for the lost ones, and more to resolve customer complaints.

On the second graph, Market Value Added represents the difference between what investors put into a company and the profits they can take out as shareholders. Companies on the top half of the chart are also those that got the highest marks for customer satisfaction.

The ACSI measurement is just one external indication of the power of customer focus. The companies profiled in this chapter stay close to their

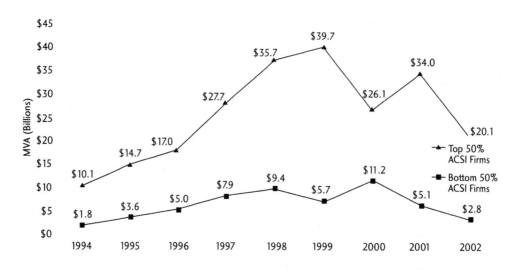

Figure 3-4 Top and bottom 50 percent of ACSI firms.

customers in a variety of ways and develop the strong customer loyalty that results in strong financial performance.

CHAPTER SUMMARY

In the new management model, business begins with *customer focus* and ends with *customer satisfaction*—two sides of the same coin. The customer requirements on which a company focuses its business on are the same requirements they use to measure satisfaction. Changes in customer satisfaction or requirements trigger changes in how business is done, and those changes affect customer satisfaction. In short, the management model that seems to work best is a closed-loop system, and it is driven by customer satisfaction.

This chapter broke customer focus into several steps that, together, lead the way to the Baldrige standard of "Customer-Driven Excellence." First, customer groups must be identified and segmented; then, the requirements of these customers must be clearly stated and fully understood. Only then can business processes be adapted to improve customer service and relationships. In this chapter, several examples are presented for each step, ending with improved bottom-line results for customer-focused companies.

The chapter also mentioned the extensive use of databases. The technological age allows companies to collect endless amounts of data about the purchasers (and would-be purchasers) of their products. The caveat is that too much information is almost as troublesome as not enough. When it is out-of-date or not especially relevant to the company's aims, the data becomes less useful as a business-building tool.

DISCUSSION QUESTIONS

1. Of all the ways that companies gather information about customers that are described in this chapter, which method do you think is the most effective, and why?
2. Some business experts say technology has failed us, because it enables a company to target its "best" customers so carefully that it ends up ignoring many other, potential customers. What do you think?
3. How would you set up a "competitive analysis team" for a retail company? What would its goals be?
4. The ACSI scores, compiled quarterly, have never fallen below 70 on a scale of 1 to 100 since the research began in 1994. If they did drop below 70, what would that indicate? If you were the CEO of a midsized company whose industry was included in the ACSI research, what would you do about it?
5. Where does employee satisfaction fit in for a retailer that is trying to focus simultaneously on customer satisfaction and bottom-line profitability? Which of the companies mentioned in this chapter (or companies with which you are familiar) seem to be the "best places to work" based on all three of these important criteria? Explain your answers.

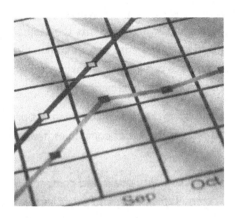

CHAPTER

4

Effective Management

There is a distinct difference between *leadership* (as discussed in Chapter 2) and *management*, which is the next area of focus. You've already learned that a company's leadership sets its vision and values, and the overall tone for how business is done. The company has done the research (Chapter 3) and knows who its customers are and what they want and need. Now it's time to use strategic planning and intelligent management to convert the vision, values, and customer requirements into company goals—and to manage the system so that the goals are pursued, day to day.

For management to be effective, everyone in an organization has to know not only *what* they are supposed to do, but *why* they are doing it. They are working to meet the goals, but they are also positioned to think strategically about how these goals can be accomplished even more effectively over time.

Therefore, the goals must be translated into *requirements* that rivet the attention of all employees on the specific improvements they can and should be making. Without these shared requirements, clearly communicated and reviewed for progress, the system is out of sync, clanking and wheezing instead of humming along with continuous improvement.

This chapter focuses on managing the quality improvement process. We examine the methods and systems that four companies have developed to accomplish the following:

• Translate their customer data, quality goals, and company values into requirements that managers, supervisors, and other employees can use.
• Use these requirements to make workable plans that align all the efforts of the organization, including quality improvement.
• Communicate these requirements and deploy the plans throughout the organization.
• Ensure that these requirements are being met.
• Update and improve their processes over time.
• Challenge or change "traditional" roles of managers and supervisors for greater flexibility.

As an example, let's briefly discuss the very first Baldrige Award winner, Motorola. Since 1988, the date of the first award, Motorola executives have given thousands of speeches about how theirs became and remains a successful company—the "big company that acts like a small company," as some have called it. For years, the standard presentation included a slide show with this theme:

We have been successful because of our management process.

There is no vacillation here, no all-encompassing list of reasons for Motorola's success—just a simple and clearly stated management process:

1. Have a set of metrics.
2. Determine results.
3. Pick a problem.
4. Address the problem.
5. Analyze the solution.
6. Move on.

"This is no magic solution," adds Paul Noakes, former vice president and director of external quality programs for Motorola—the man responsible for a good portion of those speeches. "The basic tools are there for everyone to use. The rest is a management process."

In this chapter, our corporate role models for terrific management include the Cadillac Motor Car Company, the Engelhard Corporation, Motorola, and the Ritz-Carlton Hotel Company LLC:

Cadillac Motor Car Company. This is a division of General Motors North American Automotive Operations. A Baldrige Award winner in 1990, Cadillac earned quality recognition as early as 1908, when it was the first American company to win the prestigious Dewar Trophy. Cadillac's quality leadership declined in the early 1980s, but a reorganization in 1987 spurred a transformation built on three strategies: (1) a cultural change, (2) a constant focus on the customer, and (3) a disciplined approach to planning. Cadillac says that its business plan *is* its quality plan, and it has managed to maintain and build on its luxury-vehicle image.

Cadillac appears to be targeting a slightly younger crowd with the 2005 unveiling of a slick, five-second advertising campaign to showcase higher-horsepower "V" versions of two popular Cadillac models, the XLR and STS. The company's marketing director Jay Spenchian calls the lightning-fast ads "a dramatic way of getting their attention."

Interestingly, parent company General Motors—the world's largest automaker—is also the largest health care purchaser in the United States, spending $5 billion a year on employee health-related benefits alone. Those expenses, combined with the company's huge pension fund, have resulted in a long-term competitive disadvantage over foreign automakers. This underscores the importance of each GM division working hard and driving innovation for maximum profitability, and Cadillac is no exception.

Engelhard Corporation. A corporate overview says Engelhard "converts base metals into wealth"—which means it processes them into the raw materials necessary for various types of specialized manufacturing. The company refers to itself as a "surface and metals science company," which encompasses a wide range of technologies. For example, Engelhard is a major manufacturer of catalytic parts for vehicles' emission-control systems, and it produces color pigments, performance additives, and chemical catalysts used in a wide variety of products, from cosmetics to pharmaceuticals. About half of its customers are in the United States; the rest are spread throughout the world.

Engelhard actually invented catalytic converters in the early 1970s and built a plant in Huntsville, Alabama, to manufacture them. By the early 1980s, productivity and quality were so bad that the plant was close to being shut down. Today, however, new diesel-emission regulations in many nations have meant a business boom for Engelhard-Huntsville, and the plant underwent a major expansion in 1996, and again in 2001. Among Engelhard's innovations: a high-tech filter that allows older trucks and buses to be retrofitted with pollution controls.

The Huntsville employees can proudly point to dramatic productivity gains, an excellent safety record, and low turnover rate as indicators of their success. The plant—which is now officially known as Engelhard Specialty Chemicals—has received many quality awards and citations, including the prestigious Ford Total Quality Excellence Award (only a handful of Ford's 3,300 suppliers have been so honored) and a U.S. Senate Award for Productivity, which it won in 1991. Today, Engelhard's Manager of Corporate Communications Kevin Kelly confirms that Huntsville remains the company's "flagship production facility," where new ideas are engineered and tested.

Motorola. Since winning the first-ever Baldrige Award, this leading provider of electronic equipment, systems, components, and services worldwide went on to invent the Six Sigma® methodology introduced in Chapter 1 (and now taught through its "Motorola University" organization). The company has supplied all the digital two-way radios for security personnel at the Olympic games since 1972, and it has won awards from groups as diverse as Interpol (for its contributions to international law enforcement) and the National Academy of Television Arts and Sciences (seven Emmys so far for television technology)!

Motorola employs 88,000 people in seven business segments, known as "Sectors":

- Broadband Communications (broadband products)
- Commercial, Government, and Industrial Solutions (two-way radio, voice, and data communications products)
- Global Telecom Solutions (wireless and cellular equipment)
- Integrated Electronic Systems (automotive and industrial electronics)
- Personal Communications (digital phones)
- Semiconductor Products (integrated semiconductors)
- Other Products (includes Next Level Communications, Inc.)

In 2002, the Commercial, Government, and Industrial Solutions Sector was honored with the company's second Baldrige Award.

The Ritz-Carlton Hotel Company LLC. Six years after winning its 1992 Baldrige Award, this hotel management company was bought by Marriott International, Inc.—and went on to win a second Baldrige Award in 1999! The corporate marriage has been mutually beneficial for these two ambitious partners. Ritz-Carlton moved its headquarters from Atlanta to Chevy Chase, Maryland, where it supervises the operation of about 60 business and resort hotels in 20 countries, as well as 11 international sales offices. The company employs 28,000 people worldwide.

The upscale hotelier targets primarily industry executives, meeting and corporate travel planners, and other higher-budget business travelers as its customer groups. In recent years, the company has branched out to open spas at some properties, and partnered with golf courses and luxury carmaker Mercedes-Benz to offer guests the upscale "perks" for which Ritz-Carlton has become known. At some locations, they've added luxury residential condominiums and/or vacation time-shares for sale. In 1999, the company opened The Ritz-Carlton Leadership Center to pass along its winning management concepts. More than 10,000 executives in a variety of industries have taken seminars on employee and customer retention, service excellence, and other business-building topics from the Leadership Center staff.

MAKING THE SYSTEM HUM

The four companies mentioned in this chapter have learned that, despite ownership changes and economic downturns, the way a business plans its work and manages its systems will determine its success in terms of quality improvement. That statement sounds so obvious it is almost trite, but somewhere between thinking it and actually believing it often lies a wall of disclaimers:

- Strategic planning and solid management are keys—*except* when competition is unfair.
- Strategic planning and solid management are keys—*except* when employees don't do their jobs or follow through on responsibilities.
- Strategic planning and solid management are keys—*except* when the market goes bad.

Now consider Motorola's take on it. "If we don't make a goal," says Noakes, "we've learned it's because management isn't involved enough in the process." Our role models have used several primary methods to make their systems hum. These include

- Setting challenging goals
- Developing action plans to pursue the goals
- Training people to achieve the goals

Now let's look at each company and its management philosophy.

Ritz-Carlton: Striving for "Gold Standards"

The Ritz-Carlton Hotel Company translates customer requirements into employee requirements through its Gold Standards and its strategic planning process. The Gold Standards include a credo, a motto, three steps of service and 20 "Ritz-Carlton Basics." The credo states

> The Ritz-Carlton Hotel is a place where the genuine care and comfort of our guests is our highest mission. We pledge to provide the finest personal service and facilities for our guests, who will always enjoy a warm, relaxed yet refined ambiance. The Ritz-Carlton experience enlivens the senses, instills well-being, and fulfills even the unexpressed wishes and needs of our guests.

The company's motto is "We are ladies and gentlemen serving ladies and gentlemen," and its three steps of service are

1. A warm and sincere greeting. Use the guest's name, if and when possible.
2. Anticipation of and compliance with guests' needs.
3. Fond farewell. Give them a warm good-bye and use their names, if and when possible.

The 20 "basics" include understanding and following the credo, motto, and three steps, as well as other, job-specific requirements.

Employees are expected to adhere to these Gold Standards, which describe processes for solving problems guests may have, as well as detailed grooming, housekeeping, safety, and efficiency standards. "We've taken the things our customers want most and come up with the simplest ways to provide them," says Patrick Mene, vice president of quality. "And then we continuously emphasize them. We define our employees' behavior." The Ritz-Carlton's data show that its employees' understanding of the Gold Standards is directly correlated with guest satisfaction.

Ritz-Carlton employees are charged with mastering the basics first, then improving. The requirements for improving are set through the strategic planning process. Teams that include corporate leaders, managers, and employees set objectives and devise action plans, which the corporate steering committee reviews. Quality goals draw extensively on customers' requirements, which are determined by travel industry research and the company's customer reaction data, focus groups, and surveys.

Employees also determine and respond to customer requirements at the individual level because, as Mene points out, "This is a highly personal, individual service." Ritz-Carlton's employees are trained to read customers' reactions and to detect their likes and dislikes. "You're fully deploying customer reaction detection," says Mene. Customer likes are documented on a simple form and entered into a computerized guest-history profile that provides information on the preferences of more than 250,000 repeat Ritz-Carlton guests. "When the customer returns, we know his or her personal preferences, which are distributed to the employees providing the service," Mene says. "What's unique is that employees correct and use customer reaction data to deliver premium service at the individual level. Our business management system is almost driven by the individual employees, running the business at the lowest levels."

If an employee detects a dislike, he or she is empowered to break away from the routine and take immediate positive action, to "move heaven and earth" to satisfy the customer. Any employee can spend up to $2,000 on the spot to make a customer happy. Or, the employee can call on any other employee to assist. The Ritz-Carlton refers to this as "lateral service." Such a system depends on trained, empowered, and involved employees, so the company is careful to hire perceptive people, define their behavior, and train them to serve. With more than a million customer contacts on a busy day, the Ritz-Carlton understands that its customer and quality requirements must be driven by each individual employee.

Motorola: Setting "Stretch" Goals

Motorola, Inc. celebrated its seventy-fifth anniversary in 2003—and from the beginning, it has been a very goal-oriented place to work. Motorola expects not only quality work but good ideas and improvement over time from every business unit, division, department, work team, and individual. Apparently, the philosophy has paid off! The company has documented more than $17 billion in savings to its bottom line since implementing its trademarked Six Sigma® methodology almost 20 years ago.

"I believe the fundamental reason Total Quality Management fails is because no level of expectations has been set," says Noakes. "You need *results* or people will get disillusioned—and that includes management."

Perhaps the most striking results were obtained in the time period from 1987 to 1996—the first few years after Six Sigma® implementation:

- Cumulative savings from quality improvement topped $10 billion.
- Sales increased 475 percent.

- Sales per employee tripled, while the number of employees increased 46 percent. This translates into an average increase in employee productivity of just over 12 percent per year.

To achieve these goals, Motorola had to change its system. It reduced the number of managerial and supervisory layers, and encouraged the remaining managers to function more as coaches and mentors than "police." Related functions were integrated, and employees were grouped into smaller teams to promote teamwork and, again, a greater sense of control. And the topic of quality was catapulted to the top of the agenda at every meeting—from strategy sessions to performance reviews.

Notice that every change affected the way in which managers and supervisors *managed* the process. The fundamental change in Motorola's system was to redefine management's roles and responsibilities.

Motorola's longtime "stretch goal" is 10 times improvement in quality every two years, which works out to a 68 percent *annual* improvement in whatever is being measured. Managers and supervisors are expected to reduce the amount of defects in the products and services for which they are responsible by 68 percent this year. Then they must do it again next year and the year after that. They are also expected to reduce cycle times by 10 times in five years—approximately 40 percent improvement per year. Through clearly defined goals, Motorola has focused the efforts of its managers, supervisors, and other employees on *five initiatives* that capture the company's customer focus and quality values:

1. Six-sigma quality
2. Total cycle time reduction
3. Product, manufacturing, and environmental leadership
4. Profit improvement
5. Empowerment for all in a participative, cooperative, and creative workplace

Cadillac: Planning Pays Off

In its Baldrige Award-winning application, Cadillac Motor Car Company wrote, "At Cadillac, the Business Plan *is* the Quality Plan." The business planning process that was in place when Cadillac won the award continues to spur quality improvement at Cadillac because

1. It drives an *annual review* of the division's mission and strategic objectives, to make sure they are aligned with the business environment and the mission of General Motors.
2. It guides the development and implementation of *key processes* such as simultaneous engineering and the labor-management quality network.

3. It builds *discipline* into the ongoing process of creating and achieving short- and long-term quality improvement goals.

Figure 4-1 illustrates Cadillac's planning process. It may resemble the inner workings of an automobile engine but is, in fact, a chart that details a full year of management steps and feedback opportunities, in simple steps on a timeline. It begins in June, with the executive staff reviewing current objectives to make sure they are aligned with corporate objectives. The staff then gathers relevant data (from inside and outside the organization) to assess Cadillac's strengths and weaknesses. The data includes benchmarking of competitive products and processes used by world-class companies. Key suppliers and dealers also contribute to the planning process.

Only after this thorough analysis does senior management propose business objectives for the next year in six major areas: leadership, people, quality, customer satisfaction, cost, and speed to market. The proposed objectives are reviewed across the division, and the feedback generated by this review is used to develop the final business objectives. The executive staff shares the objectives with top union leaders, company management, and employees of various internal divisions at a business planning kickoff meeting.

Next, the functional staff, plant quality councils, and human resource management develops goals and action plans that support the business objectives. "Just about everybody in Cadillac got involved in this process," recalls William Lesner, a former superintendent of manufacturing. "Plants and departments came up with their own plans to meet the division's plans." The executive staff reviews all plans, for alignment and adequacy. In December, the entire business plan is presented to all Cadillac employees at an annual state-of-the-business meeting. Implementation begins in January.

In addition to business strategy and product strategy, Cadillac has also institutionalized a "people strategy." Employees at all levels serve on people-strategy teams of 6 to 10 people, with at least one member from Human Resources. Each team looks at different issues in terms of how they will impact people—from the public's perception of Cadillac, to the development of its own workforce. The individual teams report to a senior HR Management Operating Committee.

By using the team approach and a variety of communication tools to keep its key goals and measures in front of people, Cadillac focuses everyone's efforts on activities that contribute to achieving its quality improvement goals and other business objectives.

Engelhard-Huntsville: Aiming for "Exceptional Quality"

Engelhard's version of process improvement was called *Exceptional Quality*. The entire company was trained in "EQ"—so much so that, as corporate communications manager Kevin Kelly puts it, "The EQ program has been

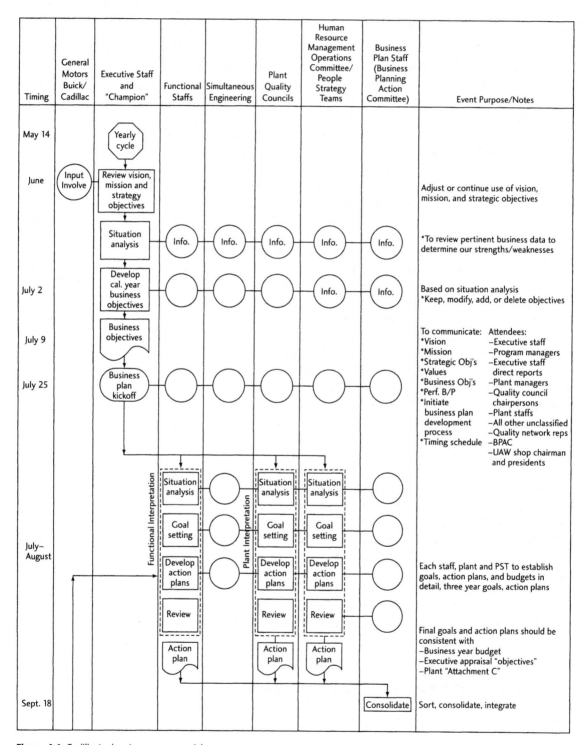

Figure 4-1 Cadillac's planning process model.

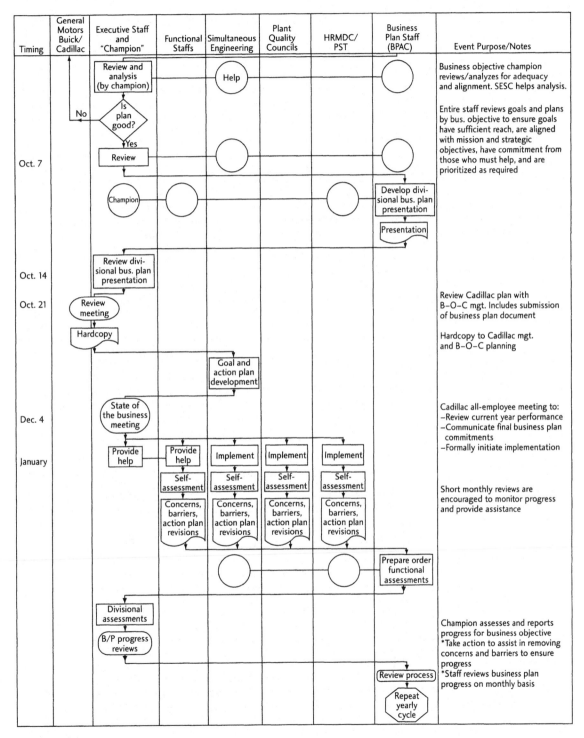

Figure 4-1 *Continued*

woven into the fabric of the company" and no longer exists as a formalized program. However, the Engelhard culture is still based on the principles that were the cornerstones cf the program: flexibility and adaptability, teamwork, the ability to train and empower each other, encouragement of innovation, and promotion of long-term relationships with customers, suppliers, and fellow employees. The twelfth principle was a pledge to "provide management support and accountability for the quality commitment and principles through direction, example, and appropriate resource commitment."

In past decades, the Huntsville plant in particular learned from experience the link between good management and success. When Joseph Steinreich became general manager of the plant in 1981, it had 590 employees. In 1982 they filed 82 grievances and lost 22 workdays because of accidents. Turnover was at 150 percent per year. Eighteen percent of product was being wasted because of poor quality. Not surprisingly, the plant was losing money. Engelhard gave Steinreich six months to turn things around or the plant would be closed.

Steinreich began by ditching the plant's confrontational management style. He instituted a supervisors' training program to foster a more people-oriented management culture. Managers and supervisors changed or were replaced. "We focused on skill building, on how to get along and solve problems," says Carl English, a former human resources manager.

More than 20 years later, employees who know the plant's history especially appreciate the dramatic changes that have occurred. Asked to list the changes during training sessions, they came up with more than 500—498 of which were positive.

In 1994, Steinreich retired and was replaced by Ken Rogers, who had been the manufacturing manager at Huntsville from 1986 to 1991. Rogers led an effort to redesign the organization around employee teams, which are now totally responsible for order fulfillment, including receiving customer orders, planning, scheduling, production, maintenance, quality control, shipping, and billing.

There have been other managers since Rogers, and business continues to grow. The plant expanded in 1996 to serve a growing worldwide market share; yet another expansion began in 2001. Engelhard is now among Huntsville's largest employers. Such growth is only one measure of Engelhard Specialty Chemicals' success. Other achievements are

- Turnover has been reduced from 150 percent to less than 3 percent annually.
- Scrap has been cut by more than 50 percent since 1994.
- The plant went without a single lost workday to accidents in 13 years.
- The plant provides 70 percent of the automotive catalysts for the Japanese market.
- Huntsville has earned top quality awards from Ford, BMW, and Honda.

Engelhard-Huntsville achieved these successes by setting specific requirements—first through a more formal, structured quality training program; and today, by empowering its managers, supervisors, and other employees to meet these requirements. Engelhard has manufacturing facilities in more than a dozen states, as well as internationally from Brazil to China, and Germany to Korea—and they all look to Huntsville to set the quality example. Annual "EQ" awards are given to individuals who live the philosophy that keeps Engelhard strong even in uncertain economic times—the philosophy that, long ago, began as an ultimatum: Turn things around, or shut it down.

HOW MANAGERS PLAN FOR CONTINUOUS IMPROVEMENT

The best strategic plans include specific measures for achieving every objective, a means for gathering and publishing data on these measures, and a process for timely review by management—and all three steps are necessary to prompt actual improvement over time.

Here is a business truism: "What gets paid attention to, gets done." Many companies find that something as simple as posting trend charts in a department immediately improves performance because people naturally want to see that their efforts are making a positive impact. The catch here is to post those trend charts not just because someone got a great idea ("Hey! Let's put up copies of some of these trend charts and let everybody know what's happening!") but because communication is built into a well-organized plan that starts at the top.

That leads us to the delineation of "who does what" in the planning process. From our real-world examples, here is what can be deduced:

- Senior executives are responsible for identifying strategies that reflect their company's long-range vision, which typically reaches five years into the future. They develop those strategies with input from people throughout the company, and often get feedback from key customers and suppliers.
- Once the corporate strategies and objectives have been determined, the planning process involves more employees. Departments, teams, and work units translate the corporate vision into specific goals, action plans, and measures. The more employees involved in the process, both in developing and carrying out the strategic plan, the greater the understanding and deployment.
- The completed plan may be circulated among major customers and suppliers for their input. The advantage of involving external people in the

process is one of *alignment*: The plan will reflect what customers need and expect, and what suppliers are able to provide and support.

Once the plan has been implemented, managers and employees report progress on action plans and objectives. The employees participate in the reporting process as members of teams that work on related issues, or as representatives of their departments.

By assigning responsibility for input and follow-up throughout the process, good managers institutionalize continuous improvement in those areas the company considers most important. The word "institutionalize" does not mean stripping the ingenuity or soul from the individuals involved. It merely refers to having an organized method by which things are done, checked, and reevaluated. The managers serve as the "translators" between the wishes and needs of senior executives (big picture) and down-line employees (daily tasks).

Of course, it is critical to identify, collect, and use the right data; otherwise, continuous improvement on the company's most important areas cannot be made. Everybody in the company "mines" and contributes the data with which they are most familiar:

- Customer service, sales, and marketing functions usually report on customer satisfaction and current and future needs.
- The human resources department describes the talent and skills that are available to achieve the company's vision, and how those talents and skills can be enhanced through involvement, training, reward, and recognition.
- The quality and finance departments outline the company's condition and the resources available for the coming year.
- Other departments provide relevant data on environmental issues, government regulations, process capabilities, supplier capabilities, and similar areas.
- Ongoing teams are formed to address major issues or problems and to summarize their progress, as well as their needs and expectations for the year ahead.

Typically, the data provided includes performance on key measures over the past year, results of competitive comparisons and benchmarking studies, survey results, and perceptions and ideas about current and future capabilities.

COMMUNICATING REQUIREMENTS COMPANY-WIDE

When asked how to manage quality, the first thing Joe Steinreich said was, "Set an example." Before his retirement, as the man responsible for initiating the Huntsville plant turnaround, Steinreich knew how important it was for managers and supervisors to exemplify the attitudes and behaviors they wish to encourage.

For example, when the EQ (Exceptional Quality) program was in its infancy, Steinreich met with his staff weekly. Every month, at one of those meetings, he asked five "monthly EQ questions" he carried with him on a laminated card the size of a credit card:

1. What are you personally doing to improve EQ?
2. What are your plans for improving the work climate in your area?
3. What are your plans for empowering your people?
4. What have you identified that needs to be fixed and how can I help you fix it?
5. What successes have you had with EQ in your area?

"I went around the table and asked each person to respond," Steinreich explained, "after I answered them first." In this way, Steinreich communicated what was important to him as a leader and to his operation. The managers took the same five questions to their direct reports, cascading the requirements throughout the organization.

Steinreich also communicated directly and frequently with employees. Every quarter, he met with all employees to discuss the state of the business, which included customer requirements and quality issues. In addition to these meetings, Steinreich and one of his human resources department managers conducted 16 to 18 roundtable discussions each year. "We selected a group of hourly people to participate, and they always asked their coworkers what they wanted or needed to know," says Steinreich. "We met for lunch or dinner. I talked briefly about the state of the company, then we went around the table for discussion and questions. If we couldn't answer a question [at the meeting], we wrote it up and posted the answer [later]." Employees made a habit of checking bulletin boards for the questions and answers.

Another form of communication helped managers and supervisors understand what employees go through to meet their requirements. The program was called "Working with the Folks." Once a month, managers and supervisors worked side by side with people in the plant for two to four hours, learning a new appreciation for the production side of the business and letting each group of people see each other in a different light.

All four of the companies profiled in this chapter emphasize *constant communication of shared values and expectations.* At the Ritz-Carlton, service standards are continuously emphasized during all work activities, beginning on day one. "On the first day of work for every employee, our president and chief executive officer personally and aggressively communicates our vision, values, and methods," said Mene. "You are expected to internalize those values and vision and to use our methods quite naturally." Service standards are reinforced during training and daily "line-ups" (brief meetings between managers and employees). The constant communication about requirements is effective.

Motorola communicates its requirements through extensive training and shared goals, from Six Sigma® quality to other initiatives. Motorola also believes that management accountability is critical. One way Motorola encourages change and communicates customer and quality requirements is through rewards and recognition. Some of these ideas have been in place since the early 1980s. For example:

- Motorola has tied 25 percent or more of its managers' bonuses to improvements in quality, customer satisfaction, and cycle time. The goal of 68 percent improvement per year clearly communicates management's requirements.
- In 1987, Motorola began paying a bonus twice a year for performance on one measure: return on net assets. If a business unit does not make its goal, no one in the unit receives the bonus. If the company does not meet its goal, no one in the company gets the bonus.
- In 1990, Motorola began a worldwide competition among teams, an idea it picked up from the Japanese. As long as a team is working on something that relates to one of Motorola's five initiatives, it can enter the competition. Some years, more than 5,000 teams compete!

The heads of all major operations are accountable for their performance. The goal is 68 percent improvement. If they are meeting the goal, there is no discussion. If the trend is on target, there is little discussion. If the trend is flat, the group identifies the causes and develops an action plan to address those that are most important. The action plan lists who is going to make what happen, and when.

Through rewards and recognition, frequent meetings, personal contact, and training, successful companies tell managers, supervisors, and other employees exactly what is expected of them. World-class performers make sure every message reflects the same central themes and key requirements. The key word here is *alignment*.

THE MANAGER'S CHANGING ROLE

So what does this mean for the mid-level manager—say, of a department? To create flatter and more flexible organizations, managers and supervisors have had to learn how to listen to their subordinates, encourage their feedback, persuade rather than demand, support their initiatives, coach, train, facilitate, and serve. This is not the job many managers envisioned. As if these expectations were not enough, the specter of "self-directed work teams" threatens to eliminate supervisory jobs altogether.

All this seems to suggest a contradiction: If the key to success is the management process, what exactly should management be doing? Answers to that question appear in this chapter and in every other chapter in this book. Managers need to understand the *system* in which they work. They need to tune that system to customer requirements and get every person and process they are responsible for humming the same tune. It is far more collaborative than an old-style "boss" role. It involves much more than issuing orders and then accepting the praise and/or heat from senior management depending on how they are carried out.

In one way, managing in this "new" style is less complicated. When performance is compared with clearly documented requirements, it becomes evident whether the requirements are being met or the employee needs assistance. The purpose of a performance review is not to fix blame, scare people into action, or punish them. Quite the opposite. Good managers work to create an atmosphere in which employees are comfortable mutually discussing the working relationship.

That does not mean evaluation of individual performance is neglected, but to close the loop here, consider what the Ritz-Carlton does. The nature of its business is certainly nothing like, say, Cadillac or Engelhard, which produce a vehicle or an emissions filter that can be used, tested, and examined. Instead, a hotel has its employees' individual performance to judge. Ritz-Carlton does this by the individual's ability to master the company's Gold Standards. Performance is measured and evaluated constantly, and assessed through opinion surveys.

Service companies have long resisted the idea of measuring performance, since at least some aspects of the product (i.e., "good service") are intangibles. When FedEx became the first service company to win the Baldrige Award, an honor it received in no small part because of its measurements system, other service industry folks were quick to claim that FedEx was really no different from a manufacturer. It handles commodities—in this case, they happen to be packages. Not at all like an insurance company. Not one bit like an ad agency. Nothing like a bank. Nope, they said, we cannot measure what we do.

"People who haven't measured," says Mene, "haven't tried. They're making excuses." The Ritz-Carlton gleans its information from training sessions, observations of performance, employee evaluations, customer evaluations, and assessments by independent groups. Patrick Mene emphasizes that the measurement of performance does not have to be statistics-controlled; it can be behavior-controlled.

"The difference between us and high-tech firms is that, when they do analysis, they have more data and more strident analysis. But even without hard data, you can still meet and talk through data analysis and prevention," Mene explains. "Nobody said you had to have Deming in your plant to look at a control chart. The only difference I find from manufacturing to service is how detailed you're going to be. Managing people isn't always detail data, it's judgment."

Process data remains at the hotel where it is gathered and is used to evaluate and improve performance. The only results that get to the corporate level are about key products, customer satisfaction, customer complaints, market share, turnover, profits, safety, and employee satisfaction. "If a hotel is worse than the norm, there's some special reason unique to that hotel," says Mene. "Usually, they can find it themselves and get it in control. If they can't, we try to help." Based on results, the Ritz-Carlton Hotels have done an exceptional job of translating customer requirements and quality values into requirements for all employees, then communicating those requirements. Ninety-seven percent of the Ritz-Carlton's customers report having a "memorable experience" while staying at one of the hotels.

CHAPTER SUMMARY

The beginning of this chapter referred to a slide in Motorola's standard quality presentation that says, "We have been successful because of our management process." It is a statement any role model in this book could make, a summary of the single overriding factor that contributes to continuous improvement and long-term success.

We examined the inner workings of four companies to find their management style is a *systematic approach* to meeting and exceeding customers' expectations. The approach includes taking the mission and vision of senior management for the company as a whole, and using as much input as possible to break these down into strategic plans that consist of specific requirements and goals. In this way, every employee at every level knows what is expected of them, and the "big picture" becomes attainable in smaller steps.

There are several keys to making a systematic approach work well. One is to involve employees at all levels in some part of the planning process. The shift in thinking is dramatic. Companies are driving out of the narrow tunnel of daily departmental supervision and discovering a panorama stretching from suppliers on one edge of the horizon to customers on the other—and all of them are encouraged to give input. The ever-changing landscape is populated with planning, extensive measurement and analysis, process improvement, and employee involvement.

A second key is to communicate the goals and requirements clearly, and often. A third key involves the managers themselves shifting out of traditional roles as overseers and disciplinarians to more flexible roles as mentors and coaches. If the work requirements are clear, employees can't blame the "bosses" for being arbitrary in performance reviews when they are not met.

In the horizontal organization, managers manage processes, not results. They become process owners, in charge of the processes that lead to customer satisfaction. As self-directed work teams have shown, people can pretty much manage themselves. It's often the system that causes the problems—so it is management's responsibility to make the system hum.

As Motorola's standard presentation summarizes on its final slide:

> *Quality is not an assignable task. It must be rooted and institutionalized in every process.*
> *It is everyone's responsibility.*

DISCUSSION QUESTIONS

1. If you could rewrite Motorola's six-point management process (from "Have a set of metrics" to "Move on") or reorganize the existing six points for retailers, what would yours be?
2. Consider the examples in this chapter, or think about other companies with which you are familiar. Then choose and briefly describe two methods you think are effective in getting employees to "buy in" to the idea of becoming more involved in the planning process. Why do you think they work?
3. Do you think the management style of facilitating and coaching is more difficult than the "traditional boss" role of supervision and discipline? Why or why not?
4. Could any of the service-oriented goals of a company like Ritz-Carlton be adapted for, say, a manufacturing company like Engelhard? Why or why not? Is quality measured differently in these two types of businesses, and if so, how?
5. How would a mid-level manager ensure that no one gets left out of the planning process? If you were a manager, how would you bring quiet or hesitant employees into the discussion? How about curmudgeons (there's one in every department) who flatly refuse to be part of the "people strategy" team? Is it necessary to *require* participation—or can that backfire on a manager?

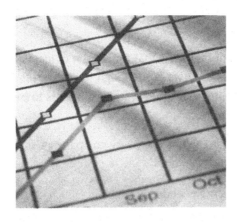

CHAPTER

5

Training

Remember McDonalds' "Hamburger University"? It began in the 1960s with less than a dozen students in the fast-food giant's management training course. McDonald's was one of the first restaurants to focus on and standardize its training techniques, and to show employees that there's a lot more to running a successful McDonald's than flipping burgers. Today, "Hamburger U." is still going strong, in 10 training centers around the world and in 22 languages! More than 65,000 unit managers have taken the courses.[1]

Whether or not a company combines its training efforts and calls it a "University"—and many of them do—training is really just another word for learning. Successful companies know that the more their employees learn—about their jobs, the products, and the company overall—the better they will become at every aspect of these jobs, including quality improvement.

A second critical aspect of training is that it is a form of morale building. It shows that a company values its workers enough to invest in them. Top-performing firms consistently treat their workers as assets to be developed, not commodities to be used.

To develop an effective training process, every company must wrestle with the questions posed in this chapter:

- What kinds of training are needed?
- Who should receive training?
- How do successful companies deliver training that actually meets performance goals?
- How do they know whether the training is effective?
- How can existing training processes be improved?

Let's meet the three quality leaders we'll examine for answers.

Eastman Chemical Company. This international firm was once a division of the well-known Eastman Kodak Company, but it spun off as a separate business in 1994—just after winning the Baldrige Award. Today, Eastman produces more than 400 types of chemicals, fibers, and plastics. None of its products are sold directly to consumers, but they are used in countless other products that consumers purchase.

The company has three divisions: Voridian is the world's largest manufacturer of the plastic (abbreviated PET) used to make soft drink bottles and food packaging. A Developing Businesses Division has been busy acquiring technology and service companies that will augment or enhance the company's business. A major chunk of the Eastman Division (where most of the inks, polymers, and adhesives are made) was sold off to other companies in mid-2004.

Eastman is headquartered in Kingsport, Tennessee, and employs about 12,000 people in more than two dozen nations worldwide.

Northern Trust Corporation. Not every company can boast a 100-year history, but this bank opened for business in Chicago in 1889. Today, it employs 9,600 people. Its ambitious plans to open 20 more branches from 2003 to 2005 bring the total to more than 100 banking locations in 15 states and seven other countries.

In an industry full of takeovers and consolidations in recent years, Northern Trust has managed to maintain its autonomy primarily by focusing on its trust business, which makes up almost half of its overall sales. Fees from trust services provide a steady income that is not dependent on volatile interest rates.

Although Northern Trust continues to lead the trust side of the banking business, it determined in 1990 that a systematic quality improvement process would improve its position. It developed a process it called "Commitment to Absolute Quality," with the goal of consistently exceeding clients' and partners' expectations while striving to become their ideal provider; and it has also created a rigorous "Gold Program" for management trainees.

Texas Nameplate Company. This two-time Baldrige Award winner is one of the smallest companies so honored—in 1998 and again in 2004! It is a 40-person, family-owned business that specializes in the design and manufacture of identification labels. You may be surprised at how many products have very specific labeling requirements, from electronic equipment to vehicles to appliances. No matter what the challenge, Texas Nameplate appears to be ready for it. Their quality goals include getting back to customers with reliable price quotes within two hours after an order is received; and shipment of finished products within 5 to 10 days. Profitability the past few years has averaged 40 percent annually. From 2001 to 2004, the number of lost TNC customers decreased from 26 to 1.

The list of awards the Dallas-based company has received reads like the brag sheet of a much larger corporation—in addition to two Baldrige Awards, there's a Texas Quality Award (1996), a Texas Business of the Year award (1997), a City of Dallas "Blue Thumb Award" for pollution control efforts (nine years in a row!), and certifications from both ISO 9000:2000 and ISO 14001, as well as Underwriters Laboratories.

DETERMINING TRAINING NEEDS

Without exception, some type of training is necessary in every company. In today's highly competitive business world, it is absolutely reasonable for employers to have high expectations of their workforce. Consider just a few of the things high-performance companies ask employees to do nowadays:

- Contribute to work unit, department, and cross-functional teams.
- Solve process problems in all parts of the company.
- Communicate with customers and suppliers, both internal and external.
- Measure and analyze indicators of performance and improvement.
- Manage processes to improve quality and reduce cycle time.
- Learn a wide range of skills to improve flexibility.
- Take the initiative in identifying and addressing improvements.
- Assume responsibility for quality and productivity.

None of these tasks is easy, and most require a host of advanced skills in such areas as teamwork, problem solving, communication, process management, and leadership. Employees cannot do any of these if they check their brains at the door. And yet, the average company spends just about 1 percent of its annual payroll on training.[2]

Before discussing the training experiences of this chapter's "all-stars," let's begin with an example from a company introduced in Chapter 4. Baldrige Award winner Motorola took nearly a decade, from 1980 to 1990, to develop a training program that did what Motorola *wanted* it to do. Initial executive training did little to improve quality, so it was back to the drawing board. Motorola then developed a five-part curriculum that included courses in SPC, problem solving, and goal setting. Every employee received about 20 hours of training—but this failed too, perhaps because the employees were not motivated to apply what they were learning, and because their managers were not receiving the same training.

From 1985 to 1987, Motorola's top 200 executives had 17 days of training in manufacturing, global competition, and cycle time. The training was then cascaded down through the company. However, when Motorola converted a facility from radio technology to cellular technology, it discovered *the wall*: elementary reading and math. Only 40 percent of the facility's employees passed a simple math test, and 60 percent of those who failed could not read the questions. Motorola surveyed its 25,000 manufacturing and support employees in the United States at the time and found that half could not do math, read, and/or write at seventh-grade levels.

When one of Northern Trust's business units wanted to learn how to attract and retain skilled, flexible employees, the company conducted a workplace study to establish benchmark performance levels and training needs. The study revealed that some of the most important skills sounded more like the topics at a school board meeting than a corporate board meeting: reading, grammar, writing, math, and problem solving.

What others can learn from the experiences of Motorola and Northern Trust is that a company would be wise not to assume any level of knowledge when it assesses the need for training, even for seasoned employees.

It may involve remedial reading and math, etiquette and food safety topics in service industries, and perhaps design of experiments and concurrent engineering in manufacturing environments. It is important to note that employees should not be ashamed (nor employers aghast) that the most basic skills are needed in order for some to progress.

Unfortunately, the rush to improve quality often leads to poor decisions about what kind of training to provide. Some of the most common mistakes are as follows:

- A customer expects a new skill from a company, so senior management authorizes department heads to begin training employees in that skill . . . without knowing whether they are ready to learn it.
- A company discovers a competitor is implementing a certain quality technique, or an executive reads an article about how such a technique "turned a business around." Training is quickly organized . . . before finding out whether the technique is a good idea and a good fit for the company.
- Something new happens—an equipment upgrade, the decision to offer a new product or offer a new service—and employees wade right into it, learning by feel. Management only considers training as an afterthought, when the process gets bogged down.
- The training covers broad quality concepts, and although it seems like good information, managers aren't really sure how each employee will apply those concepts in his or her daily work to improve quality.

These mistakes suggest that there is a more effective way to determine a company's training needs, a process anchored in the business management model. The process begins with data and information that determines current skill levels, and what is required to achieve both short- and long-range plans, satisfy customers, improve quality and operation performance, and grow personally and professionally. The human resource department is often designated to gather this information from a variety of sources, perform an analysis, and determine training needs. The nature of the assessment depends primarily on the size of the company: The smaller the company, the less formal the assessment.

Eastman Chemical opened "Eastman University" in the summer of 1997—more as an idea than a place. Its goal is to create learning systems that provide common solutions to Eastman employees worldwide. "In our culture, training priorities and support are determined by functional areas," says Edd Baldock, manager of Eastman University. "They run their own programs in terms of employee development. They analyze jobs to determine what the needs are. Eastman University is a strategic initiative aimed at developing employees as a whole."

Eastman University flows from a history of employee development, beginning with the company's roots in Eastman Kodak Company. A formal development and coaching process brings employees and their supervisors together to discuss learning opportunities and to plan future training and development. "We started out thinking these meetings would be annual, but some occur semiannually or quarterly," says Baldock. "The learning cycles have gotten so fast that you can't just plan development on an annual basis."

Another goal of Eastman University is to implement systems that accelerate the cycle time of learning. The company wants to match people and knowledge faster than in the past, a task that requires a more centralized approach.

"Excellence through Training and Development" is a cornerstone of the culture at Northern Trust. The company strives for a balance between corporate-level training and training determined by its business units. The company identifies training needs by:

1. Determining what *skills* its employees will need to achieve the company's strategic quality initiative. Its 24-hour training curriculum, "Training for Absolute Quality," includes skill building in the four key goals Northern identifies as necessary for achieving absolute quality:

   ◇ Unrivaled client satisfaction
   ◇ Continuous improvement of all processes
   ◇ Inspired leadership
   ◇ Active involvement of all Northern people.

2. Conducting periodic needs assessments to identify *topics* to be addressed. As a result of recent assessments and other data, Northern is now focusing on bringing training to employees who need it when they need it.

3. Using an ongoing *needs identification* process, which includes employees' evaluations of courses they complete and suggestions by Northern's business units and managers for new training.

4. *Benchmarking other companies* in the industry to find out what they are doing and where their training programs are going.

The skills taught as part of the "Training for Absolute Quality" course target the areas Northern has identified as essential to achieving its goals. The course is filled with individual and team exercises that help employees understand and act on each of the principles just mentioned as Northern Trust's four quality goals:

1. **Unrivaled Client Satisfaction**

   ◇ Client needs drive improvement decisions.
   ◇ All areas need an ongoing process for establishing client and partner requirements.
   ◇ Prevention of defects is essential to meet or exceed client and partner requirements.

2. Continuous Improvement of All Processes

◇ Everything is a process—and every process can be improved.

◇ Process measurements provide the facts that will guide decisions.

◇ To solve problems, look beyond symptoms so you can find and remove root causes.

3. Inspired Leadership

◇ Absolute quality management is achieved through attention to both process *and* results.

◇ We will deliver absolute quality to our clients and partners through cooperation and teamwork between areas.

◇ Managers can lead improvement by creating a climate of support and respect for all Northern people.

4. Active Involvement of All Northern Employees

◇ Everyone has a vital role in delivering unrivaled client satisfaction through absolute quality in everything we do.

◇ We exceed client expectations when all Northern people apply a systematic and disciplined approach to process improvement.

Skills improvement and knowledge of the Bank are fundamental tools for Northern people.

The course on unrivaled client satisfaction is the only course mandated for all employees. Northern is a very decentralized organization; each business unit is responsible for customizing training to its unique needs.

As with Motorola, that training ranges from basic to advanced skills. A workplace survey of more than 200 employees revealed that fundamental reading, writing, and math skills were critical to success. At the other end of the spectrum, an analysis of Northern's goals and principles pointed out the need for courses on the Baldrige criteria, benchmarking, service delivery, and team-working skills. Northern addresses the full spectrum through a comprehensive training program that reflects where employees are, and where they will need to be.

The term "development" in Northern Trust's "Excellence through Training and Development" philosophy brings up another good point—that is, today's training should be preparing employees not only to succeed at their current jobs but to think ahead to their overall career goals with the company. It is safe to say that most new employees come in not fully aware of the other types of opportunities that may await them if their new company turns out to be a good fit. Personal growth and career development are hot new training topics, both for new hires and long-term employees looking for greater responsibility.

A final important component of training should be giving retail employees the skills to set and meet their own work-related goals, not just the company's. A common criticism is that unless they are salespeople, employees get very little assistance with how to improve their work habits, stay organized, meet deadlines, and juggle priorities in a timely fashion. And, of course, in sales the results are measurable. In other types of jobs, progress may not be clearly defined and is therefore more difficult to quantify.

WHO RECEIVES THE TRAINING?

It is important that every employee receives some type of quality (and related) training, no matter what their job—a human resource manager's quality lecture at orientation time is simply no longer sufficient. One of the Baldrige Core Values is "Agility," and Texas Nameplate Company has taken it to heart, tailoring its training to allow its small workforce to meet major deadlines. When you promise any client that its job will be done and ready to ship within 5 to 10 working days or it's free, you're guaranteeing quite a bit! To meet the challenge, TNC has cross-trained more than 80 percent of its workforce to perform multiple jobs. They rotate as needed to different departments. Real-time workflow information is tracked on an intranet system and displayed on TV screens, so everyone knows what's being worked on when, and which jobs require the most urgent attention. Each employee creates and maintains his or her own Web page on the intranet, which contributes to keeping computer skills sharp, as well as keeping communication lines open when things get busy.

Cross-training not only keeps things interesting for the workers, who enjoy the variety of tasks; it also gives them a more holistic view of the company and the importance of their role in it. Before the 5- to 10-day guarantee was initiated, the average production time for an order was 14 days. Now, it's 8 days. All Texas Nameplate employees participate in monthly group meetings; managers also attend weekly meetings where quality improvement is among the topics.[3]

While cross-training is not necessary in all business environments, it can be helpful to at least include a job-swap or job-shadow component as part of a training program. It builds individual versatility and morale, as well as awareness, empathy, and communication among departments. It also improves the odds that employees, when seeing a department or process with "fresh eyes," will come up with a solution that people who do the job every day hadn't thought about.

To varying degrees, today's leading companies train all their employees in a number of standard areas. These include quality awareness, problem solving, computer proficiency and technology upgrades, reducing waste, process simplification, teamwork, and meeting customer requirements. The process is much like teaching the fundamentals to a baseball team. With that foundation in place, a variety of methods are used to identify the additional training needs of departments, work units, teams, and individuals. The additional needs differ with each "player." In baseball, all pitchers run, to strengthen their leg muscles; they practice-throw in the bullpen, to work on their pitches and develop a rhythm; and they keep track of how other pitchers approach different hitters, to learn what will get those hitters out. The nonpitchers learn and practice other skills. Within the pitching group, each individual pitcher works on additional skills only he needs, such as developing a new pitch, improving a pickoff move, or changing speeds on an existing pitch. To improve the quality of the entire team, the team's coaches work with the pitchers as a group and with each pitcher individually.

The quality of a company, like the quality of a team, depends on the continuous improvement of every member. A training program that recognizes who needs what types of specific training has an advantage over any program that consists of one basic "quality course" required for all employees. Smaller companies can be quick to respond when a single employee identifies a training need. A flat organization, dealing with established types of technology that employees know well, can also afford to focus on the immediate training needs of individuals and teams.

However, organizations that are larger, that are new to the quality improvement process, or that are involved in rapidly changing industries must first develop a quality training program that teaches the fundamentals to all employees. Then they can establish a mechanism that allows them to respond to specific needs.

For instance, every Northern Trust employee is trained in client satisfaction, but the company also has a rigorous "Gold Program" specifically for leadership development. The candidates must have a bachelor's degree with a grade point average of 3.0 or better and must either be recent college graduates or people with up to two years of work experience in the financial services industry.

If chosen for the Gold Program, participants select a career track—credit services, investments, and so on—spending 15 to 18 months in "rotations" (of 2 to 4 months) learning the different functions of that track. There are mandatory rotations in Operations and Credit Training, in addition to professional skills training in areas like negotiation, executive writing, and time management. The program ends with each candidate making an executive summary presentation to senior management—and if they're successful, a permanent job placement at Northern Trust.

DELIVERING TRAINING THAT MEETS GOALS

Increasingly, companies have discovered that training and development are specialized fields that can best be tailored to the corporate goals and strategies by a senior-level executive. With that, the position of Chief Learning Officer (CLO) has been created—often part of the human resources department, but sometimes as a stand-alone function. Depending on the company systems and products, this person is responsible for determining what kinds of training will give employees the core competencies needed by the company, and then analyzing the best ways to deliver them. Today's training doesn't have to be held in classrooms or conference rooms. CLOs develop Web-based learning programs or contract those services to educational vendors. They forge agreements with local universities for certain courses, and set up guest lectures and workshops that focus on skills or topics of interest—from PowerPoint presentations, to closing a sale, to stress management or money management, and so on. They may assist individual departments in hiring consultants for particular types of training. In some companies, the CLO is responsible for career mapping and overall workforce development, the mentor an employee can go to with questions about where to get the necessary skills for a promotion or transfer.

This brings up another decision that companies face: whether to train internally, or to trust the process to consultants who conduct training programs. One option that combines the best of both worlds is to take advantage of any training offered by suppliers and/or customers. Big companies—General Motors, Ford, Dow Corning, and General Electric, to name a few—offer training as a routine part of doing business. There are even training sessions specifically for senior executives, such as the "Insights Sessions" at IBM's Institute for Business Value, which are held on three continents. A Chief Learning Officer can facilitate these types of training experiences and partnerships.

Eastman does most of its training internally. Half of the training is done in the line units. The rest is handled by staff groups or outside trainers.

Northern Trust began by creating a volunteer corps of 175 trainers drawn from its business units to teach the course on absolute quality. "All of them had to be certified to train," says Debra Danziger-Barron, senior vice president. "They each had 70 hours of preparation time, during which they attended classes, studied absolute quality, and practiced being a trainer during videotaped sessions. They also spent about 100 hours each customizing the training materials for their business units." An *audit team* observes the training sessions to make sure the message is consistent and to help improve the training process. Computer-based, interactive training supports the instructor-led pieces.

Customizing the materials for each business unit makes the information more relevant. Asking participants to apply what they are learning as individuals and teams helps them remember information. For example, one exercise in Northern Trust's "Training for Absolute Quality" course reinforced the steps in describing a problem. The exercise asked the participant to "define a problem in one of your processes" and then to list key individuals or groups to be involved, current performance on key indicators, desired performance level, and a problem statement. After a section on identifying root causes, the participant's team was asked to choose one of the problems described previously and construct a cause-effect diagram to help identify likely causes.

Northern closed the loop with an "Action Guide" section that is rife with assignments on everything from conducting an internal partner interview to developing a plan for preventing service defects or assessing team information needs. They decided it was important that basic process improvement training came first; then more complex, continuous improvement training would build on the basics.

The on-the-job application of knowledge and skills becomes more difficult when the training is more theoretical or general, or when immediate applications are not identified and monitored. At Eastman, on-the-job application is part of the package when each line unit has its own training unit and is determining its training needs.

All these companies focus on quality during the orientation of new employees. One of the projects Eastman University developed was an employee orientation learning system called "Eastman Fundamentals," an introduction to Eastman's business, training in fundamental skills, and the company's quality expectations.

Northern Trust introduces new employees to absolute quality in a letter they receive before they start work. A half-day seminar during their first workweek presents a more detailed description. Within their first two months, new employees attend a welcome assembly hosted by Northern's chairman. He talks about his career at the bank, how the new employees fit into the process, why they were chosen, and how they carry out the bank's quality mission.

EVALUATING THE EXTENT AND EFFECTIVENESS OF TRAINING

Does the training help employees to learn? Does it help them to grow, both professionally and personally? Evaluating the extent and effectiveness of training is as necessary as providing it in the first place. This task also tends to fall into the purview of the Chief Learning Officer. It requires the identification and use of key indicators for each.

Extent is the easy one: How much of each type of training have employees received? The number of training hours per employee varies considerably, even among quality leaders. When this book was written, the amounts of time per year were as follows for a few corporations:

- Motorola employees averaged about 40 hours.
- Marlow Industries employees averaged over 60 hours.
- Milliken associates averaged about 76 hours.
- Corning employees averaged more than 90 hours.
- Solectron employees averaged over 100 hours.
- Custom Research Inc. employees averaged over 130 hours.

Of course, these time periods are only guidelines. The *effectiveness* of specific training on quality-related topics is harder to measure. Many companies tie general improvements in quality to the completion of training. Other companies are measuring effectiveness through indicators more closely linked to the training—indicators that offer a more immediate and traceable footprint, instead of trying to extrapolate the impact of one quality contributor from that of the whole herd. Typical indicators come from

- Surveys of employees, upon completion of a course, to measure such things as how appropriate the material was and how easy it was to understand
- Surveys of employees, a few weeks or months after completion of a course, to determine the degree to which the course content has been retained and applied
- Questions, in annual employee surveys, about training needs and effectiveness
- Follow-up training sessions, some time after completion of a course, to discuss problems, obstacles, and successes
- The development of measures that show the application of learned behaviors and skills on the job (statistical process control, for example)

Northern Trust has tried several methods over the years to check its training programs. Employees are surveyed at the end of a module for their opinions about its usefulness, and again six months after a course is completed to see whether their new skills are being applied. The company also relies on its certified trainers for input. "We tap into them about every three months," says Danziger-Barron. "They've played a major role in helping us develop and refine the training courses for our nonmanagement employees."

Companies such as Northern Trust, Texas Nameplate, and Eastman Chemical fine-tune their training needs by listening to their employees and external customers, studying their competitors, translating their short- and long-term goals into training needs, and soliciting input from employees and work teams. (Texas Nameplate offers customers additional incentive for their opinions—free shipping on their next order—for completing its quality survey form.)

The evolution of training from a tactical response to an urgent need, and then to a strategic initiative designed to give a company a competitive advantage, is just one more example of the dramatic shift in thinking that total quality commitment requires.

CHAPTER SUMMARY

In the new business management model, a company is obligated to train its employees—to provide them with the intellectual arsenal they need to work in teams, collect and analyze data, initiate improvements, satisfy customers, and assume all the other responsibilities that come with empowerment and involvement. Today's training does not have to take place in a classroom or conference room to be effective. Most companies have at least some form of Web-based learning available, or a combination of Web-based and in-person programs.

As the role models in the chapter and throughout this book prove, continuous improvement is possible only with the continuous and effective training of all employees at all levels. The key to effective training is understanding both the needs of employees and their corporation, and it may involve some surprisingly basic refresher courses on topics such as business writing and math. Successful companies train all their employees in the fundamentals of quality as defined by their company's goals and objectives. Then they build on the fundamentals by tailoring more specific quality training to the needs of business units, divisions, departments, teams, and individuals. The addition of a Chief Learning Officer to the human resources team helps many companies ensure that their goals and their training programs mesh.

Training should also include personal and professional development—not just job skills, but life skills and interpersonal skills that enable an employee to chart a rewarding and challenging career path within the company. Training programs may change often, to reflect and anticipate changes in customers' needs and expectations, new technologies, new markets, competition, worksite issues or problems, and employees' capabilities. The people in the system are in the best position to improve it, but they cannot unlock the possibilities without knowledge.

DISCUSSION QUESTIONS

1. Could a more effective screening process for new hires minimize the need for (and expense of) training in most companies? Which do you think would be more effective, and why: hiring people who have the skills you need to begin with or hiring a person with "potential" and training them?

2. Some common problems with training are outlined in the section entitled "Determining Training Needs." Think of an example—either from research or your own experience—and write a brief description of what happened and how the training could (or should) have been done differently.

3. If you managed a manufacturing company that was being impacted by a serious economic downturn, what types of training would you eliminate and what types would you keep? Would you cut back on training or increase it?

4. Do you consider issues like sexual harassment, diversity, and Americans with Disabilities Act awareness as suitable training topics, or are they human resource issues that can be dealt with in an employee handbook or by individual managers or departments as needed?

5. Does a fast-track management training program, such as the one at Northern Trust, discourage lower-level employees about their chances for promotion in a company if they are not part of that program? As a branch manager, how would you counter that?

ENDNOTES

1. *Workforce Management* magazine, Crain Communications, Inc., Detroit, Michigan, January 2002.
2. Research results, the Saratoga Institute, Santa Clara, California, February 1998.
3. *MRO Today* magazine, Pfingsten Publishing, LLC, Seven Hills, Ohio, November 29, 2004.

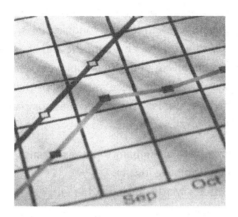

Employee Loyalty

Despite the fact that almost all adults work (and at last count, the average U.S. employee's workweek is 46 hours), there are common misconceptions in the working world about what motivates people. Most managers and supervisors believe that pay is the prime motivator of performance. As you will learn in this chapter, while salary and benefits are important, research and surveys of employees suggest they are not the primary reasons people cite for job satisfaction.

So, other than training them well and paying them well, what else can today's corporations do to build employees' trust and loyalty? The Baldrige Award Core Values for 2005 phrase the challenge this way: "Valuing employees means committing to their satisfaction, development, and well-being."[1]

Today's management model is a people-focused system that is driven by customers but fueled by employees. In tough economic times, most business relationships grow in importance: between customers and employees, managers and employees, employees and other employees, employees and suppliers. Loyal employees do better in these relationships than dissatisfied employees. In this chapter, we address five major issues companies face in their attempts to produce a loyal workforce:

- Aligning human resources with a company's strategic plans
- Earning and maintaining employee loyalty
- Using forms of recognition: awards, time, pay, benefits
- Using performance assessments
- Creating a pay structure that supports a company's quality goals

The companies mentioned in this chapter include several examples that have made employee satisfaction as high a priority as customer satisfaction: BI Worldwide, Tennant Company, and Trident Precision Manufacturing. Following is an overview of each.

BI Worldwide. This is a company that "walks the talk" and teaches others to do the same! BI calls itself a "performance services" company. It specializes in developing reward, recognition, and incentive programs to help clients improve the performance of their employees and distribution personnel, and to develop higher levels of consumer loyalty and frequency of purchase. BI calls its approach the "Customer Delight Process."

BI has nearly 1,400 associates at its Minneapolis headquarters and in more than 20 U.S. sales offices. In recent years, the company has merged with a British firm to launch its specialized research capabilities and services in Europe.

Along the way, company executives challenged themselves by entering the Baldrige competition for 10 consecutive years. They insist their goal was not to win but to learn and improve using the Baldrige guidelines in a system they call the "BI Way." In 1994, BI became the first service company to win the Minnesota Quality Award, which is based on the Baldrige criteria; and in 1999, BI followed up with a national Baldrige Award. Several of its divisions are also registered for ISO standards.

Tennant Company. One of the world's leading manufacturers of industrial and commercial cleaning equipment, floor coatings, and related products, Tennant is also headquartered in Minneapolis. It has approximately

2,300 employees (up from 1,700 just five years earlier, despite one layoff in 2000 after it acquired a German company.)

From the mid-1980s to mid-1990s, the company received an astonishing number of quality awards—more than 1,100—and its company executives have written three books on the topic of quality management. The employee recognition program is an interesting mix of history and modern updates. The profit-sharing program, service awards, and retirement protocol have all been in place for more than 45 years, but the newest recognition programs have all been developed and administered by its workforce.

Tennant has expanded its product availability in foreign markets as a key growth strategy. In recent years, the company has purchased cleaning equipment manufacturing companies in the United Kingdom, the Netherlands, and Germany.

Trident Precision Manufacturing. Trident Precision Manufacturing is a precision sheet metal fabricating company, making custom electromechanical assemblies and components for the office equipment, medical supplies, computer, and defense industries, to name a few. It is a privately held company of about 140 employees, based in Webster, New York. Owner and CEO Nick Juskiw attended a Xerox-sponsored "Leadership through Quality" seminar in the 1980s, primarily looking for ways to improve morale and reduce the company's 41 percent employee turnover rate. With that, TQM was born at Trident.

One of the five strategies that compose the company's "Excellence in Motion" initiative is employee satisfaction. Today, turnover has shrunk to less than 4 percent. The company won a Baldrige Award in 1996.

WHY KEEP EMPLOYEES HAPPY?

Do satisfied employees make a difference to a company's bottom line? A yearlong study released in 2005 by the Forum for People Performance Management at Northwestern University was among the first to quantify the link, indirectly but surely. A 1-unit increase in employee satisfaction led to a 0.31-unit increase in customer satisfaction; and every 1-unit increase in customer satisfaction created a 0.28-unit improvement in financial performance.

What constitutes a "unit" of employee satisfaction depends on the company—and the employees. But the connection is valid, says James Oakley, the assistant professor of marketing for Purdue University who ran the study for the Forum. In Oakley's words:

> There is a direct relationship between how employees feel and customer attitudes. Any company that is trying to directly impact the bottom line can measure employee satisfaction and know that improvements will drive profitability. This gives an organization a place to begin.[2]

However, in many organizations, despite a lot of positive rhetoric at annual meetings, making the transition from viewing employees as "grist for the mill" to embracing them as partners in a shared mission has happened very slowly. At the same time, competitive global markets have led many corporations to demand so much of their people that, even in the best-intentioned workplaces, stress and burnout have become serious problems.

An inescapable contributor to the modern employee's stress level is the fear of losing a job. A startling number of companies in the last 20 years have turned to layoffs as the remedy for mediocre financial performance. In the early 1990s, writing for the Cox News Service, the "Corporate Curmudgeon" columnist Dale Dauten blasted the downsizing trend, which, since then, has become a way of life in corporate America. Today, Dauten's words carry the same sting as they did more than a decade ago:

> [CEOs who slash jobs] ought to be getting up and saying: "We did such a lousy job of planning and hiring that we have more people than we have work. And we are so broke and so dimwitted that we can't come up with any way to get more work, so our only choice is to send a lot of good people home. I am ashamed, and I am sorry."

Ouch! No doubt most corporate leaders can rationalize layoffs, but that doesn't mean they were the results of sound business reasoning. And for the remaining managers, the unspoken dilemma remains: How can they build teamwork when people feel they are expendable? How can they "rally the troops" around a common vision of excellence when the troops know the only excellence that *really* matters is profit for shareholders and bonuses for senior executives?

Unfortunately, few leaders seem to recognize the contradictory nature of some of their actions. They say customer satisfaction is the primary goal but make short-term decisions focused solely on improving the bottom line. They claim that quality is an overriding value but sacrifice quality when it threatens to cost too much. They say that the company's employees are responsible for the company's success, then lay them off. They say the people who make the products and deliver the services and serve the customers are the most important people in the company, then pay themselves hundreds of times more than the people they are praising.

They don't get it. None of these contradictory messages is lost on employees. If senior management says one thing and does another, employees become distrustful, anxious, and cynical—anything but satisfied. As leaders strive to align their management systems, *they must also strive to align their messages*. If customer satisfaction is the primary goal, success is naturally measured in terms of customer satisfaction and retention. The challenge is to see employee satisfaction in the same terms as customer satisfaction.

So What Keeps 'Em Happy?

Professional mediator and motivational speaker Terry Bragg of Peacemakers Training in Murray, Utah, often starts his presentations to companies by asking for a show of hands to this question: How many people get *too much* appreciation where they work? He jokes that if a person raises their hand, it's usually because they happen to be sitting next to their boss and feel as though they have to!

"Appreciation is the closest thing to a universal motivator," Bragg believes. "It usually works better than the fancy programs we think should work better."[3]

BI calls itself "The Business Improvement Company." Its goal is to help client companies improve their results by motivating employees to produce specific behaviors. As its business matured, BI sought to prove the validity of that idea through statistical methods. It conducted studies with clients to see whether people respond better to cash or noncash incentives. Noncash wins every time.

BI also redefined the business by developing an integrated performance model that focuses on improving results. The performance model has four pieces—communication, training, measurement, and rewards—plus research. "We believe that if you use all these elements, you can change people's behavior," says Mary Etta Coursolle, senior vice president at BI. "That changed behavior may or may not produce different attitudes, but it *does* produce results." BI draws from its model to shape performance improvement programs for its clients. It also applies the model to improving the performance of its own associates.

The elements of the performance model are evident in companies intent on creating a high-performance work environment. As an example, look at Ben & Jerry's (a company profiled in Chapter 10 for its corporate citizenship). Its human resource agenda includes the following:

- Distributing guides for managers and employees (called *Coaches' Guide* and *Player's Guide*, respectively) to communicate the principles behind the company's policies

- Improving communication by having regular leadership meetings and making leaders responsible for relaying to their people the information shared at these meetings
- Adding training to fine-tune team and cooperative work skills
- Enhancing measurement by improving the performance appraisal process
- Introducing a new compensation system for production workers, to reward them for acquiring certain skills and competencies

BI's performance model captures actions that any organization can take to improve performance. But what does this have to do with developing loyalty among workers? One might assume that better performance means higher quality, faster delivery, or lower prices, but it could also mean more aggressive selling or working harder for longer hours. And if employees are working harder and longer, what does a model for improving performance mean to the employees being asked to improve?

To help answer these questions, two BI associates examined current performance models that link workplace practices with financial performance. Their goal was to develop a valid and useful model that offers insights into the dynamics of loyalty, and that shows the connections between workplace practices and financial performance. They called their new model a Loyalty Model. As shown in Figure 6-1, the model identifies three sources of financial performance:

- Workplace culture and practices
- Employee and customer loyalty
- Workplace performance

Each area in the model has been identified by management experts and research as important, all areas have been measured, and all linkages are supported by research.

Workplace culture consists of the vision, values, and beliefs that define an organization. Employees who accept the culture translate its value to customers; employees who ignore or reject the culture create disconnects between what the company says it provides and what the customer receives. *Workplace practices* are what employees do and how they do it. *Employee loyalty,* as defined by BI, means that employees

- Understand and commit to their organization's business goals and objectives.
- Make an active and ongoing decision to stay employed with the organization.
- Perform "above and beyond" behaviors to create value for customers.
- Modify their workplace behaviors to accommodate the demands of changing market environments.

Workplace culture and practices can help create or erode employee loyalty.

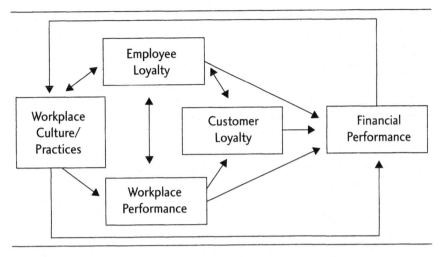

Figure 6-1 BI's loyalty model.

Workplace performance is the measure of how well products or services meet standards. Workplace culture and practices help set and communicate the standards. Employee loyalty affects how well employees adhere to those standards. In these terms, it's easy to see how the components are linked.

Customer loyalty was discussed in Chapter 3. Why "customer loyalty" and not "customer satisfaction"? Interestingly, a Xerox Corporation study found that totally satisfied customers (another definition of "loyal") were six times more likely to repurchase Xerox products than "just plain" satisfied customers. Higher rates of repurchase improve financial performance. As the model shows, long-term *financial performance* depends on workplace performance and the loyalty of employees and customers.

TAKING FUN SERIOUSLY

Empowerment, training, reward and recognition, and job security are essential to developing employee loyalty. But why should business be "all business"? Most workers love the opportunity to lighten up and have fun, at least once in a while.

Perhaps no corporate executive took this notion to heart more than Jerry Greenfield, who helped to build Ben & Jerry's on a simple philosophy: "If it's not fun, why do it?" He created the Joy Gang in 1988 to increase joy in the workplace. Among its zany activities:

- **Name That Face Contest.** Employees brought in photos from their past. They were displayed on a bulletin board for other employees to guess who was who.
- **Barry Manilow Day.** To celebrate this balladeer's birthday, Manilow tunes were played in the lunchroom, Manilow buttons were distributed, and employees voted on their favorite Manilow tune. (Of course, today this would mystify the Generation X and Y members of the staff—but it might still be fun!)
- **National Clash-Dressing Day.** Everyone seemed to revel in this celebration of the tacky, donning stripes with plaids with polka dots in a one-day homage to Really Bad Taste in Clothing.
- **Pizza & Puttin'.** This pizza party for employees was held at an indoor miniature golf course.
- **Play Day.** The Joy Gang covered lunchroom tables with white paper and left boxes of crayons, finger paints, and cans of Play-Doh for employees to enjoy.

The list is much longer, and not all the activities are goofy, but their purpose is the same: Have some fun and enjoy your coworkers. There are numerous books on the market today that feature hundreds of ways companies can inject more joy into the workplace.

At BI Worldwide, the equivalent of the Joy Gang is the "Fun QIT (Quality Improvement Team)" at various company offices. More than 200 BI associates have signed up as volunteer "fun consultants" eager to help the QIT come up with cool new events. They have included a Valentine candy exchange (an associate buys candy for any other associate, and the Fun QIT delivers it), book fairs, May "Daffodil Days," and "Dunk the Director" parties (music and disk jockey, lunch, and a big dunk tank for willing senior executives).

"It's all done in a tongue-in-cheek way," says Coursolle, "because everyone knows this isn't how you have fun!" Work is work, after all, and the *real* fun comes from learning, working as a team, doing a job well, reaching a goal, and being recognized for your accomplishments.

Fun sometimes takes a while to get used to in a business setting. For instance, in an effort to increase the number of employees recognized for good performance, the Tennant Company introduced the Koala T. Bear Award. To qualify for the award, an employee must do one of the following:

- Make an extra effort to meet or exceed customers' needs.
- Go above and beyond job requirements in a small group or special project.
- Consistently meet job standards and have a positive work attitude.

Candidates are nominated in writing by their peers or managers. A cross-functional employee committee selects the winners, which are delivered monthly—by someone dressed in a giant koala bear costume! The awards are stuffed koalas wearing "Tennant Quality" T-shirts. Some folks thought it was hokey, causing the award committee to get rid of the bear suit and just hand out the awards. But it wasn't as much fun. When so many employees asked, "Hey, where's the big bear?" the committee brought it back.

REWARD AND RECOGNITION

The role of employee rewards and recognition—such things as performance appraisals, compensation, recognition programs, and promotion systems—is to support the achievement of the company's goals. This aspect of the system is usually not among the first to receive attention, nor should it be when a company is still figuring out how to satisfy customers, manage processes, and involve employees. But successful companies soon learn to align their reward and recognition systems with their quality improvement efforts.

BI Worldwide divides reward programs into two broad categories: a regularly budgeted, formal awards system and a shorter-term, incentive-type of program designed to do a particular thing—increase sales, decrease manufacturing defects, improve a safety record, and so on. BI's theory is that a company must be able to quantify improvements, or both types of programs slowly end up being thought of as discretionary spending and are among the first items to be cut when budgets are tight.

"If they are not carefully planned and regularly evaluated," BI senior vice president John Jack explains, "they tend to become viewed as an expense rather than an investment."[4]

The typical recognition program most people think of is the formal "Employee of the Month," or a company equivalent of the Academy Awards—the Chairperson's Award, President's Award, and so on, or Company XYZ Quality Award—but there are other options to ensure more consistent (and more effective) recognition than these types of annual honors. In 1993, the Tennant Company published its own book, entitled *Recognition Redefined: Building Self-Esteem at Work*. One chapter includes a description of a survey of industrial employees conducted in 1946. Asked what factors provided the greatest job satisfaction, the workers ranked "full appreciation of work done" first. The same survey done again in 1986 placed "full appreciation of work done" second—behind "interesting work," but still ahead of job security, good wages, good working conditions, and every other factor that traditionally contributes to job satisfaction. *Employees crave recognition.* Quality leaders take every opportunity to satisfy that craving.

The distinction between rewards and recognition is that *rewards* are usually monetary and *recognition* is an action or activity that is not monetary. Examples of rewards are bonuses, cash awards, trips, and merchandise. Examples of recognition are company awards, department or team awards and special events, individual awards, and personal thanks.

Time Is Money

In today's busy world, a new type of benefit has surfaced that is neither strictly reward nor recognition. In 2004, employees of Procter & Gamble— all 98,000 of them—received a two-day vacation "bonus" in recognition of the company's excellent four-year performance. They could opt to take it as paid vacation or keep working and receive two days' extra pay.

A Houston-based company, Medical-Legal Consulting Institute, Inc., allows its employees a half day off when sales increase by 15 percent over the same month in the previous year and a full day off if sales increase by 20 percent. The additional time must be taken in the following month. "It's amazing what people will do for a day off," company owner Vickie Milazzo told *Workforce Management* magazine in 2004. "They all want to know if the company is meeting its sales goal, and they stay later and cooperate with each other."[5]

Job sharing and flextime aren't exactly "rewards," but they are increasingly popular methods that employers use to improve morale by acknowledging busy workers' need for personal time. The Colorado Department of Personnel and Administration has adopted the following well-stated definitions of these work concepts:

> **Job-sharing** is a flexible means of pooling the talents and energies of two part-time employees to perform the work of one full-time job. Employers can use this option to accommodate the changing workforce and business needs. An increasing number of workers are deciding that part-time work is most suitable in meeting their career and personal circumstances. Job-sharing allows the state to accommodate these desires while capitalizing on the skills, energy, and talent of these employees . . . Studies show that job sharers may be more productive than their full-time counterparts who are affected by stress, fatigue, burn-out, etc. Job sharing employees tend to be more motivated because of a personal interest in the success of this voluntary arrangement. Reports also say that less supervision is actually required of these employees.
>
> **Flextime** is a way to redesign or restructure traditional work schedules so the employee works daily hours different from regular office hours or works a full schedule in fewer days. Employers can use this option to accommodate the changing workforce and

business needs. Employees can use innovative scheduling to fulfill a variety of personal needs, including family responsibilities, routine health appointments, educational activities, and volunteer and wellness activities. This type of scheduling is flexible enough to be used on an ongoing or as-needed basis.

A daily flex-schedule is a flexible schedule where the employee is free to set his/her own work hours within limits established by management. There are five components:

- **Core Period.** The hours in a workday when all staff are needed (e.g., 9 a.m. to 11 a.m. and 1 p.m. to 3 p.m.), when meetings are likely to be scheduled, customer contact is heaviest, etc.
- **Bandwidth.** The hours during which managers allow flexible scheduling (includes the core period). It defines the earliest time employees may arrive and the latest time they may leave.
- **Flexible Hours.** The hours an employee chooses to work. Under one approach, work schedules can vary daily within the band without prior approval, as long as the full workweek is completed. A variation is staggered work hours when employees begin and end at individually based, fixed times that do not change daily but may periodically change on specific dates.
- **Compressed Workweek.** A full workweek is completed in fewer than five days by increasing the number of hours worked per day. The more common examples are the four-day (10 hours per day) or three-day (12 hours per day) workweeks.
- **5×4 Workweek.** A flexible schedule where four days are worked in one week and five in the next for a total of 80 hours. There are variations on this type of schedule. The key is working 80 hours over a two-week period.[6]

These arrangements are increasing in popularity every year and are designed to benefit employees without additional costs to the employer. Of course, not all types of jobs lend themselves to such flexibility, but companies looking for ways to build loyalty among workers would be wise to consider their personal and family needs in addition to the corporate goals and deadlines. Perhaps both can be accommodated.

THE TENNANT RECOGNITION MODEL

For more traditional awards and employee recognition, the Tennant Company created a *three-dimensional recognition model*—formal, informal, and day-to-day—based on research into human behavior and its own experiences and goals. To understand the benefits of each, Tennant identified a list of attributes that define a recognition program:

- It is *consistent*—delivered the same way every time.
- Some *cost* must be incurred.
- The recognition is *frequent.*
- The person providing the recognition uses *interpersonal skills* to give personal, specific information about the accomplishment.
- The recognition comes from *peers.*
- The goal is to recognize the highest *percentage* of total employees possible.
- Some *prestigious* awards are considered special and sought-after.
- Public *display*—a high-visibility event—is involved.
- The recognition must be based on *sincere* trust and respect.
- *Specific feedback* is provided to show what the person did that was of value.
- The more people involved in the selection process, the more *subjective* their opinions and judgments become.
- The recognition comes from *superiors.*
- A *tangible reminder* is left behind to remind the recipient of the reason for the recognition.
- The recognition is *timely;* as little time as possible is allowed to elapse between the action and the recognition.
- The recognition is *win/win*—everyone is a winner.

Tennant then looked at each type of recognition offered—formal, informal, and day-to-day—and determined whether an attribute ranked high, medium, or low for that type. For example, with formal recognition the cost is high and the percentage of total employees recognized is low. Tennant divided the attributes into three distinct groups, shown in Table 6-1.

The table reveals two insights: First, each type of recognition has different strengths, and second, all three types rank high in consistency, sincerity, and specific feedback. The first insight suggests that a three-pronged approach to quality recognition has a better chance of success than a program that provides only one type of recognition. The second insight suggests that consistency, sincerity, and specific feedback are critical to the success of any recognition program.

Formal Recognition

Like Tennant, most quality leaders begin with formal recognition. Intel, Carrier, IBM, Honeywell, and others have *corporate quality awards* based on quality and/or customer satisfaction measures. The awards have two primary goals:

1. To recognize employees for their contributions
2. To communicate a commitment to quality and customer satisfaction at the highest levels of the company

"We developed a reward and recognition strategy as a basis for performance management," says Joe Conchelos, Trident's vice president of quality. "The question is, how would you reward the actions you wanted?" The intent of the resulting plan was to reinforce behaviors that contribute to achieving its goal of Total Customer Satisfaction.

Trident's formal awards include the President's Award and Employees of the Month Award. Each year, the CEO selects the person he feels has done the most for the organization. The President's Award winner receives $1,500 and a plaque, presented at the company's year-end holiday celebration. There are also Employees of the Month, nominated by employees and supervisors and chosen by management. Winners are announced at monthly company-wide meetings. All Employees of the Month are eligible for the Employee of the Year Award, which also includes a $1,500 prize.

Tennant's first foray into quality recognition was in the formal arena. Candidates for a formal Quality Recognition Award are individuals or groups nominated by their coworkers. The nominations are reviewed and evaluated by a Recognition Committee, which is a cross-functional team of employees. Up to 25 individuals and 12 groups receive the awards at banquets in their honor.

Informal Recognition

This second dimension of Tennant's recognition program took shape as the company sought ways to help managers and supervisors uniformly recognize groups. Although individual recognition is more critical than "group" recognition, congratulating team efforts is still important and happens more frequently than formal recognition, and less frequently than day-to-day recognition. According to Tennant's guidelines, it depends on:

- The amount of effort the group put into the project, beyond the members' regular job responsibilities
- The amount of time expended to accomplish the task
- The importance of the accomplishment to the entire organization
- The ability of the group to set and meet goals

The form of recognition usually falls into three categories:

1. Parties or gatherings (pizza parties, luncheons, or coffee and doughnuts)
2. Outings (tours of other companies, visits to customers or suppliers)
3. Gifts or giveaways (coffee mugs, pens and pencils, or gift certificates)

Table 6-1 Attributes of Tennant Company's Recognition Program

Low	Medium	High
Formal Recognition		
Frequent	From peers	Consistent
Interpersonal skills	Subjective	Cost
Percentage of total	From superiors	Prestigious
Timely		Public display
Win/win		Sincere
		Specific feedback
		Tangible reminder
Informal Recognition		
Subjective	Cost	Consistent
	Frequent	Sincere
	Interpersonal skills	Specific feedback
	From peers	From superiors
	Percentage of total	
	Prestigious	
	Public display	
	Tangible reminder	
	Timely	
	Win/win	
Day-to-Day Recognition		
Cost		Consistent
Prestigious		Frequent
Public display		Interpersonal skills
Subjective		From peers
Tangible reminder		Percent of total
		Sincere
		Specific feedback
		From superiors
		Timely
		Win/win

Source: Used with permission of the Tennant Company, Minneapolis, Minnesota, 1998.

Managers decide what type of recognition to give, and there's an "informal recognition fund" that amounts to about $20 per person per year. The most popular purchases include food, apparel, and gift certificates. As an example, the process has been used to encourage employees to wear their name tags. Employees (whose names are randomly selected and who are "caught" wearing their name tags) get a surprise visit from Name Tag Committee members, who bestow $20 gift certificates, candy bars, cans of soda, or other small gifts. The number of employees who remember to wear name tags doubled (from 30 percent to 60 percent) over a five-year period.

Tennant's informal recognition program for safety began in 1975. It includes cash awards, special dinners, small gifts, and internal publicity. The recognition helped Tennant to achieve one of the lowest workers' compensation rates in the country and to earn public recognition for its safety efforts.

The focus of Trident's reward and recognition plan is on informal recognition. "We look at the entire organization as a team," says Conchelos, "and we have several awards for the company team. If we go an entire month without a customer complaint or a rejected part, the employees select what they want for an extended lunch period. Senior managers may cook out, lunch might be catered—whatever the employees want. If we go six months with no more than two customer complaints, everyone gets a day off. And if we go 90 days without a recordable accident, we have a pizza party. We've had several of those."

One risk of a strictly informal recognition program is that employees are wise to the fact that it is easier to reward a group or team than to single out individuals. For this reason, Trident managers and supervisors also hand out more than 1,700 items a year (gift certificates, sports tickets, and the like). These efforts are tracked, and the average Trident employee is "thanked" in some way by the company more than 10 times a year.[7]

Day-to-Day Recognition

The third dimension of Tennant's recognition program happens when one employee thanks or praises another employee. The recognition can be verbal or written and can be used by anyone—it's not strictly a management tool. Global e-mail capability makes this almost instantaneous, and as easy as typing a quick note of congratulations and clicking Send. Research shows that people value specific, individual recognition more than any other type.

A 1991 study by Nelson Motivation, Inc. in San Diego found some real discrepancies in what managers *think* people want versus what employees *say* they want in terms of on-the-job motivators. The managers listed good wages, job security, and promotion/growth opportunities as the three most important concerns of their workers. The workers ranked the following three choices highest:

- Full appreciation for work done
- Feeling "in on things"
- Empathy to personal problems

Each of these is accomplished most effectively in a day-to-day context. And ironically, each costs a company nothing.[8]

DETERMINING EMPLOYEE SATISFACTION

Recognition Redefined coauthor Rita F. Maehling once asked more than 400 Tennant Company employees attending recognition training to rank the three types of recognition in order of importance to them. Two-thirds said day-to-day recognition was most important, 28 percent ranked informal recognition first, and only 6 percent put formal recognition at the top of the list. Asked to rank where their company placed its emphasis, 46 percent felt the focus was on formal recognition, 44 percent said informal, and 10 percent said day-to-day.

"The surveys show that people craved day-to-day recognition but they weren't getting it," explained Maehling. "They want feedback. They can't function in a vacuum anymore. We need to change our culture so that regular, positive feedback is a natural reflex."

Relevant information is required to improve the system, not to fix blame. If a process goes out of control, information about that process is used to bring it back into control, not to seek out the responsible people and chew them out. This is true whether the process involves manufacturing a widget or managing people. It is the reason that companies must do a better job of collecting information about employee satisfaction.

Consider the parallels to customer satisfaction. Companies have always assumed that they knew what their customers required. However, when they were forced by competition and other pressures to get closer to their customers, they quickly discovered that their understanding was often superficial. Companies such as Solectron, IBM Rochester, Xerox, and Staples now work hard to stay on top of customer requirements because they know those requirements drive their business—and the requirements change.

The same principle can be applied to employee satisfaction. Companies have always assumed that they know what their employees require. However, as they are being forced to involve all of their employees in meeting customer requirements, they are discovering that their understanding may be rather shallow.

What can be done to improve it? Most companies determine employee satisfaction through an employee survey. Both Trident and Tennant conduct surveys twice a year; BI Worldwide has an annual survey. The companies communicate the results to all employees/associates, analyze the results, and develop and implement improvement plans.

Some firms survey a smaller percentage of employees every month, or use focus groups and interviews to get feedback. The less frequent the survey, the greater the risk of two problems: an absence of data much of the time and an abundance of data that prompts a flurry of improvement activities—but only once a year or so. During the course of a year, the attitudes of employees may change significantly, but management will not be able to measure those shifts or respond appropriately until the survey results are available.

Even exit interviews should be designed to encourage "recently former" employees to speak up about how things might be done better in the future for the people who are still on the job. Every opportunity to listen becomes a learning experience.

PERFORMANCE REVIEWS

Recognition and reward programs are generally accepted as valuable support for a company's agenda, but a consensus on performance assessments is not as easily achieved. Most businesspeople would agree that performance reviews can benefit the drive for continuous improvement—but only when they are conducted according to the principles of quality management. This includes the following conditions:

1. **The performance appraisal must be separate from the compensation system.** The purpose of a performance appraisal is to improve performance through communication. Dangling pay like a carrot changes the emphasis from improving because it is the *right* thing to do to improving because it is the *profitable* thing to do.
2. **The performance appraisal must be based on observable, measurable behaviors and results.** The identification and use of key indicators is a principle of quality management that is just as valuable to an employee who is evaluating his or her performance as it is to an employee who is evaluating the performance of a tool needed on a manufacturing line. In both cases, the goal is to improve performance, not to criticize the performer. And in both cases, the employee should help determine what to measure, then collect the data.
3. **The performance appraisal must include timely feedback.** Annual performance reviews are not frequent enough to promote continuous

improvement and defect prevention. Feedback should be specific, immediate, and positive, and related to performance the employee can control.

4. **The performance appraisal must encourage employee participation.** The manager's role in a performance appraisal is to help the employee understand the assessment, to work with the employee to develop new goals and actions, to explore opportunities for career development, and to encourage the employee to provide feedback on the manager's performance as it relates to the employee. The employee is not a passive listener but an active participant.

This method of reviewing performance is a natural extension of the principles that quality leaders have embraced. It treats employees as *valued internal customers and suppliers* who are responsible for their meeting part of the continuous improvement goals. A performance assessment that supports and encourages their contributions becomes an important tool for the quality improvement process.

COMPENSATION AND PAY STRUCTURE

Pay and benefits are the top two reasons a candidate accepts a job—but they lose some of their effectiveness as motivators when it comes to retaining people after they get the job. Today's savvy employees have come to expect health insurance, retirement accounts, paid vacations, and sick leave as part of any basic employment package. So in addition to these, companies are trying new approaches with work-life balance (and happier employees) as the intended outcomes.

According to the Society for Human Resource Management, an organization that represents 180,000 HR professionals, the following are among the new work-life "perks":

- 57 percent of companies offer some type of flextime.
- 56 percent offer wellness programs.
- More than one-third (36 percent) allow telecommuting.
- 20 percent offer on-site fitness centers.
- 19 percent offer stress-reduction programs.[9]

So-called "cafeteria plans" are also popular, in which a company allows each employee an amount of money to be spent on any of a list of benefits the employee selects. This system is inherently fair because it doesn't, for example, force childless workers to help finance a company day care center. People who need child care can pay for it with their benefits credit or spend with their own funds and use the benefit money instead for other priorities—health or life insurance, college tuition, elder care resources, counseling, and so on. The key in today's companies is giving employees choices that fit their lifestyles.

No matter what else is offered, however, most people have bills to pay. In a TQM-based company, the compensation system follows these key principles of quality management:

1. **Compensation should be customer-driven.** Pay all employees for skills that matter to the company's external customers. Doing so requires a clear understanding of what customers need and expect, and what the company does to meet those needs and expectations. Internally, both employees and managers are "customers" of the compensation system. Their needs and expectations must also drive the compensation system.
2. **Compensation should be team-oriented.** Total Quality Management requires the extensive use of teams. If any compensation is considered "at risk"—that is, if it is dependent on performance or results—it should be based primarily on achieving team goals.
3. **Compensation should be measurable.** The measures used to determine pay must be the observable results of team performance. Measures must be relevant; available throughout the process; focused on what is important to the customer; and established, collected, and controlled to a great degree by the team.
4. **The compensation system should have full employee participation.** Employees, individually and in teams, must participate in setting meaningful goals, identifying key performance indicators, and monitoring and evaluating progress. The company must provide and encourage training to help employees master these tasks.

Today's employees, whether assembly-line workers or senior executives, are concerned about whether they are being paid fairly, not just in relation to coworkers but to other companies in similar industries. In order to create an equitable and competitive pay structure, the company must first gather information in the form of a pay survey.

Pay surveys are questionnaires (by phone, e-mail, or regular mail) to determine if a company's compensation structure is truly competitive with others in an area or an industry by asking others about salary ranges for their people in similar types of jobs. There are plenty of "free" sources of this information, from trade associations to the U.S. Department of Labor, but the best results often come by hiring an outside consultant to do a customized survey. The advantages of a custom survey are as follows:

- It ensures the most current data (since sometimes the "free" data isn't the freshest, and pay results can change within 6 to 12 months).
- It allows the company to pinpoint data from other firms that, job for job, are the closest industry competitors.

- It can focus on information for exact job titles and duties. The more specific the survey questions are, the more easily a responding company can match it to a truly comparable position in their company, which increases the accuracy of the survey.

A pay survey should not be too complex or ask for too many types of information—an HR or payroll person in a responding company should be able to fill it out within a few minutes. It should include a deadline for returning the data. (Even then, not everyone who receives the survey will bother to respond.)

As with any other type of survey, if it's not used and interpreted correctly, it will be a waste of time and money. Professional consultants who specialize in HR topics can increase a survey's usefulness, and even increase the response rate, by crafting the "right" questions and targeting the "right" companies to answer it. They are also sensitive to the legal realities of surveys—for instance, companies must avoid doing anything that would make them appear to be "price-fixing" their salaries by tacit agreement. It is one thing to seek competitive information; it is quite another to conspire with other companies in an effort to set salaries at certain levels.

CHAPTER SUMMARY

Smart leaders know that *employees make the system work*. They interact with customers, translate customers' requirements into products and services, manage and improve processes, work with suppliers, determine and use measurements, compare their processes to others, contribute to their communities, and perform all the other tasks that turn a building filled with equipment into a successful business. And the new process technologies depend on people who are empowered, trained, recognized—and satisfied with their work.

To that end, senior management must serve the workforce, in the sense that it must help people learn, grow, contribute, and excel. Once in a while, it should also allow them to have some fun! This chapter mentions ways to inject humor into the workday, as well as new time-off and flex-time approaches to give employees more work-life balance.

To reward and recognize employees for their achievements and motivate them to do even better, the same quality management principles used in other processes may be put to work to determine compensation and recognition programs:

- Learn what the "customers" of the program *need* and expect. Effective programs are developed based on the needs and expectations of all employees.
- *Involve employees* in improving the compensation and recognition programs. This may include participating in discussions and opinion surveys, determining the goals and how to measure them, and creating award programs and nominating peers to receive them.

Companies must recognize and reward both individual achievements and team goals, and in order to be administered fairly, they must make at-risk pay and formal recognition dependent on *measurable* performance. Even better, have the employees establish, collect, and control the measurements.

Pay, benefits, and reward programs address some very basic human needs, such as security, acceptance, self-respect, achievement, and appreciation. Employees expect that they be fair, clearly explained, and equitably administered.

DISCUSSION QUESTIONS

1. Do you agree with the first quote in the chapter, from Dale Dauten? Why or why not? Take one side or the other on this issue, and write a few paragraphs (no more than 500 words) upholding your position.
2. Suggest a way that each of the companies mentioned in this chapter could add "more fun" to their work environments. Have you worked for a company that took "fun" seriously?
3. Do you think that giving employees time off as a reward is smart? Could it backfire on a company if the economy takes a turn for the worse and sales are impacted despite their hard work?
4. What do you think about the idea of compensation being "team-oriented"? Do you agree or disagree with it?
5. Why should a competitor company give another one salary information for a pay survey? What would be the advantage?

ENDNOTES

1. Baldrige "Core Values," 2005 Criteria for Performance Excellence, Baldrige National Quality Program, National Institute of Standards and Technology, U.S. Department of Commerce, Gaithersburg, Maryland.

2. James Oakley, assistant professor of marketing at Purdue University, quoted in *Incentive* magazine, New York, January 1, 2005.

3. Terry Bragg, "How to Reward and Inspire Good Sales Behavior," *Progressive Distributor* magazine, Pfingsten Publishing, LLC, Seven Hills, Ohio, November/December 2000.

4. John Jack, senior vice president of BI Worldwide, quoted in *Incentive* magazine, New York, March 1, 2004.

5. Joe Mullich, "A Reward Money Can't Buy," *Workforce Management* magazine, Crain Communications, Inc., Detroit, Michigan, July 2004.

6. Job-Sharing Policy and Flextime Policy, Division of Human Resources, Colorado Department of Personnel & Administration, Denver, Colorado, November 2001.

7. Jennifer Koch, "1998 Financial Impact Optimas Award Profile: Trident Precision Manufacturing, Inc.," *Workforce Management* magazine, Crain Communications, Inc., Detroit, Michigan, February 1998.

8. Jennifer Koch, "Satisfy Them with More Than Money," in *Workforce Management* magazine, Crain Communications, Inc., Detroit, Michigan, November 1998.

9. 2004 Benefits Survey results, Society for Human Resource Management, Alexandria, Virginia.

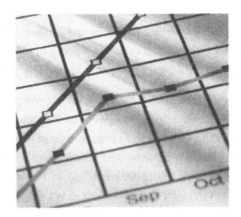

CHAPTER

7

Customer Contacts

Our discussion of customer-driven excellence continues in this chapter, where the presumably satisfied employees (of Chapter 6) meet the presumably satisfied customers (of Chapter 3) in day-to-day situations. In the new management model, companies intent on improving customer service have encouraged a greater number of employees to interact with customers on a regular basis. But is greater "personal contact" enough? As competition neutralizes the distinctions among products in many fields, companies vie to differentiate themselves through the quality of their service.

Exactly what makes excellent service? The 2005 Baldrige Award Core Values and Concepts state it thusly:

> *Customer-driven excellence is . . . a strategic concept. It is directed*
> *toward customer retention and loyalty, market share gain, and*

growth. It demands constant sensitivity to changing and emerging customer and market requirements and to the factors that drive customer satisfaction and loyalty. It demands listening to your customers. It demands anticipating changes in the marketplace.[1]

In Chapter 3, we discussed the methods by which several companies have achieved high levels of customer satisfaction. Many of the same principles are at work here; however, the focus of this chapter is on exactly *how the contact is made.* How "personal" does personalized service need to be? How is it delivered, and at what level(s) of an organization—to what level(s) of customer? And what if the business, by its very nature, does not afford much personal contact between employees and customers? As in any relationship, the success of a company's customer contacts depends on how well these issues are addressed:

- How the company defines its role in relationships with customers
- How it communicates this role internally, and to customers
- How it carries out the responsibilities in the relationship
- Whether it decides to outsource customer-contact functions
- How problems are solved when they are discovered
- What the company learns from the complaints it receives

Implicit in each of these points is the need to continuously improve. For example, FedEx (a company introduced in Chapter 2 for its outstanding leadership) cites three rules for achieving a quality perspective in customer contacts:

1. We must take the customer's viewpoint.
2. We must emphasize the emotional issues by making the product or service emotionally attractive.
3. We must look at everything that affects the customer.

These are relationship issues, even more than they are business issues. If all of this sounds too touchy-feely, consider this: Today's leaders know their employees can either set an engaging and helpful tone with customers or watch them run off with the first company that does.

Solectron, one of this chapter's role models and a two-time Baldrige Award winner, has an exemplary system for staying close to its customers. It updates and modifies its programs with input from *all customers, every week.* How is that possible? Let's find out, by examining customer contacts in three diverse companies: Solectron, Robert Wood Johnson University Hospital Hamilton, and Thomas Interior Systems.

Solectron. This manufacturing services company operates one of the world's largest surface-mount facilities for the assembly of complex printed circuit boards and subsystems. Its customers include companies that make computers, workstations, disk and tape drives, and other equipment. Solectron has a total of more than 60,000 employees; about 3,500 work in the United States. In the United States alone, benefits information for employees is translated into 18 languages and dialects!

The company is grouped into four business units: Global Operations, Technology Solutions, Global Services, and Microsystems. A rare two-time Baldrige Award winner (in 1991 and 1997), Solectron also wins numerous annual awards from customers for superior performance. Its Austin, Texas facility has won the Texas Quality Award, the Charlotte plant won the North Carolina Quality Leadership Award, and its Panang (Malaysia) facility won the Prime Minister's Quality Award, a Malaysian honor similar to the Baldrige Award, in 1997.

Robert Wood Johnson University Hospital Hamilton. One of the newest Baldrige Award winners (in 2004), RWJ Hamilton is located in Hamilton, New Jersey, where it serves a community of more than 350,000 residents. RWJ Hamilton is one of seven acute-care hospitals owned by the Robert Wood Johnson Health System.

As New Jersey's fastest-growing hospital, occupancy rates at RWJ Hamilton grew from 70 percent in 1999 to 85 percent in 2003. Primary services include cardiology, orthopedics, obstetrics, and surgery, as well as an emergency room that sees 52,000 visits a year.

RWJ Hamilton has 1,734 employees, who support a medical staff of more than 650. In 2004, a Center for Health and Wellness was added 4 miles from the hospital, that focuses on health education, community wellness programs, and physical therapy.

In addition to a Baldrige Award, RWJ Hamilton ranked first in nine categories in a 2002 Gallup Community Survey, including customer loyalty, best doctors, and best nurses; 73 percent of people surveyed say they are likely to visit again if their medical needs require a hospital.

Thomas Interior Systems. This finely tuned, family-owned business has been providing office planning and furnishings services to organizations of all sizes since 1977. It has two locations in the Chicago metropolitan area and about 40 employees.

The goal of owners Tom and Paul Klobucher is for the company to be an industry leader. "We sell office environments," they say, "but our number one product is customer satisfaction."

Apparently, the customers agree. Thomas Interior Systems has completed more than 15,000 projects, furnishing over 15 million square feet of office space and installing $400 million of products.

DEFINING THE CUSTOMER RELATIONSHIP

Successful companies in all types of industries are doing everything they can to bring their customers into their organizations—even literally. They are reorganized to be

- Customer-focused, instead of function-focused
- Driven by customer requirements, rather than operational requirements
- Relationship-oriented, rather than product- or service-oriented

The challenges are multiple: to create relationships without blurring the ethical lines between business and personal contact; to be concurrently quick and thorough, caring, and professional; and to exceed customers' expectations rather than simply meeting them; to name a few.

Before we introduce the customer contact methods of the three companies listed in this chapter, we'll mention another worth considering. In the early 1990s, Metropolitan Life developed what it called a "personal quality training program" for its insurance agents as well as others in the company. MetLife concisely identified six personal attributes that contribute to solid customer relationships:

1. Treat customers as you want to be treated when you are a customer.
2. Take personal responsibility to see that customers' needs are met.
3. Constantly seek to improve by learning as much as possible about your job so as to serve your customers more effectively.
4. Share your knowledge, skills, and time with others, offering help and assistance to customers and coworkers.
5. Have a positive outlook and be persistent in meeting customers' expectations.
6. Communicate effectively with customers and fellow employees.

With this list, MetLife recognized the power of personal contact. In fact, the attributes would be equally valuable in any type of relationship. It is striking to notice the similarities between MetLife's attributes of personal quality and the ways quality leaders such as Engelhard-Huntsville and Ben & Jerry's relate to their employees (see Chapters 4 and 6), or how Bose relates to its key suppliers (see Chapter 9), or the ways USAA relates to its community (see Chapter 10). MetLife's attributes have the feel of universal truths—like the behaviors that contribute to a good marriage or the wisdom we might pass along to our children. And yet they were the result of an extensive study of *customer expectations.* As the foundation for solid customer relationships, they are the point where intuition and intellect meet.

Of course, a common problem for large companies with multiple business units is having to implement by persuasion rather than mandate. Smaller companies can standardize their approaches more quickly and implement them throughout the company. In either case, it helps to have written policies.

At Solectron, the standards for customer contact are listed in a *Customer Service Guidelines Manual.* Compared to MetLife's general attributes, Solectron's specific standards may sound arbitrary and rigid. However, each company's standards reflect the expectations and requirements of its customers.

Solectron's 120-plus original equipment manufacturing customers are served by plants in the United States, Mexico, South America, Europe, and Asia. With such a small customer base, Solectron's employees constantly interact with the same customers. Solectron has translated its customer service requirements into *standards* that include the following:

- If unexpected problems occur, notify the customer as soon as possible; identify the problem and its impact, and propose an action and scheduling.
- Answer phone calls within four rings; respond to messages from customers within two hours.
- Acknowledge receipt of customers' problems as soon as possible; respond within 24 hours with a solution, an action plan, or a date for a plan.
- When a customer calls to complain, listen carefully; do not argue. Encourage the customer to talk, apologize for any inconvenience or misunderstanding, give assurance for satisfaction, ask for suggestions, and take action immediately. Follow up by calling back within four hours.
- Any Solectron person contacted by a customer represents Solectron. Do not blame Solectron's problems on any individual or department within Solectron. Resolve the issue internally and apologize to the customer on the company's behalf.
- All ongoing customer partnerships must have weekly formal exchanges with the customer.

Listen. Act. Take responsibility. Meet (or exceed) expectations. Be courteous. Communicate. The essence of Solectron's standards fits well with MetLife's attributes of personal quality. The definitions of these standards must vary with customers' expectations and the organization's structure, but the principles behind them are similar.

COMMUNICATING WITH CUSTOMERS

Good relationships require constant communication. At Thomas Interior Systems, only about a half-dozen employees do not have direct, daily contact with customers. With such broad exposure, the company recognizes the need for employees to be generalists, familiar with customer requirements and with every element of Thomas's business. It responds to the need with a Customer Focus Process—about 40 hours of training a year, to give every employee background in such subjects as product lines, specifications for major lines (i.e., carpeting, panel systems, electrical requirements), project management, delivery and installation, estimating, design, computer issues, and business math. All training is managed by employee teams, the units through which Thomas operates. Each team has a weekly meeting to focus on customer and operational requirements and performance. Team administrators also meet weekly to coordinate activities across team lines and to share learning.

At one point, Thomas decided that some extra face-to-face contact with customers would help both sides better understand the other, as well as give the company new clues about how to improve service. So periodically, every person in the company visits a customer—specifically *not* the ones they normally serve. While on-site, each associate is instructed to ask three questions about how Thomas Interior Systems could improve.

"We get a lot of good information from this," says president Tom Klobucher. "We take the top five expectations and revise our customer satisfaction surveys to reflect them."

In recent years, Thomas has discovered what its time-crunched customers want most is convenience. They have office buildings to furnish and not enough time to make the hundreds of decisions (with a dozen or so vendors) that this may require. The company used this learning to develop its "Total Resource Office Alliance," a group of 20 firms with expertise in many different areas that complement Thomas's office furnishings business. Now, a Thomas sales representative can make recommendations, get cost estimates, and even oversee complex projects for customers that require telecommunications, artwork, security systems, and other details beyond the 300 product lines Thomas Interior Systems normally offers.

In health-related businesses, the customer may be operating in crisis mode—for instance, in the emergency room of RWJ Hamilton hospital. The "customer needs" in this case are immediate, and the employee must take the reins (or, in this case, the clipboard) and assess the situation quickly and calmly. More than 70 percent of inpatient admissions at RWJ Hamilton start in Emergency, and the hospital received astonished reactions (from skepticism to applause) when, in 1998, it instituted the "15/30 Program." It's a guarantee that any patient coming into the emergency room will see a nurse within 15 minutes and a doctor within 30 minutes or their treatment is free. An average of one patient a month receives free service, out of about 4,300 visits.

15/30 is part of RWJ Hamilton's "Patient-Focused Model." For those who require an inpatient stay, it includes daily care plans that are created with input from the patient. The plans are not just medical charts. They include the person's cultural and language choices, opinions on lifestyle and quality-of-life issues, and organ donation wishes, to name a few.

At Solectron, business is done across continents and requires a more formal process for customer communication. Surveys are sent to every customer every week. Before a customer is surveyed, Solectron finds out who, within the customer's organization, has the best information on how Solectron is performing. That person is asked to reply to the survey. The company faxes or e-mails a one-page Customer Satisfaction Index (CSI) survey to these key people every Friday. The form asks one question each about quality, delivery, communication, and service. Customers respond with a letter grade (A to D) and any comments, then send back the completed form, usually within a day.

The CSI coordinators who receive the completed surveys at Solectron know from experience when a response suggests a problem. The coordinators are responsible for contacting the responsible division and explaining the problem, so that a plan of action can be discussed at a weekly meeting that includes senior executives and customer-contact people. Each meeting starts with a corporation-wide summary of the previous day's quality results, then turns to a review of the week's performance. Depending on the number or severity of the issues, managers spend up to half an hour describing the problems, analyzing causes, and proposing solutions. The purpose is not to put managers on the spot but to make customer issues highly visible.

"We want our customers to tell us weekly about anything they are dissatisfied with, and it doesn't matter whose fault it is," says Sae Jae Cho, director of customer satisfaction. "We want to make the problems visible to the management at this company. Not many problems last more than a week or two."

Solectron has found that most problems are caused by poor communication. The solution is often as simple as contacting the customer to make sure everyone agrees on what the problem is, then changing the communication process so that the lapse does not happen again.

As with all parts of the customer relationship, communication is the key to making customer surveys work. Companies that try to increase the frequency of surveys are often deterred if customers complain about how much work is involved, or when the return rate is consistently low. This typically indicates a problem with the survey, not the customer.

When Solectron encountered similar resistance, the various plants began inviting customers to attend the weekly meetings. "When they see that they aren't filling out a form just to fill out a form, and that the information they send back is used to improve, they tend to become believers," Cho explains. If a customer still resists, a division vice president visits the customer's president to explain the value of the process. The fact that every Solectron customer participates in the weekly survey suggests that customers believe the value outweighs the minor hassle.

Solectron began its weekly customer satisfaction index in 1987. In the first five years, it raised its average score from 86 percent to 96 percent. To understand how impressive that 96 percent is, consider the scoring values:

$$
\begin{aligned}
A &= 100 \text{ percent} \\
A- &= 90 \\
B+ &= 85 \\
B &= 80 \\
B- &= 75 \\
C &= 0 \\
D &= -100
\end{aligned}
$$

It would not take many Ds to bring the average down. By surveying its customers weekly and acting on their concerns immediately, Solectron prevents Bs from turning into Ds, retains satisfied customers, and gains new customers through referrals.

The survey is only one of many ways Solectron stays close to its customers. Customer focus teams review quality and current delivery schedules during weekly meetings. At some of the meetings, top executives of customer companies are asked to make presentations. Each quarter, a team headed by the senior executive who represents the customer's interests at Solectron visits the customer to discuss ways to improve existing projects and plans for future projects. A top-to-top executive survey is done twice a year, and an annual third-party survey provides objective data for comparison.

Outsourcing Customer Contact Functions

None of the three companies profiled in this chapter outsources customer contact functions, but no discussion of the topic would be complete without mentioning this trend. The current catchphrase is "**global sourcing,**" and it is among the most controversial business issues of the past decade. At this writing, no less than a dozen states are considering laws to restrict, or at least discourage, outsourcing government contract jobs to workers in other nations.

In a study released in March 2004, 45 percent of the 500 senior finance and human resources executives surveyed said their companies either currently outsource some business functions or are considering it "within the next three years." Half of the companies said the function "most frequently globally sourced" is customer relations. An average of 13 percent of their job functions were performed overseas, with another 12 percent being considered for "relocation" in the near future. For most (43 percent), outsourcing is a fairly recent move, beginning in 2000 or later.

The primary reason executives gave for outsourcing was cost reduction—92 percent cited it as their company's top motivation. 54 percent also mentioned "productivity improvement," and 38 percent said it allowed them the opportunity to staff customer service functions all day, every day.[2] The availability of a multilingual workforce is also attractive.

For the most part, the functions that are "offshored" are routine transactions. Proponents of outsourcing say this allows U.S.-based companies to focus their talent "at home" on the higher-paying sales and operations jobs, and frees up resources for research and development, allowing them to remain competitive. Having workers in a foreign country helps that country's economy, which is good public relations for the company and may pave the way for increased business in the region.

"Back home," however, the impact on customer contact can be major. A company must be willing to relinquish a certain amount of control over work provided by others under contract, and the sheer distance involved makes it almost impossible to monitor their activities. Language and culture can be potential barriers, as well as sufficient training for the new labor pool. There is a certain amount of risk from terrorism and political instability in some areas. Among the most underreported facets of global sourcing are the very different ways that commerce is conducted in some foreign markets, where bribes and kickbacks are "business as usual," part of a politically corrupt system. A United States-based company certainly doesn't have to cooperate, but it can be put in some touchy situations in these cases.

Interestingly, while most of the companies in the Hewitt Associates survey said they evaluate labor costs (88 percent) and analyze potential returns on investment (79 percent), only 40 percent analyze the tax structure, economic, and political climate of the countries to which they send the jobs.

Another kind of outsourcing that is extremely common is the local use of certain vendors or contract labor to perform such necessary tasks as printing, billing, building maintenance, recruitment, catering, vehicle fleet management, and so on. These types of arrangements are, for obvious reasons, not part of the "global sourcing" controversy.

However, whether it is a local accounting service or a technical support call center based in China, a company must always consider the potential impact on its customers as well as the bottom-line cost savings when it

OUTSOURCING—WHERE ARE THE JOBS GOING?

The top locations currently used for global sourcing include

- India   60 percent

- China   36 percent

- Mexico   32 percent

- Canada   15 percent

- Ireland   14 percent

(Percentages total more than 100 because some companies outsource jobs to more than one country.)

The areas of greatest outsourcing expansion from 2005 to 2007 are expected to be Southeast Asia and Eastern Europe.

Source: 2004 survey results, Hewitt Associates, Lincolnshire, Illinois.

hires another firm to handle part of its business. A final word from the Hewitt Associates survey: 23 percent of the respondents (U.S. companies that outsource to foreign countries) said the move has had a "positive impact on their brand," while 11 percent said it had a negative impact. And 30 percent indicated there had been a negative impact on morale in their own workforce.

USING CUSTOMER INPUT

Most companies understand that the simple act of offering a questionnaire, survey, or "report card" has the subtle effect of letting the customer know their feedback is valued. Some companies seem to stop right there. Sure, someone probably reads the completed surveys and follows up on the most serious issues raised. But if the data is not compiled and monitored for progress (or lack thereof), a survey becomes a public relations tool, and not an especially effective one at that. Ongoing research and analysis are necessary to aggressively seek a competitive advantage—an advantage that is really the point of surveying customers in the first place.

How do our "all-star" companies handle the input? RWJ Hamilton has created a database called "Voice of the Customer" as a place to gather all customer and/or patient information. The sources include:

- Customer satisfaction surveys
- Physician referral trends
- Demographics of the area
- Information on competitors
- Any other market research

To capture customer feedback, Thomas Interior Systems relies on its customer satisfaction surveys and on employee participation in the weekly team meetings. About one-fourth of the surveys are returned, and every employee either reads or hears about every response. Results for each question on the survey are compiled and tracked monthly. If employees hear directly from customers, they bring those issues to the weekly team meetings for discussion and action. All action items are addressed at the team level first, then across teams as necessary, before they are elevated to the management level.

Solectron enters all of its weekly survey information into a database, to track numbers and plot trends by customer, category, division, and so on. On the evening before an executive meeting, the CSI coordinators compile this information for the next morning's presentation.

And what about the people who fill out the surveys? Today's customer wants to be part of the process that makes improvement happen. They are keen observers, and in an era of information overload, any of them can access the Internet to purchase other goods and services from other sources or, at least, research their options and be well prepared to debate quality, price, contract terms, and other important issues.

What do we know about meeting (or exceeding) their needs based on the customer contact methodology and follow-up protocols of the three companies profiled in this chapter?

- Solectron engages its customers by inviting them directly into the plants for meetings. This instantly builds Solectron's credibility, "disarming" disgruntled customers and making use of their brainpower (free of charge) to help solve problems.
- Frustrated by endless waits in doctors' offices and intimidated by medical technology and terminology, customers (patients) feel powerless and even victimized by a health care system that often treats them as "cases" or insurance policy numbers instead of individuals. RWJ Hamilton spoke directly to these strong emotions in the creation of its 15/30 and Patient-Focused Model programs.
- The Total Resource Office Alliance is a value-added service that Thomas Interior Services might never have taken the time to create without learning of the need for it from customers. Thomas was doing a great job of selling office furniture and did not have to take on the extra work of forging new partnerships. But being driven by customer requirements instead of its own operational requirements, Thomas has created

the opportunity to gain more customers (with referrals from the other businesses in the Alliance) as well as assist its own client base more effectively.

In summary, if a company asks for honesty from its customers on a regular basis, they are likely to deliver. The feedback may include a few things company executives secretly wish they didn't have to hear. On the other hand, this candid communication builds an atmosphere of mutual trust, helps a company tailor its services to its target customers, and spurs business growth as a result of referrals.

LEARNING FROM COMPLAINTS

Customers should be encouraged to communicate and complain in any way they choose, but there must also be a formal process for logging and handling complaints. For example, at Solectron any grade of B– or worse on a customer survey is considered a complaint and is formally logged into the company's system. Solectron sends an acknowledgment to the customer that it has received the complaint and is addressing it, then pursues one of two problem-solving modes:

- If something is out of control in the process, the company does whatever is necessary to bring it back into control. There is a formal process to find out what happened and to take steps to prevent it from happening again.
- If the process is in control but the customer is unhappy, it tightens the tolerance limits on the process, using statistical tools.

All complaints are tracked until they are closed. This brings up the desired end result of customer contact: a fountain of ideas for continuous improvement. Sampling products on a production line cannot achieve the same results as listening to customers. Sometimes, the problem is not with the product—it may be with the instructions or improper use of the product in the field. It may be that customers' expectations of it are different than the company's intention. Personal feedback from actual humans is the only way to pinpoint these types of issues.

There are four ways to categorize issues raised in surveys and/or complaint processes. Each focuses on eliminating the root cause of the original complaint.

- **Repair.** A part or product that is broken or damaged when it arrives at the end user must either be repaired or replaced. This category does not alter the process by which the item was made, nor does it change the design of the item itself. It is a short-term, individual solution to an individual complaint. When undertaken, the results are almost immediate—the item is replaced, case closed.

- **Renovate.** Outdated production methods or pieces of equipment are replaced by newer technology, and/or technological advances allow something that was made by hand to be made (faster or more consistently) by machine. Again, the process itself does not change, nor does the product. It is simply made differently. Renovation is costlier (at least up front) and sometimes riskier than the old, tried-and-true way of doing the job.
- **Refine.** In this case, once again, the process or product is not changed but improved. Usually, this involves making a process more efficient or effective. It often happens over time, not all at once, such as in the Kaizen theory of process improvement.
- **Redesign.** This is the "back to the drawing board" phase at which a company decides its customers will never be truly happy with a product "as is," or perhaps it has a compliance issue—not meeting a safety requirement, for instance. If it's a service, it just isn't selling. A team is gathered at this point and charged with using the most current complaint and/or customer needs data to come up with something new.

Translating complaints to make them useful to a company's quality assurance (QA) efforts has been divided into a helpful six step process by John A. Goodman and Steve Newman, the president and director of research, respectively, for TARP, the Technical Assistance Research Program in Arlington, Virginia. Following are brief outlines of them:

1. **Evaluate Problem Severity.** Determine whether the problem is really worth worrying about. What kind of marketing impact does it have on the company? Does it impact customer loyalty or the company's market share? If not, do QA resources need to be allocated to it? Goodman and Newman suggest there are several aspects to a complaint that will indicate the severity of the problem: if the customer threatens to switch brands or service suppliers; if the dissatisfaction is enough that the complaint is sent to senior management; and (if it's a survey) whether the customer would recommend the product or service to others. If not, there's a serious problem.
2. **Extrapolate to the Marketplace.** If the "problem severity test" is met, the company must estimate the possible number of occurrences in the marketplace. Since a high percentage of dissatisfied customers never complain to the company—they may complain to others, then choose to do business elsewhere—this can be difficult. Rounding up similar complaints from field offices or sending out a direct survey are two ways to accomplish this.

3. **Estimate Revenue Impact.** How many customers will be lost because of the negative experience and also the negative word-of-mouth that will result? TARP research indicates about 37 percent of non-complainers will remain loyal if the problem is small. Ironically, about 10 percent of complainers, even if they are not satisfied, will remain loyal simply because someone listened to them and empathized with them.

4. **Compare the Data to Internal Measurements.** If the number of complaints is going up but the internal measures of quality (repair rates, system downtime, service call schedules) haven't changed, the problem may be in the directions or labeling, or in the installation or service procedures.

5. **Determine the Cause.** Goodman and Newman say detailed data collection is not done in most companies, so the complaints are often too general and QA must interview customers more extensively to pinpoint a cause. This takes time. A classification system that "codes" incoming feedback as it is received would be helpful.

6. **Determine the Solution.** The most effective solution is, of course, the one that eliminates the problem. However, in the real world, a company's QA staff must look at all options in terms of cost-effectiveness—how much time and money it takes to repair or replace the item, redesign it, relabel it, and so on.

Goodman and Newman also have some good overall advice about how to deal with complaints: First, remember that a new complaint does not always indicate the existence of a problem, only a suggestion that further investigation is warranted. Second, complaints tend to increase when customers are given a new "complaint vehicle," such as a toll-free hotline. And finally, complaints often flag short-term concerns. In these researchers' words, "They indicate smoke, not the existence of fire."[3]

CHAPTER SUMMARY

Successful companies use every opportunity to learn more about what their customers need and want. In some cases, they work to make their customers feel that they are part of their organizations, to the extent that this is possible. Some include customers in their strategic planning process, because they understand that customer requirements will drive the results. They plan to stand out from competitors by exceeding the customers' expectations.

Constant communication solidifies customer relationships and ensures a better level of honesty when problems arise. Communication is much easier when

- Customer contact is continuous.
- As many employees as possible are involved.
- A variety of communication vehicles are used.
- Formal processes are established for listening, analyzing, and responding to complaints.

Outsourcing is a growing trend in customer service. This chapter detailed both the reasons it is commonly used and the potential downsides for meaningful customer contact and a sense of "personal service."

When customer feedback indicates a complaint or problem, this chapter introduces ways to pinpoint and solve the problems cost-effectively from a quality assurance standpoint.

DISCUSSION QUESTIONS

1. How important is telephone etiquette in the maintenance of good customer relationships? Do you think automated answering devices help or hinder customer contact?
2. As noted in this chapter, some companies survey customers weekly or monthly, some whenever they deliver products, and there are other systems as well. What would you say is the optimum frequency for a customer survey?
3. Would you agree with Solectron that most customer service problems are really communication problems? Why or why not?
4. How would a manufacturing company reach better levels of understanding between customers and employees if most of the employees had no customer contact at all?
5. Do you feel outsourcing is beneficial or detrimental to United States-based companies? Explain your answer in 500 words or fewer.

ENDNOTES

1. Baldrige "Core Values," 2005 Criteria for Performance Excellence, Baldrige National Quality Program, National Institute of Standards and Technology, U.S. Department of Commerce, Gaithersburg, Maryland.

2. "Global Sourcing Trends and Outcomes," *Corporate Restructuring and Change Practice*, Hewitt Associates, Lincolnshire, Illinois, March 2004.

3. John A. Goodman and Steve Newman, "Six Steps to Integrate Complaint Data into QA Decisions," *Quality Progress* magazine, American Society for Quality, Milwaukee, Wisconsin, February 2003.

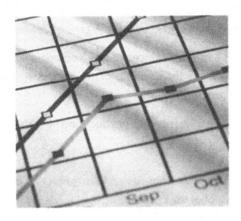

Design of Products and Services

The design of products and services is the most customer-focused activity most companies undertake. In the design process, external requirements are translated into internal requirements, and customers "throw the switch"—or nowadays, perhaps "click the mouse"—that activates the business. The design process constantly forces companies that are truly customer-driven to reevaluate customer requirements and their responses to them. It is a cauldron of opinions and ideas stirred by customers, suppliers, and employees at virtually every level of a company.

Popularly known as *concurrent engineering*, this process encourages everyone involved in product development—designers, engineers, customers, and suppliers—to contribute *simultaneously as a team*. Is this difficult to accomplish?

Without a plan, you bet it is. Even *with* a plan, with team members in different cities and/or on different continents, an extra degree of difficulty is added.

In this chapter, we will use the experiences of three companies known for excellence in this field to examine the design process. Each enterprise offers new insights into the following topics:

- Translating customer requirements into product and service design requirements
- Ensuring design quality
- Reducing **cycle time** (the time from design to introduction of a product)
- Design teamwork in a global workplace
- Improving the design process

We will address these points a little differently here than in other chapters. Because each of our three models has a distinctive design process, it would be confusing to jump from one to the other in order to make a particular point or draw a general conclusion. Instead, we will present each company's process individually. All three touch on the similar aim of achieving design quality by using both internal and external input, as well as up-to-the-minute technology, to satisfy customers.

Intel Corporation. Intel is the world's largest semiconductor company, and #53 on the list of Fortune 500 companies. About 80 percent of the world's personal computers contain an Intel-branded Pentium or Celeron microprocessor. Headquartered in Santa Clara, California, Intel employs more than 80,000 people—up from 50,000 five years ago—in almost 300 offices and manufacturing facilities. Building of a new $2 billion production plant in Ireland was announced in 2004. In the United States, *Working Mother* magazine included Intel on its 2003 list of Top 100 Best Workplaces for working moms; PC *Magazine* recognized Intel in 2004 with two awards for technical excellence. The company also gets high marks for its hiring and training programs for workers with disabilities.

The impact of the global economy is seen in the fact that about three-fourths of Intel's business comes from continents other than North and South America; roughly half of its sales are in Asia. You can't stay on top of an industry without extensive research and development efforts. Intel spends more than $5 billion a year on them, and in 2004, the company introduced a total of six new desktop processors and "chipsets" that connect a computer's processor, I/O slots, and system memory, allowing data to flow between components.

"Our goal is to be one generation ahead of the rest of the industry in process technology," said CEO Craig Barrett in Intel's 2003 Annual Report. But 2005 brings big changes for Intel, as the high-energy Barrett reaches the company's mandatory retirement age. Barrett then becomes board chairman, and COO Paul Otellini takes over as president and CEO. He will be the first non-engineer to run the company in its 35-year history.

American Express Financial Advisors. Through a network of 750 offices around the United States, the business products segment of financial powerhouse American Express offers financial planning, insurance, and other investment advisory services to individuals and businesses. More than 100 financial and investment choices are included in the AEFA product lineup, including mutual funds, life insurance, annuities, and securities brokerage services. The company employs 5,000 people at its headquarters in Minneapolis and at regional offices, and supports 10,400 advisors, independent contractors who sell the company's products. Total sales for 2003 (the most current year available) exceeded $6 billion.

GfK Custom Research, Inc. This company was known as Custom Research, Inc. when it won the Baldrige Award in 1996. It has since become the U.S. subsidiary of the GfK Group, an international market research organization with more than 5,000 employees and headquarters in Nuremberg, Germany. As part of this global family, GfK Custom Research can work in cooperation with research partners in any of 90 countries, although it is responsible primarily for research and product development for U.S.-based clients. The American office is based in Minneapolis, with 120 employees stateside. U.S.-based annual revenue topped $32 million in 2003.

GfK-CRI professionals work with their client counterparts to design research projects that will provide information the clients need to make good business decisions. "Research should empower you, not overwhelm you," says the company Web site. Most projects deal with some aspect of new product development, including testing new concepts, products, packaging, advertising, and pricing, as well as tracking products' popularity and strategizing with clients to target and reach customers more effectively.

PRODUCT DEVELOPMENT—THEN AND NOW

The traditional method of product development worked much like a relay race. The product passed like a baton, from one group to the next, on its way to the "finish line" or launch date. The sequence used to look something like this:

- Sales and marketing identify a customer need and define the requirements to meet that need.
- They tell engineering what they want.
- Engineering develops a product in a series of steps that can take several years.
- When engineering finally has a model that marketing is happy with, it "tosses it over the wall" to manufacturing.
- Manufacturing figures out how to produce it.

This **serial design process** (or **sequential engineering**) seems to work well on paper, but in the real world, it is lengthy and fraught with chances for miscommunication and duplicate efforts. Decisions are made at various stages without the benefit of valuable input from affected parties. When this input is finally received, designs must be reworked, new models created, new tests ordered, and new production schedules arranged.

By comparison, companies that use **concurrent engineering** find it typically cuts the time from conception to production in half, reduces costs, and improves quality. Concurrent engineering improves quality by "building it in" in the early stages of development. In fact, many companies refer to it as **quality by design**. The process takes into account the manufacturability of products and deliverability of services; it anticipates quality issues and initiates corrective action *before* the design is completed. This proactive, prevention-based approach has proven to be a more effective way of improving quality than rolling out an almost-perfect product and fixing problems as they are discovered in the marketplace. Judy Corson, one of two partners who founded the original Custom Research, Inc., puts it succinctly: "Quality pays—and it's more fun! Doing things over is not."

Intel's Chairman of the Board Andrew Grove has said, "When companies lose their proprietary advantages, speed seems to be what matters most." To keep up the pace, as Intel regularly introduces new microprocessors, it continues to work behind the scenes on its next three generations of products. Remember, however, that this *is* the real world, where even the most forward-thinking plans are not perfect. In 2004, Intel was forced to delay the release of one product—a slightly faster Pentium 4 processor—by more than six months as it worked out fabrication problems.

Involving all relevant departments (and a company's true experts from those departments) in product design simultaneously has cost-saving benefits, too. Although only 5 to 8 percent of a product's cost is spent in the design phase, these critical decisions lock in 60 to 80 percent of the total costs. A change in the design that may cost $1,000 early in the process can cost millions as production nears.

Through concurrent engineering, companies strive to involve customers throughout the development cycle. If the goal is to translate their requirements into products and services, it makes sense to keep them close, so the design team can run new ideas and changes past them. The improved communication is one of the key reasons that concurrent engineering works. The challenge for global companies like GfK-CRI and Intel has become how to keep communication flowing across time zones and geography. Even with sophisticated technology, real-life considerations (like the lack of overlapping work hours on different continents) must be taken into account.

The idea of forming cross-functional teams to design products and services is equally applicable to service companies. They too share the goals of reducing cycle time, cutting costs, and improving quality. The primary difference is that the variability of a service is often in the hands of the person or team providing it.

For example, if a customer sits down with a bank loan officer to talk about borrowing money, the loan officer must determine the type of loan to recommend. This requires building a relationship with the customer, learning what he or she needs and translating those needs into a loan package that fits his or her situation. Indeed, the list of options from which the bank officer chooses may also have been generated during a loan "design" process. However, the officer's *relationship with the customer* is often more important to satisfying and retaining that customer than the loan itself. As one of our corporate examples, American Express Financial Advisors, has discovered, its clients' primary requirement is a long-term relationship with one financial planner whom they trust. More than a decade ago, the company redesigned its entire organization specifically to improve this relationship, as you'll read in a moment.

Before delving into the design processes of our model companies, you should note what "quality by design" is *not*. It *does not mean* simultaneously designing and producing—rather, it means not producing anything until the design is complete and agreed upon by all parties. It *does not mean* inspecting products more often, or at more points along the way in a manufacturing process. And if it is not handled by a team of specialists, working with reliable research and adequate resources going in, the design process cannot guarantee enormous savings of time or money, let alone a better-quality product.

INTEL: COMPETITION AND COLLABORATION

When Intel introduced the Pentium processor in 1993, experts hailed it as the most important product in the company's history. But in technology-related businesses, a company must act a bit like a professional football coach, depending on the star quarterback for the current schedule but ever mindful that there are a few interesting college prospects who could be the keys to the team's future. The star is the star—until someone better is developed. And someone better *will* be developed.

Although there have been numerous processors since the first, after years of industry kudos, in May 2004 Intel stopped work on the next generation Pentium 4 and another product known as Xeon. Instead, the company redirected its resources to another Pentium product with a later release date.

"They were probably a couple of years in design," William M. Siu told *Scientific American* magazine in November 2004, as the manager of Intel's desktop platforms group who pulled the plug on the projects. The company acknowledged that the Pentium 4 microarchitecture had reached the end of its life earlier than planned.[1]

Of course, the company was already hard at work on the next big breakthrough. Intel develops its next stars through a design process that relies heavily on input from three sources: the people who use computers run by Intel chips, the computer manufacturers (Intel's customers), and the host of experts at Intel, from architects and engineers to marketing staff members.

The company has a formal process for soliciting the views of its end users: A consortium, consisting primarily of information systems managers, meets every four months in the United States and Europe, and every four to six months in Asia. Participants are queried about what they want from products, how they use their computers, and what applications they use.

Intel's customers (the largest are Dell and Hewlett-Packard) are also surveyed about their needs, distribution channels, and so on. Intel's internal experts combine this customer and end-use input with their own experience and knowledge to brainstorm possible design solutions. The design process begins by posting open-ended questions to these experts. As their ideas are narrowed to specific types of products, Intel begins to bring customers back into the design loop to test the experts' perceptions. The general feeling is that, early in the planning stages, the issues are complex, technical, and not particularly interesting to customers. The design teams would rather show them something farther along in the process.

Of course, exceptions are made as necessary. For instance, Hewlett-Packard engineers worked side by side with Intel's to create the Itanium 2 servers in 2001. The collaboration was worthwhile for both companies, but at the time, it presented a potentially sticky situation. After all, Intel was working with a major customer to develop a product that would also be used eventually by a number of HP competitors. To avoid the appearance of favoritism, it was necessary to view the HP engineers much like temporary, contract workers. Intel's technical marketing organization acted as a buffer for the engineers, answering competitors' questions and providing reassurance while the design team concentrated on its work.[2]

Typically, Intel does not directly involve *suppliers* in the product definition phase either—that is, unless a question is raised about whether (and how) a new technology might affect a supplier's capabilities. In this case, the supplier is represented on the design team by an internal representative of the supplier who works on-site at Intel. (This type of on-site partnering arrangement is becoming more common and is discussed in greater detail in Chapter 9.)

Collaboration obviously has its merits. In 2001, Intel announced contracts with four leading manufacturers to form the Embedded Electronic Manufacturing Services Providers (EEMSP) program. For Intel, the organization's dual goals are to share design and technical expertise while building loyalty for Intel products among the engineering teams of its collaborators. Today, the list has grown to six companies on Intel's EEMSP team—including Solectron, profiled in Chapter 7.

High-performance companies are also bringing more internal groups into the design process. You may have heard the expression "laying the silo on its side," meaning a company is striving to create a more horizontal organization by overcoming the functional **"silos"**—the marketing department, the engineering department, the manufacturing department, and so on—that have traditionally dictated how the company operates. Some companies pull together people from these different silos into one physical area to work on a specific product, product line, or service. For manufacturing design, these cells become the hub for the company's concurrent engineering activities.

Once a product has been defined, Intel moves to the design phase, which follows a product implementation plan (PIP). The PIP identifies the critical steps of the development cycle, including design completion, customer samples, approval, and product certification. Designs are reviewed regularly: weekly by the design team, monthly by management, and quarterly or semiannually by the executive staff. An ongoing review ensures the product continues to meet specifications, is still manufacturable, and will still perform as expected, so that when it is actually produced, it will meet all customer and internal specifications.

Internally, one of the biggest challenges for Intel has been global team collaboration. In 2004, an internal company survey on the topic found that about two-thirds of Intel employees are involved in some sort of *virtuality*— for example, team members meet across time zones, across business groups, or across cultures, to name a few of the variables. And, while almost all team members speak English, there are different dialects and cultural considerations that can slow communication.

The survey found that while being "geographically distributed" has had almost no impact on team performance, the cultural differences can pose a challenge. Other sources of frustration have been the use of different communication tools (i.e., not everyone uses the same tools to collaborate on a task, and the tools may not be interoperative), and that two-thirds of Intel employees belong to multiple teams simultaneously, making it difficult to schedule meetings and keep track of the large numbers of documents and records generated in team projects.

The survey results were part of a multiyear study that is typical of the thorough way Intel approaches challenges, and pertinent to the whole point of this chapter—that good design solutions require a great deal of collaboration and research. The authors of the project, Cynthia Pickering and Dr. Eleanor Wynn, PhD, compared 21 different collaboration tools on the market, and found that no one vendor offered all the key attributes necessary to meet the authors' concept vision. Their project conclusions are far too detailed to quote in full in this chapter, but they included in-depth analyses of the following:

- The communication needs and desires of Intel's people
- How teams and meetings are managed from a process perspective
- What is required to make a virtual team collaboration workspace truly useful
- What types of technology are necessary to support team collaboration
- A five-year "roadmap" to achieve the concept vision

One interesting example mentioned in the report to help bridge the social and cultural gaps is the idea of an "Electronic Person," a personal profile that each team member can use online to communicate with others. An employee can post a photo, résumé, data about when and where they can be reached for meetings, the current time of day wherever they happen to be, and even "emoticons" to indicate what kind of mood the person is in that day. This enhancement is expected to be fully launched by 2006. Other ideas include asynchronous meetings (in which each team member has particular parts of a task to complete and post by a certain deadline, without all having to meet at once) and roaming voice conferencing.[3]

At present, Intel is working hard to improve the design process for the next generation of chips by 2006. They will contain two "cores" (engines that perform computing functions) instead of a single core. By running more cores at a slightly slower pace, the chips won't generate as much heat—which is better for the computer. It's only one of the innovations the Intel design teams are surely working on, somewhere in the world, at this very moment.

AMERICAN EXPRESS FINANCIAL ADVISORS: DESIGN QUALITY AND CYCLE TIME

American Express Financial Advisors has been in a good news/bad news dilemma. The good news is, its affiliation with financial giant American Express gives it instant name recognition and credibility. The bad news is, its parent company is still known primarily for credit cards and travelers checks rather than financial planning.

In 2004, AEFA set out to change this with its biggest-ever advertising campaign. It spent more than $20 million in a few months getting the word out about its multitude of services, both on television and in print venues—more than the company spent in all of the previous year.[4] The goal of the ads, which continued in 2005, is to "brand" the American Express Financial Advisors' products. Branding is critical because, of course, financial planning is a relationship-oriented activity in which people trust the achievement of their financial goals to an individual advisor, as well as the company that supports the advisor.

AEFA suspected as early as 1986 that it needed to focus on this relationship to succeed. It got serious about it in 1990. By then, the company had made several sincere efforts to improve client relationships, but none had taken root. Business was good by industry standards, but not as good as the company knew it could be. Senior management decided the only way to break through the barriers to change was to redesign the entire system, and the best way to drive the change was through a new cross-functional team created solely for this purpose.

The 31-person team focused on four objectives:

1. Retain 95 percent of clients.
2. Retain 80 percent of the financial planners who had at least four years of service, and 97 percent of its Senior Financial Advisors.
3. Achieve annual revenue growth of 18 percent. (In 2003, it was about 10 percent.)
4. Bolster the company's position as industry leader. (Chief competitors are Merrill Lynch, Smith Barney, OppenheimerFunds, and other financial planning service providers.)

The team spent almost a year interviewing clients, advisors, managers, and staff members to get a thorough picture of the existing system. They benchmarked companies such as Motorola, Microsoft, and Wal-Mart to find out how other firms handled similar processes. When their research was completed, they developed a list of process- and system-oriented recommendations, most of which were implemented over the following decade.

Although sales and employee retention were the ultimate goals, the recommendations wisely focused on serving the needs of clients. AEFA asked advisors to form groups that would make a broader level of knowledge available to their customers. Additional training positioned its advisors as true experts in the world of personal finance, which seems to become more complex by the minute. Today, each client still has a primary advisor, but if the client needs more specialized information about a particular topic, such as tax planning or education funding, the primary advisor may defer to another advisor in the group who has that expertise. This also means that when the primary advisor is not available for any reason, someone else from the group can step in for the moment.

To support the groups of advisors, AEFA reorganized its field management, which had a traditional hierarchical structure, into coordinating teams based on geography, demographics, and numbers of clients. A group vice president leads each team.

To serve field managers' and advisors' needs for information, AEFA then identified just about anything an advisor would need to serve clients. This included upgraded technology so that routine functions like name or address changes can be completed instantly online. Computer programs also give the advisor the flexibility to tailor presentations to a client's preferred way of receiving information—columns of numbers or with pie charts and graphs, longer explanations or shorter ones, and so on.

With the reorganization of the company, every advisor became a product designer, of sorts. He or she gained the authority to bring other experts into the design process—other advisors or headquarters personnel—with the end product being a plan to meet each investor's requirements. AEFA also redesigned its processes and products to improve service to its clients and advisors. Client service processing is an example. AEFA used to have a different service area for nearly every type of product it sold. If clients or advisors had questions, they might be passed to several departments before they got one that could help. To improve service, the company looked at this process from the client's perspective, then created service teams that could answer all product service questions from clients and advisors in one call. It also organized its coordinating teams around specific geographic regions so that each team's operating hours match the region it serves.

In addition to its functional silos—marketing, finance, legal—AEFA also has *product silos*. The life insurance group develops its own products, as do the annuity group, the mutual fund group, and the other product groups. The process is not always seamless. In 2004, the company was criticized for entering the 401(k) retirement account market late, almost three years after Congress allowed it and major competitors had been offering it. However, a plan was created based on advisor and client feedback, and at least 1,500 investors are anticipated to have American Express 401(k) accounts by 2006.[5]

Currently, the company is working hard to target the business of the so-called mass affluent market—that is, people who are not considered "wealthy" but who have amassed between $100,000 and $1 million and are looking for intelligent investments. It's a lucrative niche market worth an estimated $6 trillion.

As examples of what a service-oriented product includes, the latest AEFA plans, unveiled in 2002, contain the following benefits:

- **Gold Financial Services.** For investors of $100,000 to $500,000. This program includes face-to-face meeting time with the AEFA advisor, tax advice, retirement and college planning, plus a no-fee credit card, home loan discounts, higher interest on savings accounts, and a free personal Web site on which they can check their balances and pay bills online.
- **Platinum Financial Services.** For investors of $500,000 to $1 million. This program includes any of the "Gold" offerings, plus more complex advice on estate planning, charitable giving and business transition strategies, trust services, and so on. It also includes some luxury perks, such as concierge services, airline tickets, and more.

A financial advisor must take additional training to be able to offer these packages to investors; for the Platinum program, only Senior Financial Advisors are eligible to sell it. The target market is folks who are doing pretty well in the financial scheme of things but are just not "rich enough" to get much attention from high-powered bankers and stockbrokers. The face-to-face meeting time was determined as a critical factor in customer satisfaction. This combination of caring advice from a "real human," along with the prestige of the American Express name, could be exactly what AEFA needs to boost business. The company literally has a division called the "Affluent Client Group."[6]

AEFA began honing its competitive edge 15 years ago, when it redesigned not only its processes, products, and services, but the entire company and culture. Today's strides prove that, even when initial efforts are successful, the job is never quite finished.

"The objectives of the reorganization were client retention, advisor retention, revenue growth, and image in the industry," says Ora Kaine, AEFA director of National Implementation and Advisor Services. "We have found that the redesign has improved all four areas."

GfK CUSTOM RESEARCH: RESEARCH "BY DESIGN"

According to independent surveys, Custom Research Inc. (CRI) is a leader in its industry. It has been customer-driven since it was founded in 1974, and that customer focus permeates its design process.

GfK-CRI, as it is known today, provides a small but critical piece of much larger projects for its clients. It does the market research for large companies that want to find out more about their customers' preferences before they make any expensive decisions. These corporate clients have four key requirements of their research: It must be accurate, on time, on budget, and relevant to their questions. For every research project it accepts, the project team assigned to carry it out works with the client to define what these four criteria mean *for that specific project.*

Almost every project involves custom-designed research. It is the service company equivalent of a "job shop." Because each project is unique, the company organizes its services into four modules, listed alphabetically with brief descriptions as follows:

- **Brand Equity and Positioning** utilizes GfK-CRI's brand management research tools to evaluate how much *brand equity* (the value of its name recognition, reputation, quality attributes, etc.) a product has in the marketplace and/or how much potential it has, as well as who (and how keen) the competitors are.
- **Customer Satisfaction and Loyalty Tools** include effective ways for client companies to improve customer relationships, find out how loyal *their* customers really are, and determine returns on investments for these efforts. This research is backed up with creation of statistical models, and GfK-CRI's ability to integrate and analyze data from multiple sources.
- **New Product Development** includes just what its name indicates—concept and package testing and in-home use testing, leading to sales estimates and needs assessments. Methods include everything from focus groups to Internet-based surveys.
- **Strategic Segmentation** helps client companies come up with the ideal customers for their products, which will determine how they market products based on the target groups' needs and preferences.[7]

For each project, the client company can choose from this "menu" of services to design their own "product" that consists of the specific research services that they seek. The process includes meetings between client company, a GfK-CRI senior executive, and the account manager, who works directly with the client to determine the scope of the project. A summary of the meeting is circulated to the team members who will work with that client. The senior executive also summarizes the client's requirements in a letter, which is sent to the client for verification. The letter (revised if necessary to reflect client feedback) becomes the basis for planning and action by the project team and for the team's service standards and account plan.

Communication between customer and supplier is nothing new, but for small service companies—law firms, advertising agencies, and medical practices, to name a few—defining specific client requirements on paper and verifying their accuracy with the client are rarely done with any consistency. GfK-CRI does it every time. It is especially critical in an industry that deals with feelings, perceptions, and concepts, not concrete products.

The result is a *project design,* based on the client's expressed requirements, to guide the project team's efforts. The follow-up document is a *plan of action,* created by the account manager and project team. It includes the research design, data collection and tabulation details, statistical analysis, and final report, along with timetables, responsibilities, and cost estimate—in short, what's going to be done, by whom, in what time frame, and at what cost.

A critical element in the success of a research project is the design of the questionnaire that will be used to collect the data. The results must satisfy the client by accurately reflecting what the target audience thinks and feels about the subject. Since 1997, GfK-CRI has done more than 1 million consumer interviews online, and it has trademarked some of its proprietary research templates and tools (with names like "Emotional Brand Intelligence" and "Criterion" concept testing) for their ability to perceptively pinpoint consumers' thoughts and behaviors.

"We've identified four to eight fatal flaws that can render the project useless," says partner Jeffrey Pope. "We have checkpoints that will reveal if any of these flaws are present in our questionnaires."

Questionnaires are also presented with a small sample of people, including the client, to evaluate the effectiveness of the design. "We have a lot of checks and balances built into the design process," adds partner Judy Corson, "such as having the client review the questionnaire, determining how to code any open-ended questions, and finding out what the client wants in the survey report."

Every quarter, a United States-based steering committee compares the performance with its clients' four key requirements: Was it accurate? Was it delivered on time? Was it on budget? Did it exceed the clients' expectations? Account teams also review their performance quarterly for major accounts. This relentless drive to measure and analyze its performance, together with the company's constant communication with clients, has produced exceptional customer satisfaction.

The GfK Custom Research experience offers three lessons for similar firms:

1. **Be explicit about what the clients expect.** "We've sat down purposefully and periodically with our clients to discuss their requirements. It's rare they don't tell us something we need to learn," says Pope.
2. **Measure customer satisfaction.** The research isn't done just because the project is done. The company sends a short questionnaire to every

client on every project, asking about the client's overall level of satisfaction, and it conducts periodic telephone surveys of its major clients. Follow-up means "service after the sale." It reinforces that the company cares about its reputation and its customers.

3. **Tie internal measures to customer requirements.** GfK-CRI has established such internal measures as Project Quality Recap Reports. On each project, every team member documents problems or errors on questionnaires, data tables, reports, and timing. Companies in "high-touch" service industries often like to claim that what they do cannot truly be measured. GfK-CRI has shown that it can be—and should be, if continuous improvement is the goal.

CHAPTER SUMMARY

In the new business management model, the design process has been taken from the hands of an elite corps of engineers, or a marketing department, and delegated to a host of internal specialists. To gather these specialists, teamwork has become commonplace. People from marketing, engineering, manufacturing, and other "silos" collaborate as a product is created, to address every aspect of its design, production, delivery, and service—and this is critical: *before any facet of production begins*.

In some cases, companies invite customers into their teams to better understand what customer requirements really are and how well their ideas are responding. They pull key suppliers into the process, to benefit from their special knowledge and to assess their capabilities.

The quality-by-design process is an interesting combination. It may be an intensely creative and sometimes freewheeling exchange of information and ideas, but it retains its structure and its focus on very specific goals: to meet or exceed customer requirements, design quality into the product or service, and "get it out there" to customers or end users faster than before. Indeed, as shown in the examples from Intel and American Express Financial Advisors, companies are not seen as on top of their game when they delay getting new products to market, even for the "right" reasons.

To differing degrees (based on the types of products), all three companies profiled in this chapter put the responsibility for product design in the hands of specialists who work directly with the clients. Compared to the traditional one-size-fits-all mentality, this allows translation of customer requirements into products and services that meet those requirements *exactly.* Equally important, the requirements and steps to be taken to meet them must be consistently documented and approved or modified along the way, by team members and the client. No surprises at the end!

Meeting customer requirements. Improving quality. Reducing cycle time. In the new management model, the design process has the most critical role in achieving these goals.

DISCUSSION QUESTIONS

1. What's wrong with the *serial design process*, as described early in this chapter? For some types of products, wouldn't it work just fine? Why or why not?
2. Why would a company "lay the silo on its side"? Is it still important to *have* a corporate hierarchy if you are trying to foster teamwork? Could a smaller, service-oriented company perhaps do without one?
3. What do you think of Intel's "Electronic Person" communication idea? What else would you suggest to prompt team spirit across cultures and time zones?
4. How does teamwork minimize the risk of human error in each of the three companies in this chapter?
5. Look at any company for which you have worked, and describe how it handles the product or service design process. What improvements would you suggest now that you've read this chapter?

ENDNOTES

1. W. Wayt Gibbs, "A Split at the Core," *Scientific American* magazine, a publication of Verlagsgruppe Georg von Holtzbrinck, Stuttgart, Germany, November 2004.
2. Erik Sherman, "OEMs Inside: How Intel developed the Itanium 2," *Electronics Design Chain* magazine, a publication of Reed Electronics Group, New York, Winter 2002 issue.
3. Cynthia Pickering and Eleanor Wynn, "An Architecture and Business Process Framework for Global Team Collaboration," Information Services and Technology Group, *Intel Technology Journal*, Intel Corporation, Santa Clara, California (Volume 8, Issue 4, 2004).
4. "AmEx advisers no longer a secret," *Crain's New York Business*, a publication of Crain Communications, Inc., New York, November 11, 2004.

5. Jenna Gottlieb, "New American Express 401(k) Seen Late to an Eager Market," *American Banker* magazine, a publication of Thomson Media, New York, November 10, 2004.

6. Kristin French, "Pursuing the Almost-Wealthy," *Financial Planning* magazine, a publication of Thomson Media, New York, December 1, 2004.

7. "Honomichl Top 50" *Marketing News*, a publication of the American Marketing Association, Chicago, Illinois, June 9, 2003.

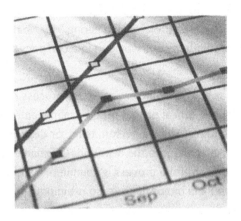

Managing Processes and Suppliers

All work involves some sort of process, and most processes cut across vertical slices of the functional organization. Process-oriented thinking forces companies to ask, "Exactly how are we going to do this, step-by-step?" This, in turn, prompts employees performing individual tasks to see where their "step" fits into the larger picture. There are processes for understanding customer requirements, for communicating requirements throughout an organization, for determining and tracking key measures, for strategic planning, for involving employees, for measuring and improving customer satisfaction, and for all other key elements that define a company's "work."

There are even processes for managing the processes! For example, to improve quality, a company first must determine which of its core business processes are used to satisfy customers. These processes, in turn, must be made as effective and efficient as possible. Some companies call this "process in-novation," "core process redesign," or "reengineering." By whatever name, process management often affects every person in a company and every task performed.

In this chapter, we look at how several companies use process management to satisfy their customers. A critical part of process management is managing the "handoffs," those points at which a person, team, or department com-pletes the work and passes it along to the next unit. Companies seek fewer, faster, defect-free handoffs until the process is complete. Handoffs may also be external, involving suppliers or contractors, so it's important to build these relationships into the processes. The topics include:

- Identifying and improving processes
- Popular process management tools used in today's corporations
- What makes a good customer-supplier relationship
- Selecting suppliers
- Giving and receiving supplier feedback
- The pros and cons of *inplant representatives*

The interesting thing about processes is that inevitably they must change with the times. Companies' priorities, the economy, the industry, and the products themselves all undergo changes. Therefore, the processes require maximum flexibility—or, in the words of the Baldrige Award criteria, agility—to remain effective over time. Our corporate role models that have managed to accomplish for the chapter are Ames Rubber Corporation, Bose Corporation, Raytheon, and Wainwright Industries.

Ames Rubber Corporation. In business since 1949, Ames produces rubber-covered rollers, molded and extruded parts, and elastomeric (syn-thetic polymer) products. It serves customers in a wide range of industries, but its specialty parts are indispensable in copiers and printers. Ames also makes components for the aerospace and pharmaceutical industries, and gas masks for the U.S. military. All products are made to order to customers' design specifications.

The company has about 200 employees in its three New Jersey plants. One is a subsidiary (called Amesil, Inc.) that manufactures silicone tubing, hoses, and connections. In 1972, Ames also reached across the Atlantic to form a joint venture company with England's Avon Rubber, with plants in the United Kingdom and the Czech Republic.

Ames won the Baldrige Award in 1993 and is ISO 9001:2000-certified. In 2004, a 28-year employee, Charles A. Roberts, became company president. In the same year, Avon-Ames Ltd. introduced its newest line of color-copy fuser rollers in Europe, designed to last more than twice as long as traditional copier rollers. The technology is also scheduled for U.S. release, with Ames' bottom-line growth predicted to be at least 50 percent by 2009.[1]

Bose Corporation. Bose designs and manufactures high-quality audio products for home and commercial use. It is perhaps best known for its Wave radio, which was introduced in 1993; the current model plays CDs as well. Bose also makes state-of-the-art sound systems for auditoriums and retail stores, speakers for stage performers, and more. Bose has also partnered with manufacturing giants (including Zenith, IBM, and General Motors) over the years to improve sound quality in televisions, personal computers, and car stereo systems.

Bose is a privately held company that bears the name of its founder, Dr. Amar G. Bose, the MIT electrical engineering professor who founded it in 1964 and still serves as CEO. The company has 8,000 employees at manufacturing locations in the United States, Canada, Australia, South America, Asia, and Europe.

Bose has hundreds of suppliers, but only a few with which it has pioneered a supplier relationship concept known as JIT II in the 1990s. Bose has since created the nonprofit JIT II Education & Research Center to help companies learn about and apply the concept, about which you will learn more in this chapter.

Raytheon. It would be difficult for the casual observer to keep track of all the transformations this company has undergone! In 1992, it won a Baldrige Award as Texas Instruments Defense Systems and Electronics Group with about 12,000 employees. Then, TI sold its defense business to Raytheon, and Raytheon also merged with the Hughes defense business. For a time, the Baldrige-winning division was called Raytheon TI Systems (RTIS); now the whole company has been renamed Raytheon Systems Company (RSC).

Now that we've got that straight, Raytheon designs and manufactures advanced defense systems and electronics technology, primarily for the U.S. Department of Defense. Employing 78,000 people, the company makes just about every military and Homeland Security component imaginable, from missiles to airport security systems, command-and-communication vehicles, surveillance and reconnaissance equipment, and turboprop aircraft, to name a few.

Formed during World War II, it is one of the world's largest defense electronics contractors and its ranking in 2004 was just shy of the Fortune 100, at #107. In recent years, the U.S. war efforts in Afghanistan and Iraq have turned the company's financial picture around from losses in 2001 and 2002 to profits in 2003, with $20 billion worth of new Defense Department contracts in 2003 alone.

Wainwright Industries. Wainwright is the sole producer of piston inserts for automobile manufacturers, but it also manufactures a broad range of high-volume, close-tolerance metal stampings and assemblies for automotive and aerospace customers, including housings for power seats, car windows, and antilock brakes.

Located in St. Peters, Missouri, Wainwright is a privately held company with less than 300 employees. It won a Baldrige Award in 1994 and was honored as one of *Industry Week's* 10 best plants in 1996, along with numerous awards for "Best Manufacturing Practices" since then. The plant received QS-9000 certification in 1997. Not a bad record for a company that, a few years earlier, had cut workers' hours to only three days a week after being hit hard by an economic recession. Wainwright underwent a radical transformation that included

- Doing away with time clocks and putting all employees on salary
- Doing away with blue- and white-collar workers by putting everyone in uniforms
- Allowing any employee to look at the company financials, any time
- Reassigning workers during slowdowns and/or retraining them for other jobs

Wainwright instigated its Continuing Improvement Process in 1991. Since then, an average of 65 recommendations from members of its workforce have been implemented per year.

IDENTIFYING PROCESSES

Before examining how our benchmark companies manage their processes and work with suppliers, let's identify a couple of terms and concepts. First, a **process** is a group of related tasks that yields a product or service—in this case, to satisfy a customer. Demonstrated graphically, a process would look like Figure 9-1, the COPIS model. The acronym is in reverse order, to show more clearly how the model is customer-driven:

$$\text{Customers} \rightarrow \text{Output} \rightarrow \text{Process} \rightarrow \text{Input} \rightarrow \text{Suppliers}$$

Many companies craft their own models to show a similar process. At the time of its Baldrige Award application, the Texas Instruments division that is now part of Raytheon came up with the depiction in Figure 9-2. No matter how they are shown, the approach is the same: Identify what is important to the customer, identify the approach, and measure the results. For many, however, this common-sense idea still generates major resistance from individuals, departments, and entire businesses.

Why? What companies often find when they embark on a process improvement method is that they put a great deal of effort into debating, identifying, mapping, benchmarking, and planning the improvements . . . only to discover they are just barely beginning to make headway. At first it is exciting, but soon people become discouraged and start to question the value of the effort. The more they realize their own jobs or attitudes may have to change, the less they want to shake up the system, even in the interest of improving quality. The larger the organization, the longer it can take to see meaningful results—and this means years, not months.

On the other hand, almost everyone realizes that a company needs the best possible raw materials in order to put out the best possible products. So one good way to improve quality is to take a closer look at the process for choosing suppliers. This is beneficial for two reasons. It forces the company to rethink how, where, and why it is obtaining goods and services, and to decide how these relationships could be improved. And suppliers that

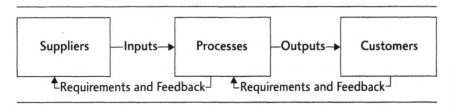

Figure 9-1 The COPIS model: How processes satisfy customers.

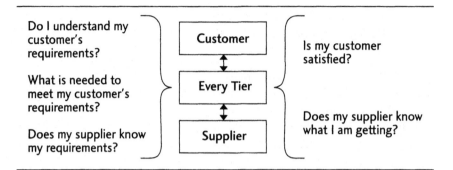

Figure 9-2 The customer–supplier relationship at RTIS.

have already instituted their own quality improvement methods and goals may have valuable ideas to share.

Who are "the suppliers"? Primarily, they are other companies from which goods and services are obtained at some stage of production, delivery, and use of a company's products and services. Depending on the industry, they may be called vendors, manufacturers, distributors, dealers, contractors, franchisees, strategic allies—or any combination thereof. We have chosen not to address issues specific to each type of supplier but to present general ideas and strategies that can apply equally well to all of them.

Before we introduce supplier relationships into the picture, let's discuss good process management in general.

Process Management Tools

We've already introduced IBM's trademarked Six Sigma® training in Chapter 1. Six Sigma is a process for improving processes, and in the 1990s, it was the approach used by the TI division that is now part of Raytheon to win its Baldrige Award. As you now know, "six sigma quality" translates roughly to no more than 3.4 defects per million opportunities. It is reached by defining these six points:

1. Identify the product you create or the service you provide. (*What do you do?*)
2. Identify the customers for your product or service, and determine what they consider important. (*For whom do you do your work, and what do they expect?*)
3. Identify your needs to provide a product/service that will satisfy the customer. (*What do you need to do your work?*)
4. Define the process for performing the work. (*How do you do your work or process?*)
5. Make the process mistake-proof, and eliminate wasted effort. (*How can you do your work better?*)

6. Ensure continuous improvement by measuring, analyzing, and control-ling the improved process. (*How perfectly are you doing your customer-focused work?*)

The purpose of this deceptively simple routine is to help employees de-fine, measure, control, and improve their processes. However, even after a process has been improved, it is still subject to significant variations known as **out-of-control occurrences** or "**noise.**" To bring the process back into control, this group applied another process they called the "QC Story." Companies worldwide use this eight-step process to identify the root cause of a problem and implement improvements:

1. Select the problem.
2. Understand the current situation.
3. Identify the root cause.
4. Plan improvement.
5. Execute improvement.
6. Confirm results.
7. Standardize the improvement.
8. Study remaining problems and/or make future plans.

The steps resemble the "DMAIC" theory of Six Sigma (see Chapter 1), with a couple of extra steps added. Today, Six Sigma is still the quality im-provement process at Raytheon—saving the company an estimated $275 million in its first three years—but it has been augmented by other systems used to manage entire projects, and even hundreds of projects simultane-ously. They include

- **Earned Value Management System (EVMS, or EVM)** is a set of processes and tools required by many government agencies, including the Depart-ment of Defense, the Department of Energy, NASA, and the Office of Management and Budget. The theory behind EVMS is that a budget is es-tablished for each task in a process, and as the work progresses, that portion of the project's total budget is "earned" a step at a time. It's a way to track ongoing costs, catch overruns, and make corrections long before the end of a project. It is also extremely useful in meeting the antifraud provisions of the Sarbanes-Oxley Act of 2002, which lays out rules for internal controls for financial reporting.[2]
- **Capability Maturity Model Integration (CMMI®)** is a proprietary product of the Software Engineering Institute (SEI), a federally funded research and development center sponsored by the U.S. Department of Defense and operated by Carnegie Mellon University. CMMI is a sophisticated, specialized version of process management for engineering applications. There are several components to CMMI that improve scheduling and quality, including supplier sourcing as an area for cost-cutting. The "ma-turity levels" of the processes are rated from 1 to 5, with 5 indicating the

process has achieved best practices in its area. CMMI can be introduced in one area of a company at a time ("staged"), or the program can be rolled out all at once ("continuous").[3]

- An **Integrated Product and Process Development System (IPDS)** is a compilation of every process, method, and tool that a company uses in its projects. For example, for a new project, teams are created called Integrated Product (or Process) Teams (IPTs) at the "doing level" of each process. Their job is to work together to see that all groups—departments or functions, special interests, suppliers, and so on—are active and equal contributors to the process, not just monitors of it. IPTs are formed not only for manufacturing a product but for customer support, training, logistics, and other activities necessary to launch it successfully when it's finished.[4]

Does all this sound like an awful lot of meeting and planning? Perhaps. But these methods keep people from different functions and their suppliers in direct communication with each other and allow them to work toward predictable performance metrics, on a timeline and a budget schedule.

In an address to the 14th Annual Integrated Program Management Conference in 2002, Raytheon Company President William H. Swanson (he is now Chairman and CEO) called EVMS "perhaps our most critical management tool." Here is an excerpt from his presentation, used with his permission:

> We're a global technology, defense, and aerospace leader. We have approximately $17 billion in sales, and we're one of the nation's largest defense contractors.
>
> We've been in business for 80 years. As I said, we have over 77,000 employees, we manage about 8,000 programs, and we submit over 10,000 proposals per year.
>
> What you should take away from these numbers is that we are a large company comprised of many individual programs. I like to describe us as a mutal fund of programs.
>
> And the company's success is driven largely by the success of our programs. Many of these programs are highly complex and technical, ranging from underwater torpedo guidance systems to space-based infrared sensors, and everything in between.
>
> And although we have lots of talented people, we can't assume we'll find an all-star to run each of our 8,000 programs. So we have to use common sense, not rocket science, to manage them.
>
> We have to use discipline and processes that are repeatable across our programs.[5]

As Swanson points out, the process a company chooses to manage its projects must be flexible enough to use in many different situations.

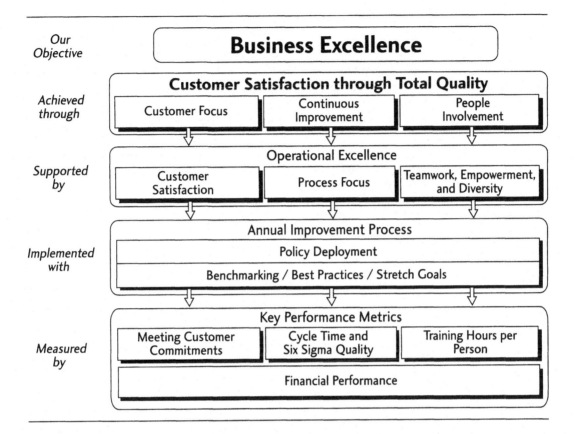

Figure 9-3 The TI-Best system.

The end result of such a process is to satisfy customers by performing projects faster, less expensively, and/or more intelligently by enabling a team or company to measure its performance as the work progresses.

Many companies also have an annual process they use to define what constitutes "Business Excellence" (or whatever similar term they come up with). The performance of each process or project is compared to this standard. Figure 9-3 shows a simple system in which customer, process, and people strategies are cascaded through an organization.

PROCESS IMPROVEMENT

We've discussed some of the popular systems and terms for creating and managing processes. But actually improving them doesn't always require a fancy system or a big company. It can be as simple as picking your priorities and identifying them with green flags when they're on target or red flags when they need improvement.

Management attention has never been lacking at Wainwright Industries. In the past, however, much of the attention focused on financial results and not on the people and processes that produced those results. Once senior leaders decided to change that, their attention shifted from the results of their processes to the processes themselves and the workers who perform them.

As Chairman and CEO Don Wainwright put it, "We realized that it takes three things to promote ownership: focusing on the customer, involving employees, and maintaining a high level of training. We realized that people are responsible for managing themselves—that they don't need micro-managing."[6]

Since then, these have been Wainwright's master goals:

	Master Goals	Key Quality Indicators
1	Safety	Safety record
2	Employees	Internal satisfaction
3	Customers	External satisfaction
4	Quality	Six Sigma quality
5	Net income	Business performance

"It's amazing how, with safety first, employees second, and net income last, the numbers keep going up," plant manager Michael Simms observes. Within five years of instituting the changes, Wainwright had reengineered the processes for making one of its principal products—metal-stamped housings for electric motors. Lead time, for instance, dropped from almost 9 days to 15 minutes. Defect rates were reduced tenfold. For customers, the benefits translated into an on-time delivery rate of 98 percent (compared with 75 percent previously) and a 35 percent reduction in product cost. On-the-job accidents decreased 82 percent. Attendance is at 99 percent. Sales rose from $20 million in 1990 to $28 million in 1995. They currently top $30 million.

What in the world happened? First, Wainwright began looking at process improvement as two separate vehicles: one, as a normal part of everyone's daily job, and two, as a more formal team activity. Wainwright manages its process through standard control methods, such as Statistical Process Control (SPC), and through the strong desire of its people to improve. All key processes at Wainwright have been mapped, and the requirements for each have been identified. All employees have been trained in root cause analysis, the tool used to evaluate and improve the key processes.

"Mission Control" is the conference room at the plant in which quality and performance charts and graphs are displayed for all to see. They include monthly satisfaction index scores (grades of A to D from customers), along with weekly customer feedback reports and updates on the plant's progress on its stretch targets. All information is linked to the company's key indicators, and the results are easy to spot: A green flag means Wainwright is on track; a red flag means that improvement is needed. If there's a red flag, you can bet there's an "action team" working on it.

Further, every customer has a "champion" in the plant. Within 48 hours of a customer expressing a concern or complaint, the champion will form a team of people who are most knowledgeable about the customer and/or the process. Depending on the size of the issue, the team takes quick corrective action or initiates a more significant process change effort. The team lets the customer know what's happening throughout the improvement process.

ENSURING SUPPLIER QUALITY

We can also learn something about good suppliers from Wainwright. Like many companies, in addition to being a customer and expecting top quality from its suppliers, Wainwright is itself a supplier. One of its largest customers is General Motors, which has a plant nearby where utility vans are assembled. About 10 years ago, Wainwright built a quick-response warehouse facility specifically to meet GM's needs. The warehouse contains not only Wainwright-built parts but about 1,500 other components from 50 different suppliers. Multiple Wainwright trucks deliver to GM daily.

Some companies would consider it a hassle having to manage a separate warehouse and all the logistics that go with it. But Wainwright saw it as a chance to become indispensable to an excellent customer; to get an inside look at the true needs of that customer and to grow new business as well by creating relationships with its other suppliers. Wainwright developed a similar program to work with Boeing, another of its top customers.

Several of the gurus of Total Quality Management have insisted that customer-supplier relationships are like family units, in which everyone works toward the same goal and has a stake in it, but their independence and identities are preserved and respected. Dr. Kaoru Ishikawa, whose theories were mentioned in Chapter 1, was a proponent of this thinking. He outlined the relationship thusly:

- It is the customer's responsibility to provide clear and comprehensive requirements to the supplier so the supplier will know exactly what is expected.
- It is the supplier's responsibility to produce the quality of goods or services that will satisfy the customer.

- Together, they should decide on the methods they will use to evaluate quality.
- Together, they should agree on a contract that includes terms for all facets of the relationship—quantity, quality, delivery methods, prices, payment terms, and what to do in case of any disputes or problems.
- They should exchange information and work together on teams as needed to improve quality.
- They should always have the best interest of the end user in mind.

Before mapping out the relationship, however, a company must answer some very basic questions about a topic known in the business world as *sourcing*—that is, where raw materials or particular services come from:

- Do we really *need* an outside supplier? Can we make this item (or perform this service) ourselves? Is it something we can do better/cheaper/faster in-house? For example, some companies use travel agencies to make all of their business travel arrangements; others have their own in-house travel department.
- Should we use a single source for an item, even though several are available?
- Should we rely on multiple sources, splitting the business between them?
- How often should we rethink our supplier relationships?

While sourcing decisions would seem like common sense, the business world does not always embrace sensibility. How many times are tasks undertaken in a certain way "because that's the way it's always been done?" How many suppliers are used because "we've worked with them for years?"

The importance of improving supplier quality and performance grows as companies pare down to their core competencies. Companies that want to be lean and agile in ever-flatter organizations strive to do only what they do best and to outsource the rest, ideally without sacrificing quality, schedules, or cost. This is possible only when a company abandons its adversarial relationships with suppliers and establishes long-term partnerships.

Generally this happens slowly, as companies do business together and learn to trust and understand each others' systems over time. For example, prospective Wainwright suppliers begin with a two-step Vendor Certification Process: The supplier fills out a report that details all of its controls (how it measures quality, designs processes and specifications, tests products, chooses subcontractors, and so on). Then a Wainwright employee visits the supplier's facility for an onsite inspection. The process rates vendors as "Approved," "Preferred," or "Certified," depending on the results of the two steps.

Wainwright goes further, giving feedback to the "Approved" and "Preferred" vendors to get them to the "Certified" level. Only a few reach it. The point of the system is not to constantly improve the vendors (although that's a valuable side benefit). The point is to assess them all fairly and accurately—which is key to any supplier evaluation process.

At Ames Rubber Corporation, specific requirements are given to suppliers. "We're a job shop," says Ed DiPetrillo, Ames's purchasing manager. "We're always building to somebody's blueprints."

In addition to the job specifications, Ames measures suppliers on quality and delivery. Using Six Sigma and Lean manufacturing disciplines, there are department goals for where Ames expects suppliers to be by category, such as metals, components, or raw materials. The goal is to hit 99 percent, a single number that is a combination of the vendor's quality (60 percent) and delivery (40 percent) ratings. Ames tracks each supplier's performance in these two areas and shares it with them monthly.

Rather than haggling, Ames also relies on suppliers to offer their best prices. Ames has benchmarked pricing to get an idea of market prices, but it doesn't play one supplier off another just to get the best deal. Ames has found that its corporate culture and the high degree of technical knowledge in its purchasing department have given it greater credibility in dealing with suppliers. "We are a very open, honest company," DiPetrillo explains. "We treat people the way we want to be treated. By having that open relationship, we expect to get their best price."

Ames has built such relationships with less than two dozen key suppliers, down from 42 in 1990. The company made a deliberate effort to slim down its supplier base in order to accomplish the following goals:

- Increase clout. (Major customers get more attention than the rest of the pack.)
- Simplify the interaction. ("It's easier to deal with one person versus 10," says DiPetrillo.)
- Reduce costs. (Prices go down for purchasing in greater volume from fewer sources.)
- Build partnerships.

A **partnership** is a long-term relationship, a commitment between two or more entities to produce a particular product or achieve a specific goal. In this case, although contracts are negotiated and signed, the term "partnership" does not mean forming a separate corporation in the legal sense. There are, however, some built-in legal concerns. One is that partners do not leak proprietary information to competitors or to the news media. This type of openness and honesty does not exist automatically. Corporate partnerships take time to develop, and even after they do, customers must be clear about the boundaries of the relationship in their contracts.

BRINGING SUPPLIERS INPLANT

One of the leaders in redefining supplier partnerships is Bose Corporation. In 1987, Bose took the venerable **Just-in-Time (JIT)** manufacturing concept and created what it called **JIT II.**

"For eons there have been sellers selling and buyers buying, and it's basically been adversarial," says Lance Dixon, now executive director of Bose's JIT II Education & Research Center in Framingham, Massachusetts, where the system is taught to businesspeople from around the world. "We determined that we had sellers selling to us and they weren't really selling; we had been 'sold' on their companies for years. And we had buyers who weren't really buying. I knew there had to be a better way to do this."

Dixon's idea was to have representatives of key suppliers work full-time in Bose's facilities. The representatives operate at the buyer level and are empowered to use Bose's purchase orders to place orders at their own companies. They are invited to attend any design engineering meetings involving their companies' product area, with full access to Bose's facilities, personnel, and data. JIT II eliminates the buyer and salesperson. The **in-plant representative** (or "inplant," for short) becomes the link between Bose's planning department and the supplier's production plant. Dixon calls it "insourcing."

The only limitations on an inplant are the same limitations placed on Bose's own buyers. They place orders for standard cost items whose price has already been calculated, and each representative has a purchase limit. Orders above that limit require a signature from a purchasing supervisor. The normal controls that the typical purchasing systems and purchasing manager place on a buyer function quite well.

Bose is currently in JIT II relationships with 12 suppliers. There is only one JIT II supplier per commodity, although Bose continues to use competing suppliers as necessary for the same commodity. A supplier may be a candidate for JIT II status when they exhibit the following qualities:

- General supplier excellence, the best in a given commodity.
- Dollar volume over $1 million. (Four of Bose's current suppliers have revenues under $20 million.)
- Good delivery record.
- Experience with large numbers of purchase order transactions.
- Computer skills and evolving technology, but not necessarily at a revolutionary pace.
- Good cost levels already being achieved.
- Operations in a Bose area that does not involve key trade secrets or sensitive technologies.
- Good engineering support already being provided.

Both Bose and the supplier receive incentives for beginning a JIT II relationship. The participating supplier's business with Bose typically increases by 35 to 45 percent, and Bose's savings in overhead alone are about $1 million a year. For example, when Bose moved from a JIT relationship to a JIT II relationship with one supplier, it reduced inventories to one-eighth of the already-low levels achieved through JIT.

The key to making JIT II work is the in-plant person. As part of Bose's system, the inplant spends much of the time getting information, analyzing and critiquing Bose's plans, and working with Bose's engineers on product development using existing materials.

"You want engineers to design state-of-the-art, innovative, exciting products using routine, standardized parts, which goes against human nature," Dixon explains. "The idea of calling in suppliers to contribute to concurrent engineering also goes against human nature, because engineers get busy, they move fast, and sometimes they don't take the time to talk to outside people. And if you bring in the suppliers too late, it's not concurrent engineering. Now imagine a dozen people, all experts in their given commodities, roaming engineering and offering their assistance."

As an example, Dixon points to one in-plant supplier that Bose asked to reevaluate a design for a speaker enclosure. The supplier suggested a resin change that saved Bose $50,000 a year.

Inplants have an interesting edge over more traditional employees—a dual career path. They can advance in their own company or choose to work for Bose after one year. After Bose established its in-plant representatives, it discovered that improvements occurred not only in purchasing but also in planning, engineering, importing, and transportation. For example, Bose's JIT II transportation suppliers share access to their computer systems that control material movement. For 98 percent of manufacturers, material en route to their factories is considered "still in the pipeline." Bose considers it inventory, because it can track that material anywhere in the world. At the other end of the pipeline, suppliers no longer need to stash piles of buffer inventory. You might say Just-in-Time has replaced "just in case."

Bose's success with JIT II has generated a great deal of interest in the past decade. Most of its suppliers now use it in their marketing with other customers. JIT II is not for everyone, however. It requires a true leap of faith between companies. Many companies are simply not ready for the openness and long-term commitments required for JIT II to work. (The Bose agreement, for instance, is an *evergreen contract*—no end date and no bidding. Now that's faith!) And yet, even Bose still purchases more than half of its materials from non-JIT II suppliers.

CHAPTER SUMMARY

How does a company "do what it does"? What are the processes? Because all work is part of at least one process, *process-oriented thinking* changes how people approach their work. Employees who learn teamwork and problem-solving skills can manage and improve their processes.

Business relationships are built among employees, customers, and suppliers alike. Poor connections between or within these groups sabotage the system and impede improvement. The companies in this chapter use many of the attributes normally thought of as individual traits and apply them to their business model: treating people as you want to be treated, taking responsibility, improving yourself, sharing your knowledge, having a positive outlook, and communicating effectively. These values must be applied consistently, and the results measured fairly, across all of the groups.

As discussed in earlier chapters, quality leaders rely on training, recognition, teamwork, and empowerment to dramatically improve quality and performance. Such initiatives are equally effective with suppliers. The companies in this chapter take the time to analyze suppliers' business strengths, weaknesses, commitment to process improvement, and willingness to accept feedback.

Collaborative processes like JIT II are proof that the lines between customers and suppliers are blurring as companies become more "horizontal." Their focus on core competencies elevates suppliers' roles and importance from customer-vendor to partnership arrangements that include the sharing of risks and rewards, and a focus on mutual goals, including quality.

DISCUSSION QUESTIONS

1. Thinking about your present employer (or the job you've had most recently), write each of the steps in two different quality-related processes used on that job. What is/was your role in the process?
2. Select one of the major process improvement systems Raytheon uses— CMMI®, EVMS, IPDS, or Six Sigma—and find out more about it. Who else uses it? What makes this system stand out from its competitors?
3. What factors would you look at when rating a supplier's performance? How would you handle a decrease in performance if the supplier had an understandable reason for it?

4. Single source, multiple source, or do-it-yourself? Let's say the issue is printing, and you are a purchasing manager. How would you determine whether it was smarter to buy a state-of-the-art printer and print materials in-house or negotiate a contract with one or more printing companies?

5. If you ran a company, how would you feel about the use of so-called *evergreen contracts*? What are the pros and cons of such an arrangement between a customer and supplier?

ENDNOTES

1. Brad Dawson, "A Step Ahead," *Rubber & Plastics News*, a publication of Crain Communications, Inc., September 20, 2004.

2. Ruthanne Schulte, "Use Earned Value to Comply with Sarbanes-Oxley," *Projects@Work* magazine, Fairfax, Virginia, April 10, 2004.

3. CMMI® background information from Web site of Carnegie Mellon Software Engineering Institute, Pittsburgh, Pennsylvania, www.sei.cmu.edu/cmmi, January 5, 2005.

4. Vaughn Pleasant, Program Management Specialist, "AFMC Integrated Product Development," *Results of the Aeronautical System Division Critical Process Team on Integrated Product Development*, U.S. Air Force, Washington, D.C., November 1990 (reviewed August 1996).

5. William H. Swanson, president, Raytheon Company, in remarks to 14th Annual Integrated Program Management Conference, Tyson's Corner, Virginia, November 18, 2002.

6. Michael A. Verespej, "Best Plants of 1996," *Industry Week* magazine, a publication of Penton Media, Cleveland, Ohio, 1997.

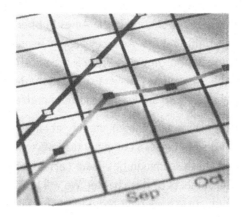

1 0

Corporate Responsibility and Citizenship

Companies should manage their reputations as carefully as they manage their employees, their new product development, and their other assets. For many people, however, the connection between business management and corporate citizenship is perplexing. What does it actually have to do with *quality*? What do environmental issues have to do with improving performance? Community involvement is nice—but is it necessary? And if so, how much is "enough," when a company is juggling so many other priorities?

When quality leaders are asked *why* their companies participate in volunteer or advocacy programs, their responses tend to fall into two categories: (1) because it is profitable or (2) because it is the right thing to do. An example of the first response is 3M, which has saved an average of $4 million every year for more than two decades through its "Pollution Prevention Pays" program. An example of the second is the Ames Rubber Corporation (introduced in Chapter 9), through its "Ames Outreach Team" that encourages employees to volunteer. And they do—in 125 organizations, for 1,300 hours a month. Ten of the "Teammates" have a special volunteer responsibility as tutors for fellow workers who are learning to read and/or write.

Every company has relationships with the community at large—local, state, national, and global—and sometimes, a company discovers almost by accident that one or more of these "communities" have certain, often unspoken expectations that are the subjects of this chapter. We will look at how three businesses in different industries have built reputations for taking the lead in corporate citizenship, charitable pursuits, and public goodwill; and we'll use their experiences to answer these questions:

- How do companies address the topics of responsibility and citizenship?
- What expectations does the public have of today's companies?
- What impact does globalization have on corporate responsibility?
- How do companies handle controversial social issues?

Like the decision to make quality improvement a corporate priority, decisions to make public responsibility and citizenship a priority require enlightened leadership and an ongoing cultural transformation. As the benchmarks show, what is good for the public can also be a good business strategy. The efforts of numerous companies are mentioned in this chapter, but the efforts of four in particular—Ben & Jerry's Homemade, Inc., SAIC, 3M, and USAA—are profiled.

Ben & Jerry's Homemade, Inc. The quirky junior high school buddies who started making ice cream in a Vermont garage in 1977 have been at the forefront of community service (and, as you'll see in this chapter, social activism) for two decades. The company commits to spending 7.5 percent of pretax profits through its Ben & Jerry's Foundation, which uses the endowment to grant millions of dollars annually to "not-for-profit grassroots organizations, which facilitate progressive social change . . ."[1] The company now sells frozen confections in a dozen countries (international sales account for about 12 percent of revenue) and owns and/or franchises more than 230 "Scoop Shop" retail outlets.

Ben Cohen and Jerry Greenfield made their fortunes and mulled over several buyout offers over the years before finally selling their business in 2000 to Unilever, a $45 billion international consumer products company, for $326 million. As acquisitions go, this one was controversial because its owner now seems to be the antithesis of the folksy, hippie culture that the original founders worked so hard to create.

By 2002, Ben & Jerry's had experienced two layoffs and two plant closures in its home state of Vermont—but Unilever has committed to continuing the work of the Ben & Jerry's Foundation and donated $5 million to the organization as part of the buyout. The Unilever veteran who is now Ben & Jerry's president formed a "Culture Club" to reassess workers' needs and continue to find ways to inject fun and creativity into the workplace.

   SAIC. Like Ben & Jerry's and USAA, the Science Applications International Corporation began as a small group of individuals (in this case, scientists and engineers) in 1969. Today, it is the largest employee-owned, United States-based research and engineering firm, with more than 45,000 employees and offices in more than 150 cities worldwide. Its home office is in San Diego, California; 2003 profits were $6.7 billion.

SAIC is the parent to a variety of companies and projects that are difficult to categorize but might be summarized as putting high-level technology, research, engineering, and computer skills to work on incredibly complex problems, mostly for the federal government. Almost all of its work, in fact, is government-contracted. For instance, SAIC built the security command center for the 2002 Olympic games in Salt Lake City, Utah; it provides technical expertise for disaster cleanups, creates new data security systems for eCommerce, and operates SAIC Frederick, a leading center for cancer and AIDS research for the National Cancer Institute.

SAIC founder Dr. J. Robert Beyster retired from the company mid-2004. Among his legacies is the Foundation for Enterprise Development, a nonprofit organization that teaches the social and economic benefits of entrepreneurship and employee ownership to companies and governments.

   3M. This Minnesota-based company manufactures more than 50,000 products for industrial, commercial, health care, and consumer markets around the world. Its business is grouped into seven operating divisions: consumer and office supplies; display and graphics; electro and communications; health care; industrial business; safety, security, and protection; and transportation. It is perhaps best known for consumer products, such as Post-it Notes, Scotch tapes, and Scotchgard fabric protectors, but these are not its primary profit makers. Other 3M products include asthma inhalers, insulation, reflective sheeting, and recording tape, to name a few. As you'll learn in this chapter, 3M's chief social cause is environmental awareness.

The company is also known for its encouragement of innovation. 3M requires that products less than four years old account for a certain percentage of its sales each year. (In 2000, for instance, it was 33 percent.) 3M employs about 67,000 people in 60 nations (down from nearly 75,000 five years ago). About one-half of the company's revenue comes from sales outside the United States.

USAA. In 1922, a group of Army officers founded a small insurance company to overcome the dilemma of being seen as "hard to insure" because they were military personnel and, therefore, always on the move. When U.S. Navy and Marine Corps officers were allowed to join, the company adopted its current name: United Services Automobile Association, or USAA.

Today, however, car insurance is only part of the USAA empire. It is the fifth largest automobile insurer and fourth largest homeowners' insurer in the country. It owns and/or manages assets of $79 billion and has 21,000 employees (62 percent are women) in the United States and Europe.

Other types of insurance are also offered (health, life, and so on). In 1980, USAA added a discount buying club, and in 1985, the USAA Federal Savings Bank opened, offering credit cards, investment services, and retirement counseling to its 5 million members.

USAA sells virtually all of its products by telephone, direct mail, and online, which offers maximum convenience to its military clientele because of the transient nature of many of their jobs. Its Corporate Creed, created in the 1990s, is to "serve each other with integrity and dependability." To that end, both advocacy and volunteerism are built into the corporate culture. USAA has been selected as one of "America's Most Admired Companies" by *Fortune* magazine and *Working Mother* magazine's "100 Best Companies for Working Mothers"—both for seven consecutive years.

PUBLIC RELATIONS AND PUBLIC SERVICE

The process of incorporating public responsibility and citizenship into the workplace is not unlike the way a company incorporates quality improvement. It begins with an understanding of customer requirements and then translates those requirements into a *vision*, a *mission*, and *goals* for the company.

The major difference is that the definition of "customer" must include all of an organization's stakeholders: the people who buy its products and services; stockholders, employees, and suppliers; and the people in the communities where the company is a "citizen." Employees also live in these communities, so a company that pays attention to the needs of the community is actually attending to a part of itself. Separating work and home, business and nonbusiness activities is tired thinking. The new management model takes a more *holistic view* of employees' roles in their company, their community, and the company's role *in* the community. Such a view challenges businesses to listen and be responsive to a broader range of needs and opinions, but it also rewards them by acting in and for their employees' best interests.

First, let's clarify the difference between responsibility and citizenship:

- **Corporate responsibility** refers to basic public expectations, such as conducting business ethically, following the laws, and protecting public health and safety and the environment.
- **Corporate citizenship** means leading and supporting publicly important purposes, such as education, community services, industry and trade practices, and quality improvement. This is sometimes referred to as *social responsibility*.

Will it grow the business? Is it good for employees? Is it good for shareholders? Is it good for the image of the company? Can we afford to do it— or are we being required to do it, either by law or by competitors' efforts? As it turns out, "doing the right thing" can be mighty complicated when you are a corporation. "Right"—for whom?

And yet, there are plenty of reasons to embark on a campaign to improve the quality of a company's image, as surely as it improves its products. In recent years in the financial industry, just as an example, 24 CEOs and other top-level executives have been fired, $1.8 billion in legal settlements have been paid, seven people have been arrested, and two companies have disbanded, among brokerage houses, banks, and other investment firms.[2]

Most of us are fed up with news headlines about greed and graft and scandal. Consumers and investors are demanding not only that companies produce quality goods and services, but that they demonstrate fiscal responsibility and a concern for quality-of-life issues: decent wages and benefits for workers; use of safe, wholesome ingredients that have been properly tested; sensitivity to environmental issues; and so on.

This trend is known as **socially responsible investing (SRI)**. People want to trust and believe in the companies with which they do business—all types of business—and SRIs vote with their dollars, steering clear of companies they perceive are not using sound judgment or making ethical decisions. Of course, "sound" and "ethical" are often relative terms in the minds of consumers. A closer look at the social values of targeted markets or customer groups may be necessary to pinpoint the issues and values that are important to them. For the purposes of this chapter, we've narrowed the field down to some of the most common topics: ethics, health and safety, the environment, charitable causes and volunteerism, and political and social advocacy.

A Code of Conduct

Where public responsibilities are concerned, the topics of business ethics and public health and safety are practically no-brainers. Regardless of a company's management philosophy, it should conduct business ethically and do everything possible to protect public (and employee) health and safety. From a new management model perspective, that means

- Establishing the company's expectations for these areas—in concrete terms, not vague generalities about fairness and respect.
- Training employees to understand and act on their responsibilities. Training cannot be sufficiently stressed in this area.
- Ensuring that all processes (manufacturing, food processing, transportation, and so on) meet all applicable health and safety laws. Depending on the industry, this can include a wide range of precautions, from safe food temperatures and plant sanitation, to selection of raw materials, to documenting truck drivers' pre- and post-trip federal inspections.
- Identifying and measuring the appropriate indicators of responsible behavior and actions.
- Offering an impartial method for discussing the inevitable "gray areas" that come up in day-to-day business situations, and for reporting problems without retribution.
- Clearly defining the consequences of unethical or unsafe practices.

It is important that businesses put these parameters in writing and make them part of the corporate culture, in everything from new employee orientation to the establishment of workplace ethics committees and employment review processes.

When it comes to building ethics directly into a company, SAIC does an especially good job, as seen in its corporate credo and the three key principles on which its ethics policies are based:

1. Ethical behavior at SAIC is an individual, as well as a management, responsibility.
2. SAIC wants its employee owners to act in an ethical manner.
3. Employees must disclose violations of our common ethical standards.[3]

CREDO—SAIC

We, as Science Applications International Corporation Employees, are dedicated to the delivery of quality scientific and technical products and services contributing to the security and well-being of our communities throughout the world. We believe high ethical standards are essential to the achievement of our individual and corporate goals. As such, we fully subscribe to the following commitments:

To Our Customers:

- We shall place the highest priority on the quality, timeliness, and competitiveness of our products and services.

- We shall pursue our objectives with a commitment to personal integrity and high professional standards.

To Our Fellow Employees, Present and Prospective:

- We shall promote an environment that encourages new ideas, high-quality work, and professional achievement.

- We shall treat our fellow employees honestly and fairly; and we shall ensure equal opportunity for employment and advancement.

- We shall share the rewards of success with those whose honest efforts contribute to that success.

To Our Vendors, Suppliers and Subcontractors:

- We shall be fair and professional in all our business dealings and shall honor our commitments to our business partners.

- We shall endeavor to select vendors, suppliers, and subcontractors who will adhere to our ethical standards and commitment to quality products and services.

To Our Neighbors:

- We shall be responsible citizens, respecting the laws and customs of each community in which we live and conduct business.

To Our Shareholders:

- We shall conduct ourselves so as to enhance and preserve the reputation of our company.

- Consistent with the commitments expressed above, we shall strive to provide our shareholders a fair return on investment.

The policies themselves are compiled as a handbook, which is posted on the company Web site for anyone to download. SAIC also has seven different channels through which employees can disclose and discuss ethical problems or concerns, including an Employee Ethics Committee and Ethics Hotline.

For higher-level management, there is an additional "Code of Ethics for Principal Executive Officer and Senior Financial Officers." An Ethics and Corporate Responsibility Committee, which consists of at least three directors, meets as necessary to review and enhance the policies, monitor the work of the Employee Ethics Committee, and evaluate the effectiveness of SAIC's ethics training and compliance programs. This top-level committee is also authorized to hire expert advisors if needed.

The straightforward manner in which the rules and procedures are spelled out leaves no doubt about SAIC's commitment to ethical business conduct. Quoting again from its Corporate Governance policy:

> We are also aware that improper conduct by any one employee affects the reputation of all employees. Therefore, each of us has a special duty to lead by example and insist on only the highest business standards from all other SAIC employees. Our conduct must not only look right, it must be right. The company cannot tolerate unethical behavior in pursuit of its business goals.[4]

The highly sensitive nature of SAIC's work for government agencies in security, aeronautics, and medical fields underscores the clients' needs for protection of proprietary information. In this case, setting high legal, ethical, and moral standards is not only the "right" thing to do, it's the only way to provide quality service to the customers.

ENVIRONMENTAL RESPONSIBILITY

Doing business without harming the environment is perhaps the area of public responsibility that causes companies the most anguish. Faced with "global greening" and the watchdog groups that report perceived "offenders," businesses often board the environmental bandwagon with no clear sense of where it will take them. By contrast, quality leaders steer their companies toward environmental stewardship by applying the same principles of quality management that we've discussed in other chapters. The application is so appropriate that it spawned its own name (and yes, another abbreviation): **Total Quality Environmental Management (TQEM).**

The Global Environmental Management Initiative (GEMI) is credited with coining the term. GEMI was founded in 1990 by senior environmental health and safety officers of several major U.S. companies (including Procter & Gamble, AT&T, Eastman Kodak, and Florida Power & Light) and is still going strong as a leader in discussing the environmental consequences of corporate activities and sharing the latest "green" management techniques. In 2005, GEMI's board of directors includes several senior managers of companies in this book, including FedEx, Intel, and Motorola.

Companies may call it **sustainability** or **environmental stewardship**, or perhaps *corporate conservation*. But monikers aside, what does it mean? In June 2004, an article in the journal *Environmental Management* defined it thusly (see Figure 10-1, from the same article):

> Sustainable business practices go beyond corporate governance, codes of conduct, and engagement with stakeholders. A genuine commitment to sustainability requires adopting a broader view of full life-cycle implications of business decisions, including new product development and supply chain management. Practical interpretation of sustainability requires evaluation criteria. For example, a sustainable product or process might be defined as one that constrains resource consumption and waste generation to an acceptable level, makes a positive contribution to the satisfaction of human needs, and provides enduring economic value to the business enterprise.[5]

Well, that's a whole new way of looking at a widget, isn't it? And it is distinctly more complex than deciding to recycle the mixed paper at the office. Again, it takes planning, research, processes, and a well-organized structure for a sustainability program to be effective and meaningful. For example, if you think of pollution as a defect, then the goal of Total Quality Management is to eliminate defects. With a nod to Six Sigma® thinking, that would involve defining the problem, measuring the performance, analyzing the gap between where you are and where you want to be, implementing a solution, and controlling it from there.

3M's corporate values include a commitment to "respecting our social and physical environment." The goals 3M has identified to carry out this value are

- Comply with all laws, and meet or exceed regulations.
- Keep customers, employees, investors, and the public informed about operations.
- Develop products and processes that have minimal impact on the environment.
- Stay attuned to the changing needs and preferences of customers, employees, and society.
- Bring uncompromising honesty and integrity to every aspect of the organization.

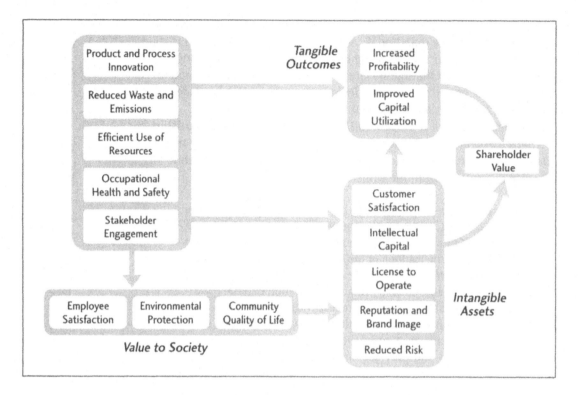

Figure 10-1 Overview of pathways linking sustainability to shareholder value.

When 3M started its 3P program, the board of directors adopted the following corporate environmental policy. It reads, in part:

3M will continue to recognize and exercise its responsibility to:

- Solve its own environmental pollution and conservation problems.
- Prevent pollution at the source wherever and whenever possible.
- Develop products that will have a minimum effect on the environment.
- Conserve natural resources through the use of reclamation and other appropriate methods.
- Ensure that its facilities and products meet and sustain the regulations of all federal, state, and local environmental agencies.
- Assist, wherever possible, governmental agencies and other official organizations engaged in environmental activities.

To turn these goals into action, senior management created specific policies, objectives, and implementation standards. The policies include going beyond regulatory requirements, preventing pollution at the source, conducting detailed environmental audits, and phasing out all ozone-depleting chemicals and PCBs.

From Intention to Action: The 3P Program

3M has more than 7,000 core manufacturing processes based on about 100 core technologies. It is a customer-focused, technology-leveraged company, but the size and nature of its business present challenges when it comes to protecting the environment. When organized and focused, however, they also present opportunities.

In 1975, no major American corporation had attempted a company-wide pollution prevention program when 3M began *Pollution Prevention Pays*—3P for short. "What we did with Pollution Prevention Pays parallels the entire Total Quality Management process," recalls Tom Zosel, a consultant who managed the program at the time. "When we looked at all the regulations that were coming, we knew we couldn't do it all from the end of the pipe, with pollution control. We had to design out the environmental problems, which means we had to build a pollution prevention ethic into the corporation."

Zosel and his team presented 3M's management with two choices: (1) You can spend this much for pollution control or (2) you can ask people to prevent the pollution by design, up front. Management took the second choice, in part because innovation and change are 3M's strengths.

Since 1975, the basic concept and goals of the 3P program have remained constant. It is run by a *3P Coordinating Committee*, which represents 3M's engineering, manufacturing, and laboratory organizations and the corporate Environmental Engineering and Pollution Control unit. Most of the individual projects are initiated when employees recognize a specific pollution or waste disposal problem. A cross-functional team is formed to analyze the problem and develop solutions. The team submits a proposal to the affected operating division, which decides whether to commit funds, time, and other resources to it.

Employee involvement has been key to the program's success, and it has resulted in even more of the innovative thinking for which 3M is known. As one engineer put it, "Our goal is that everything that comes into the plant goes out as a useful item."

In 2002, 3P programs prevented almost 36 million tons of pollution. The company's 2005 goals are the most ambitious ever—reductions in waste and air emissions by 25 percent, and reductions in items on the federally tallied Toxics Release Inventory (TRI) by 50 percent—over 2001 levels. Three of 3M's facilities (in California, Nebraska, and South Dakota) have received "Star" certifications for their high workplace safety standards from OSHA.[6]

Although 3M was the leader, many successful companies have stumbled onto the fact that pollution prevention can save significant amounts of money. Time after time, manufacturers change a process because it is environmentally better only to discover that it is also economically better. If waste is not generated, the company doesn't have to pay to manage it.

Environmental stewardship also includes conservation of resources, such as power and water, the use of "green" materials, and/or avoidance of harmful ones. In recent years, corporate initiatives that have made business headlines include

- Lowe's Corporation announced a five-point policy in 2000 to ensure that "all wood products they sell will come from well-managed, non-endangered forests," including phasing out the sale of wood products that come from endangered or "old-growth" forests around the world, working with suppliers, and raising consumer awareness of the issue. The announcement came within weeks of competitor Home Depot's unveiling of a similar policy.[7]
- Staples announced a commitment starting in 2003 to phase out paper derived from endangered forests and increase the proportion of post-consumer waste (PCW) and so-called "alternative fiber content" in the paper it sells to 30 percent—a fancy way of saying it will use and sell more recycled paper.[8]
- Boeing, General Motors, and Raytheon are among the companies using the Chemical Management Strategy (CMS) program developed by the Chemical Strategies Partnership, a nonprofit group dedicated to reducing chemical use, waste, risks, and costs.[9]

Globalization also requires a company hold its suppliers to the same standards, even if they are operating in countries where environmental, health, safety, and labor laws are not as strict. How many headlines have you seen about companies criticized and/or boycotted for products made in "sweatshops," or opening plants in countries with fewer pollution controls?

In short, the environmental bandwagon is here, and companies everywhere are being challenged to get on or be left behind. Companies fail to meet their public responsibilities when they look at them as costly activities delegated to a few people to control, clean up, and keep quiet. A quality improvement approach involves everyone and can even turn these costly hassles into opportunities.

CHARITABLE CAUSES AND VOLUNTEERISM

Companies don't always have to throw dollars at social or environmental problems. They can use the enthusiasm and manpower of their workforce to build community relations.

For example, at community activities in the San Antonio area, it is easy to spot USAA employees by the special shirts they wear. USAA has a corporate culture that puts superior service to its members and customers first—but being a good neighbor is not far behind. The company's former chairman and CEO, retired Air Force General Robert T. Herres (who ran USAA from 1993 to 2002), organized all community support activities, including philanthropy and volunteers, under a vice president of community relations who reports directly to the company president.

The USAA Volunteer Corps matches its employees with nonprofit agencies that need additional helpers to achieve their humanitarian goals. More than 4,500 USAA volunteers contribute almost 200,000 hours annually to their communities. Employees are notified of opportunities by newsletter and can volunteer hours for whatever activities they wish to support. A computer database tracks the numbers of volunteers and the hours they spend.

USAA also keeps people focused on the ultimate results of corporate citizenship by making it part of the company's planning process. USAA has identified six key result areas (KRAs): (1) service, (2) financial strength, (3) product value, (4) relationship building, (5) strategic assets (people and technology), and (6) public outreach. By including public outreach with other company priorities, USAA establishes its importance for all employees. The company develops annual and five-year plans specifically for its outreach efforts, translating its goals into measurable actions and objectives, which in turn has built good citizenship into the corporate culture. Its education outreach is especially impressive: a nationally recognized mentoring program, a major commitment to the Junior Achievement program, math tutors, pen pals, and others, all making contributions to the San Antonio community. Through USAA's example and training, 68 groups of other volunteers from military bases, businesses, and government offices provide almost 3,000 additional mentors to the city's at-risk students.

No matter how small or large the company, volunteerism is a great opportunity for building morale as well as the corporate reputation for caring. Some additional community involvement options include

- **Scholarships and grants.** The Bose JIT II Education & Research Center gives $5,000 scholarships to students of purchasing and supply management, in addition to offering internships. Many companies set up scholarship programs. Funds can be offered to any student who wishes to apply, or children of employees. 3M gives "Ingenuity Grants" of up to $3,500 to teachers who find inventive ways to learn math, science, and economics; and they donated the funds for Mississippi State University to teach Six Sigma® to engineering students.
- **Group projects.** Companies build teamwork and boost morale when they take on projects as a group. Whether it's building a Habitat for Humanity house, planning a holiday party for kids of prison inmates, or committing to lunch hours delivering Meals on Wheels, the benefits are internal as well as community-minded.

- **Support of the arts**. The 3M Foundation donated more than $1 million for development of the Museum of the American Indian at the Smithsonian Institution and paid for construction of the Science Museum of Minnesota.

The key to making any of these efforts work is setting up a quality process. Public service is an ongoing commitment. In order to be effective (and measurable) as a value builder and a morale builder, it must be consistent. Someone must serve as liaison between company and community, and do the planning and follow-through to meet the stated goals.

Personal Recognition

Recognizing employees for their commitment and ingenuity is an important component of a successful corporate citizenship program. In 3M's awards program for the 3P program, the projects must demonstrate the following criteria:

- Prevent pollution, not control it.
- Offer some other environmental benefit besides preventing pollution.
- Save money for 3M.
- Include a technical accomplishment.

3P doesn't exclude innovative improvements that are not technical, or new programs that prevent pollution but cost money; however, they are not formally recognized. Depending on the innovative nature of their accomplishments, people get awards, plaques, or certificates. Project managers' names are put into a drawing for $500 gift certificates.

FedEx gives humanitarian awards to workers who "promote human welfare, particularly in life-threatening situations," and a Golden Falcon award to employees who demonstrate "exceptional performance or unselfish acts that enhance customer service." Winners have included a technician who rescued a girl who had been abducted, and a manager who expedited delivery of donor organs.[10]

Advocacy as a Social Force

USAA is not known strictly for its volunteer network. The company also uses its economic clout and membership base to weigh in on public policy issues. In 2003, for example, USAA members were asked by the company to support the Fair and Accurate Credit Transaction Act (FACT) in Congress, as well as state legislation that would tighten auto insurance regulations in New Jersey. As Bill McCartney, USAA's senior vice president for government and industry relations, puts it:

> USAA's participation in these public policy debates is vital to our ability to provide our membership with the products and

services they expect and deserve. We do so to protect and enhance the business environment in which we operate and, ultimately, facilitate the financial security of our members and their families.[11]

And do you remember the powerful television documentary *Scared Silent*, about child abuse? It was produced in the early 1990s with funds from USAA. When child abuse agencies asked for something on abuse that could be shown to children, a follow-up program called *Break the Silence* was also produced. Hosted by actress Jane Seymour, the documentary won a George Foster Peabody Award for broadcasting excellence in 1995.

USAA does one more type of outreach to its members—financial. In December 2004, the company lowered its automobile insurance rates (from 10 to 30 percent) for members living on or near military bases in 14 states. The war in Iraq has had a devastating financial effect on many military families, who were already living frugally. The rate reduction targeted 400,000 of USAA's 3.6 million insured vehicles—at a time when their owners (and USAA's prime customer base) could really use the help.

THE UPS AND DOWNS OF ACTIVISM

Ben & Jerry's Homemade, Inc. could be seen as an example of all the best—and some of the worst—things about community involvement. Since its Ben & Jerry's Foundation was formed in 1985, a team of employees has met three times a year to review grant proposals—and there are plenty. To be considered for a grant (of $1,000 to $15,000), a group must have non-profit, or 501(c)3, status with the Internal Revenue Service, and its proposal must meet these guidelines:

Grant applicants need to demonstrate that their projects will:

- Lead to societal, institutional and/or environmental change;
- Address the root causes of social or environmental problems; and
- Lead to new ways of thinking and acting.

Projects must:

- Help ameliorate an unjust or destructive situation by empowering constituents;
- Facilitate leadership development and strengthen self-empowerment efforts of those who have traditionally been disenfranchised in our society; and
- Support movement-building and collective action.

Applicants should:

- Develop a plan for long-term viability;
- Articulate a clear analysis of the underlying causes of the problem; and
- Outline specific goals and strategies of their organizing campaign or program.[12]

The foundation makes it clear that its goal is *social change*, not social service. There's a list of programs it *does not* fund, including scholarships, religious programs, international programs, and research projects. In one recent cycle, 37 groups received grants (mostly $10,000 apiece)—from New Mexico's Center for Economic Justice (working "to counter corporate-driven globalization," for a boycott of World Bank bonds), to Oregon's Green House Network (working to stop global warming), to the Florida Clean Water Network (for a "Stop the Pipe/Save the River" campaign against a paper mill on the St. John's River).

As you can imagine, many of these causes are at least somewhat controversial. And then there are the inevitable ironies that arise when longtime policies and immediate priorities collide. In recent years, Ben & Jerry's has dealt with its share of public relations nightmares. A few examples:

- Ben & Jerry's once pledged to keep its executives' salaries no more than seven times the pay of its lowest-paid employees—a policy that was promptly scrapped with the Unilever buyout.
- Despite its eco-friendly reputation (and flavor names like "Rainforest Crunch"), the Center for Science in the Public Interest blasted the company in 2002, claiming that its "All Natural" label belied the artificial ingredients listed in the small print. CSPI urged the U.S. Food and Drug Administration to take enforcement action.
- The company is on a boycott list on the law enforcement advocacy Web site www.officer.com for cofounder Ben Cohen's contributions to the "Free Mumia Jamal" retrial efforts, on behalf of a Philadelphia taxi driver convicted of shooting a police officer in 1981.
- The corporate watchdog "Oligopoly Watch" cites the company's "illusion of independence" since being purchased by Unilever, which it says "has maintained the funky, privately-held image . . . but internally, decisions are being made as in any other division of a big company by people who think like Unilever."

Oligopoly Watch also mentions a new entrant onto the "ice cream for social consciousness" scene—Star Spangled Ice Cream, which promises to donate 10 percent of earnings to conservative causes, specifically to counter the charitable activism of the Ben & Jerry's Foundation.[13]

People who work for the "new" Ben & Jerry's are no doubt proud of their company. They can still wear blue jeans and bring their dogs to work.

Day to day, they still market ice cream and manage to have fun. Their latest effort, called "Get Connected," is an attempt to increase interaction between the employees and customers. The company president, Yves Couette, says their level of commitment and passion "has been a real eye-opener for me."[14]

The point here is that even the best intentions can backfire on a company in terms of public perception. Any company that embarks on any type of charitable, environmental, or social effort, no matter how noble or badly needed, must be prepared to think about the flack that may fly as a result. And there are plenty of groups aiming at the corporate world, ready to report the ironies and missteps—as well as their roles in "uncovering" them.

CHAPTER SUMMARY

Many companies question the extent of their public responsibilities and their roles as corporate citizens. They know they have to satisfy their customers, reduce waste, and cut costs to succeed. They understand that, in the global business world, this means understanding customer requirements, making plans, involving people, and managing processes. But what does corporate citizenship have to do with any of these process-related goals?

Our quality role models believe that taking the lead in publicly important areas is an essential part of a successful system—even if it sometimes results in negative publicity. These areas include supporting education, volunteering for and funding community services and arts organizations, contributing to industry initiatives to reduce waste and pollution, and promoting intelligent resource management.

All of these are forms of quality improvement. They require leadership commitment; goals, planning, and processes that net a clear direction; and employee involvement. Like any quality improvement effort, they also must be measured for effectiveness and periodically reevaluated.

Does all this concern really pay off for shareholders? In a Baldrige Award application, "Leadership and Social Responsibility Results" count for only 70 of the possible 1,000 points. However, there are plenty of other measures that are indirectly impacted by a company's (and its employees') sense of corporate citizenship—"Customer and Market Knowledge," "Employee Well-Being and Satisfaction," and "Human Resource Results," to name a few.

The fact is, whether the motives are financial or altruistic, the results of being community-minded leaders tend to be the same: The more you give, the more you get in return. Among the returns with immeasurable value are the pride and satisfaction of each individual who contributes their time, money, and heart.

DISCUSSION QUESTIONS

1. Should a company force its smaller suppliers to meet the same environmental standards as its larger suppliers, even if it would place a financial hardship on the smaller ones? How might this type of issue be resolved?
2. List the issues that you believe should be addressed in a company's credo or ethics statement. Should there be separate statements for senior executives and the overall workforce? Why or why not?
3. Whose responsibility should it be to analyze a company's ethical efforts (financial, environmental, charitable, and so on) for possible public relations problems?
4. Look online for the watchdog groups on a particular issue, and write a short paragraph each about at least three of them. What are their goals? How large and/or effective do they appear to be?
5. Do you think a company should require a certain amount of volunteer participation from all employees? Allow them to volunteer on company time? Why or why not?

ENDNOTES

1. Ben & Jerry's Foundation Guidelines, South Burlington, Vermont, 2005.
2. "Scandal Scorecard," *Money Management Executive* magazine, a publication of Thomson Media, New York, May 3, 2004.
3. "Corporate Governance: Code of Ethics," SAIC, San Diego, California.
4. "Credo," SAIC, San Diego, California.
5. Joseph Fiksel, Jonathan Low, and Jim Thomas, "Linking Sustainability to Shareholder Value," *Environmental Management* magazine, a publication of the Air & Waste Management Association, Pittsburgh, Pennsylvania, June 2004.
6. The Domini 400 Social Index, Domini Social Investments, New York, May 2004.
7. "Lowe's Launches Forest Protection Initiative," *SocialFunds.com* newsletter, a publication of SRI World Group, Inc., Brattleboro, Vermont, August 11, 2000.
8. William Baue, "Staples Commits to Recycled Paper," *SocialFunds.com* newsletter, a publication of SRI World Group, Inc., Brattleboro, Vermont, November 15, 2002.

9. Jill Kauffman Johnson, "Reexamining the Supply Chain," *Pollution Engineering* magazine, a publication of BNP Media, Troy, Michigan, November 2004.

10. Ronald J. Alsop, "How Some Employers Are Better Than Others," *CareerJournal .com*, a publication of Dow Jones & Company, Princeton, New Jersey, 2004.

11. "USAA members benefit from advocacy," news release by USAA, San Antonio, Texas, December 12, 2003.

12. Ben & Jerry's Foundation Guidelines, South Burlington, Vermont, 2005.

13. Steve Hannaford, "The real Ben & Jerry's story," on Web site oligopolywatch.com, April 15, 2003. © 2004 by Steve Hannaford.

14. See endnote 10.

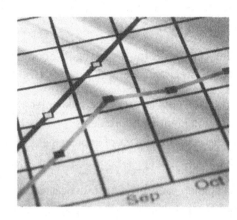

Data Collection and Benchmarking

High-performance companies understand that they can manage only what they can measure, and that is just as true for such areas as marketing, administration, and legal as it is for manufacturing. As Fred Smith, chairman and chief executive officer for FedEx, has put it, "We believe that service quality must be mathematically measured."

Indeed, one of the Baldrige Award Core Values and Concepts is "Management by Fact." The term refers to an organization that can back up its claims with verifiable data, and one that makes decisions based on intelligent analysis of accurate data. Also included in this chapter is the concept of *benchmarking*, which means taking the data a step further by comparing one company's performance to others—either competitors or the company's own "best practices"—to learn from the other and determine where there is room for improvement.

Again, we look inside several companies for their insights about developing and using data measurement systems, including these topics:

- Translating customers' requirements into process parameters
- Monitoring key processes and identifying problems
- Analyzing trends and measuring the impact of improvements
- Using benchmarking to improve quality

We'll also identify several common tools used in statistical research, to familiarize you with the types of charts and graphs that make various kinds of data easier to understand—as long as you know how to read them, that is!

The companies in this chapter—Carrier Corporation, Kennametal, and Seitz Corporation—are three manufacturers, although their data analysis and benchmarking experiences translate well to retail, or any industry.

Carrier Corporation. This world leader in HVAC (heating, ventilation, and air conditioning) products is a subsidiary of multinational giant United Technologies Corporation, but it has humble beginnings that reach back more than a century. The company's founder, Willis Carrier, started an entire industry when he invented an "apparatus for treating air" in 1902. With headquarters in Farmington, Connecticut, Carrier has 40,000 employees in more than 170 nations.

A new president was named in 2000; Jon Ayers was promoted from Carrier's Asian Pacific operation. The same year, Carrier bought Electrolux Commercial Refrigeration, giving it additional know-how in the refrigerated retail display case business, both in the United States and in Europe.

In 2003, the company kicked off a huge new agreement with Sears, Roebuck and Company—Carrier's International Comfort Products Corporation is now the exclusive manufacturer of Sears' famous Kenmore brand appliances, and Sears is the exclusive retailer of Carrier brand HVAC equipment. Carrier also makes high-tech climate-control products and support systems for the aerospace industry.

Kennametal. This Pennsylvania-based company made it big in World War II, when its metallurgist founder, Phillip McKenna, created a super-tough alloy for manufacturing cutting tools for machine metal work. Today, Kennametal has four divisions and still produces tools for cutting and drilling, plus items like grader and snowplow blades.

The company has 13,700 employees and $2 billion in annual sales, half of which are generated outside the United States. Over the years, it has purchased two dozen more manufacturing facilities in China, India, and Germany. Its most recent acquisition (in 2005) is Extrude Hone Corporation, based in Pennsylvania but with plants in Germany and Ireland, as well as the United States.

Stateside, Kennametal's plant in Solon, Ohio, has received acclaim for its system of self-managed work teams. About 600 employees work at the state-of-the-art facility, which has been named one of *Industry Week* magazine's "Best Plants." The team approach to quality improvement has produced significant improvements in on-time delivery, cost reductions, and shorter lead times. We'll focus on the processes at Kennametal-Solon in this chapter.

Seitz Corporation. This company makes high-tech plastic gears and components of all types—such as the paper feed tractors for printers and copiers—on injection molding machines that range in size from 35 tons to 770 tons. It has an in-house tooling department, and much of its work is custom, contract manufacturing and assembly.

Seitz is a family-owned business that employs less than 200 people. The company's annual sales exceed $20 million, but that wasn't always the case. In the 1980s, Seitz was a struggling company with sales of $5 million. It credits its turnaround to benchmarking, and by 1992, Seitz had won a State Blue Chip Enterprise Initiative Award as "the best example of a small business that effectively used resources to overcome adversity and emerge stronger."

Today, in addition to U.S. headquarters in Torrington, Connecticut, Seitz has a "global arm" in Changzhou, China. Both plants are QS-9001-certified. In 2000, the company also decided to enter the home automation market, producing automatic devices to open and close window shades and shutters as its first product line.

THE ART AND SCIENCE OF DATA COLLECTION

The emphasis on measurement of data in the corporate world does not mean there is no role for experience and intuition in business processes. It's just that intuition is harder to explain and quantify, and easier for others to challenge when things aren't going perfectly. The best-run companies use their employees' gut-level hunches and creativity—but they back it up with facts and figures. In fact, the better their measurement systems, the better their product and process quality. A data measurement system helps align and integrate the quality systems. As Joseph Juran wrote, "Once we have established a system of measurement, we have a common language or metric. We can use that language to help us at each and every step."

You might assume a measurement system would be simple to administer—collect the data, put it on a graph or chart and take a look at it, and figure out whether it's good news or bad news—but there's a lot more to it than that! Since every company is different, its teams must start from scratch, answering these questions:

- Exactly what are we measuring? What (and how much) data and information should we collect?
- How do we know the measurements are accurate, reliable, and useful?
- How do we aggregate and analyze the data to actually improve customer satisfaction, quality, and operational performance?
- How do we institutionalize the measurement system so everyone understands it, uses it, and appreciates the input?
- If we're going to benchmark, is our system adaptable enough to be able to make useful comparisons between our results and other companies' data?

A company's measurement system, like its entire management system, must be driven by the customers. As the company determines its customers' needs and requirements and decides how it will meet them, the measurement system can be created to align all these activities with the ultimate goal of improving customer satisfaction. Ideally, the measurements should be developed by those who will be using them, but often—especially in high-tech manufacturing settings—they are based on the requirements of important customers and their specifications. It makes sense, because again, the goal is customer satisfaction.

The last point on the bulleted list just displayed is one reason companies sign on to use standardized approaches. One of the most popular is the **Balanced Scorecard**, which was mentioned briefly in Chapter 1 and has been outlined in a book of the same name by Dr. Robert Kaplan and Dr. David Norton. Their system doesn't throw out traditional financial measurements, but it adds to them by looking at (and measuring the effectiveness of) a company from four different perspectives, as shown in Figure 11-1.

Historically, service companies have had weak measurement systems that focused almost exclusively on financial indicators. After all, not all characteristics of a product or service are measurable—or are they? Even manufacturing companies with strong production metrics have failed to measure nonmanufacturing processes. The problem is probably not that these processes cannot be measured, but that some are difficult to measure.

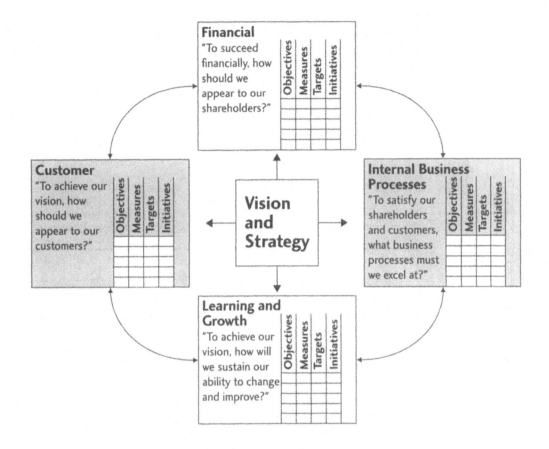

Figure 11-1 The balanced scorecard and measurement-based management.

What kinds of things should be measured? Table 11-1 is an example of a few categories and the possible information that might be gleaned from them.

Measurements may be made as comparisons to past performance, to present standards, or to future goals. A combination will net the most insightful results.

When Kennametal's Solon plant got serious about measuring, employees soon decided they had chosen too many things to measure! The list was pared down by focusing on customers' requirements and expectations, based on what is truly critical to managing each process—for instance, compliance-related measures.

For most processes, two or three key measurements are plenty to have to deal with at once. The Solon facility has a master list of about 50 key performance indicators (KPIs) in use throughout the operation, including support functions such as human resources. The business unit teams select their measures from the KPI list. A coordinator keeps track of the measures and works with the teams to establish and track them.

Table 11-1 Samples of Measurements for Different Processes

Area to Be Measured	Types of Measurements
Customer satisfaction	Number of complaints, types of complaints, percentage of on-time deliveries, amount of time taken for complaint resolution, customer surveys, number of warranty claims
Production or manufacturing	Actual performance versus goal, amount of downtime due to machinery repairs, how often inventory is turned, amount of time required to make one unit, cost per unit, number of returns or "reworks"
Sales and marketing	Number of customers, number of sales calls per week, incremental sales over previous month (or same period last year, etc.), new product sales versus total sales, actual sales versus goal, accuracy of orders placed versus orders delivered

Most important: Every measure must have a goal associated with it. "Measuring without a goal doesn't accomplish anything," explains Paul Cahan, the former plant manager and director of global steel operations. "Through the use of measures and realistic goals, you can improve performance."

Like Kennametal-Solon, the business units at Carrier also use measurement to identify and solve problems. "Each business unit identifies its top five problems, where they are in solving them, implementing action, and standardizing procedures so they don't recur," says Larry Sweet, vice president of operations at Carrier. "From a corporate point of view, we're driving a culture of consistently focusing on relentless root cause."

Like other users of the Balanced Scorecard, Carrier has constructed its own corporate scorecard that covers its own core business processes. The Balanced Scorecard jargon for this is putting priorities into "buckets" (as in, "How full, or empty, is this bucket?") The key buckets for Carrier are listed here, with a note about what types of measurements are made for each:

- Engineering productivity (metrics associated with the product development process)
- Product reliability (measures such as customer failure rate and warranty costs)
- Product quality (measures such as factory defects and supplier defects)
- Product delivery (measures along the whole supply chain)
- Customer satisfaction (an annual survey of dealers and distributors)
- Employee satisfaction (an annual survey)
- Cost productivity (total cost of purchased material, which includes such things as logistics)
- Financial (traditional measures of financial performance)

Before adding a new bucket to the lineup, Carrier does a pilot project to see whether the measurements associated with it will be useful in the long run. Sweet points out that Carrier moved away in the 1990s from a focus on company-wide measurement. The results are more useful at the process level, to help the team members on that process drive improvement. There are so-called Global Councils that identify and use metrics for cross-functional processes.

The company also uses the Baldrige Award criteria as the metric system for assessing business units that compete for an in-company Willis H. Carrier Global Quality Award. The formal Baldrige Award application requires an enormous amount of work, so Carrier developed a short diagnostic questionnaire based on the criteria to make the assessment process less lengthy and more accessible for its individual business units.

The common pitfalls of data collection include

- **Amassing too much data.** Having too much data becomes a hassle and results in a lack of focus on what is really critical and a mountain of unnecessary information to wade through.
- **Collecting too little critical data.** If it's not important information, or not collected consistently, there won't be enough "meat" in it to draw valid conclusions.
- **Measuring progress too often.** Unnecessary effort and cost are used in order to get the results.
- **Not measuring often enough.** If there are problems, they are not identified promptly.
- **Measuring vertically.** Nicknamed *stovepiping*, this tendency to compare different teams or departments on the same measure ends up pitting one against another. Unless the idea is to foster competition, it is wiser to measure horizontally.

In fact, nothing will sabotage a measurement system faster than using data to evaluate an individual's performance. Data are indicators of a process's performance, not a person's performance.

MAKING THE DATA USEFUL

Once systems are in place for collecting and analyzing key quality and performance measurements, the company's next step is to communicate them to the people who can use them. Skimping on this step is like buying a sleek sports car without the key—it's a great-looking system, but it's not going to get you very far.

To communicate data effectively, most companies use graphs and charts to determine whether (and how closely) two measurements are related to each other. Visualizing the metrics makes them easy to understand

and analyze, and also easier to store than stacks of customer survey forms or ponderous reports.

There are several types of "visuals" commonly associated with quality improvement processes. Kaoru Ishikawa (first mentioned in Chapter 1) said that 95 percent of a company's problems can be solved by charting them with these tools. Take a look at them and see if you agree! All nine of these charts, as well as some of their explanatory verbiage, are from *Quality Toolkit*, a 2001 manual prepared by Anthony Coppola. They are reproduced with the permission of the Reliability Analysis Center, sponsored by the Defense Technical Information Center (DTIC), operated by Alion Science and Technology Corporation in Rome, New York; and used with permission. (Figures 11-2 through 11-10 are the copyrighted property of Alion Science and Technology.)

Flowcharts

As shown in Figure 11-2, a **flowchart** shows the steps in a process, or actions that transform an "input" to an "output." When someone talks about **mapping** a process, this is the map. It is a significant help in analyzing a process, but only if it is truly accurate—that is, it must reflect the actual process used, rather than what the process owner thinks it is or wants it to be. The differences between the actual and intended process are often surprising and provide many ideas for improvements. Then, when the process flow is satisfactory, each step becomes a potential target for improvement, and priorities are set by measurements.

After a basic flowchart is created, it may be necessary to use separate flowcharts to break down some steps even further, into separate processes. Notations may be made on flowcharts about how much time each step takes, whose responsibility it is, and so on.

The flowchart in Figure 11-2 shows a simple management review process. Can you tell from the chart where there are possibilities for delays? For miscommunication?

Ishikawa Diagrams

Named for the famous Japanese scientist who created them, these are also known as **cause-and-effect diagrams** or, for obvious reasons, **fishbone diagrams.** The function of this tool is to map out either the factors that may be causing an undesired effect (such as a defect) or the factors needed to bring about a desired result (such as a winning proposal).

The major factors are identified as the "fishbones" directly off the "spine" or center of the diagram. (In the diagram in Figure 11-3, they are Methods, Manpower, Materials, and Machinery.) Then, each factor is subdivided into the processes or components that must be investigated to determine the

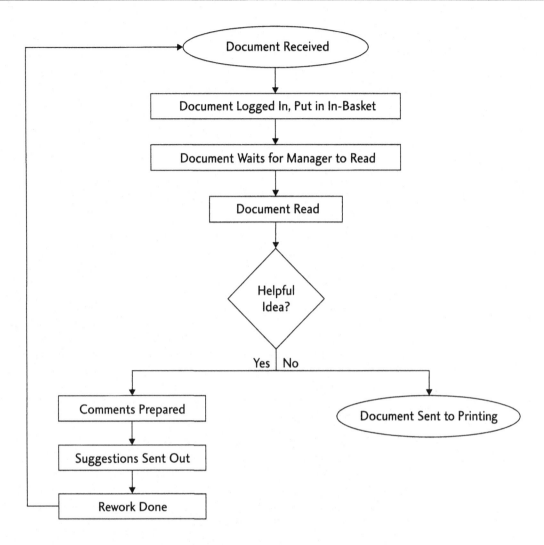

Figure 11-2 Flowchart of management review process.

cause of a problem (in this case, defects in a factory's wave solder process) or the components necessary for success in a certain process. Figure 11-3 is a partial Ishikawa diagram. How would you complete it?

Checklists

A checklist is one of the simplest ways to collect data. It can be set up by shift, by hour, by day, by type of machine, by person operating it, and so on. In most industries, checklists are computerized. A restaurant, for example, can use a checklist to keep running totals of how often each entrée on a menu is ordered every day, and use the data to determine which items should be removed from the menu because they're slow sellers, or how much food to order by day based on the popularity of each dish.

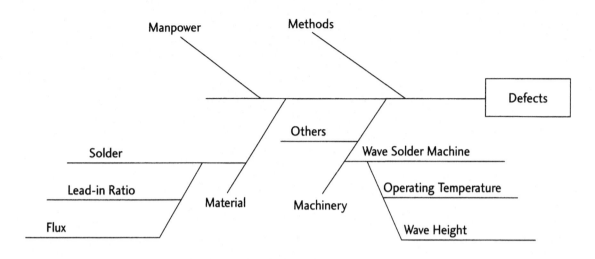

Figure 11-3 Partially completed Ishikawa diagram.

The key to a usable chart is that every factor on the chart must be mutually exclusive. For instance, in Figure 11-4, each of the defects listed is a completely separate problem, and the days of the week are also unique. This chart is another measurement of defects for the same soldering process shown in Figure 11-3.

Pareto Charts

In Chapter 1, we mentioned the *Pareto Principle*, Juran's suggestion that a few problems cause the most trouble and/or loss in any organization, but that most are small and can be repaired with vigilance. To delineate the few from the rest, they can be graphed on a diagram known as a **Pareto chart,** which is a type of **bar chart.** Like a checklist, it can be set up to measure just about anything—in fact, the data on the checklist in Figure 11-4 is the same as Figure 11-5, just put into Pareto format.

Each of the "boxes" that represents data on a bar chart is called either a *bar* or a *bin*. A set of Pareto charts created for the same data (in this case, using different possible causes of the defect) is called *stratification*. Figure 11-6 (on page 200) shows the wave solder problem in three ways—by production line, by shift, and by type of product being soldered. The produc-

Figure 11-4 Checklist for defects found.

Defect	Monday	Tuesday	Wednesday	Thursday	Friday	Total
Solder	I	II		I		4
Part	II		I	II	I	6
Not-to-Print	III	II	I	III	II	11
Timing		I	I		I	3
Other		I				1

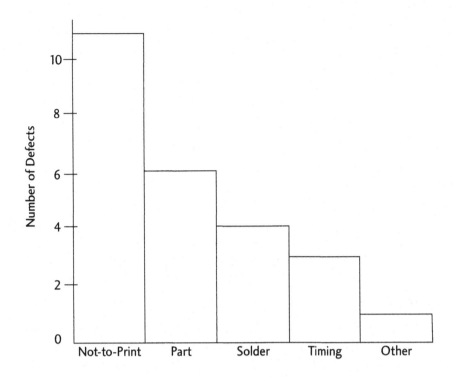

Figure 11-5 Pareto chart.

tion line and shift data look fairly consistent, but product type #3 appears to have the highest number of defects. Stratifying the data has pinpointed that product for investigation or improvement.

Histograms

The **histogram** is also a type of bar chart. The area of each bar is proportional to a number it represents—in this case, the length (in inches) of a rod. If the "ideal" (shown as X at the bottom of the chart in Figure 11-7) is 1 inch in length, the histogram shows that most of the rods are pretty close (from 0.9 to 1.1) to the ideal length. However, the chart also shows quite a variance overall, from rods that are one-half inch too short, to rods that are one-half inch too long. In a real manufacturing situation, would you say this chart reveals a problem, or not?

Scattergrams

The **scattergram** is a graph rather than a chart. Like a chart, it is a means of showing the relationship of two parameters. It is created by simply plotting each point of data on a chart, with one parameter as the x-axis and the other parameter as the y-axis. If the points form a narrow "cloud" (close together), the parameters are closely related and one may be used as a

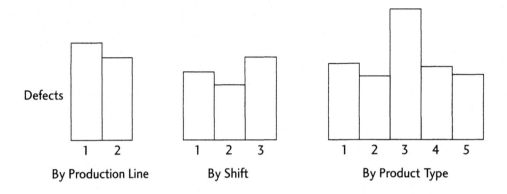

Defects

By Production Line   By Shift   By Product Type

Figure 11-6 Stratification.

predictor of the other. This is called being "strongly correlated," as seen in Figure 11-8. The other scattergram, Figure 11-9, shows a weak correlation.

Control Charts

The final and perhaps most complicated tool for measuring quality-related data is the **control chart**, although it is based on simple principles. A control chart is made by taking samples from a process, measuring them, and then plotting the measurements in sequence along a horizontal line that represents the mean or average measurement for that item or parameter. Measurements that fall far below or far above the mean are "out of control," indicating a problem with the process.

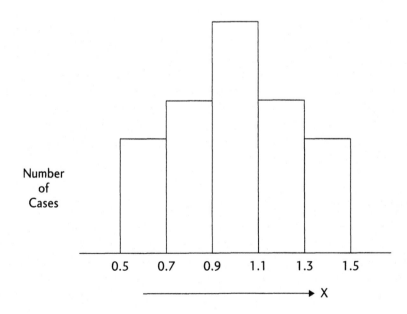

Number
of
Cases

0.5   0.7   0.9   1.1   1.3   1.5

X

Figure 11-7 Histogram.

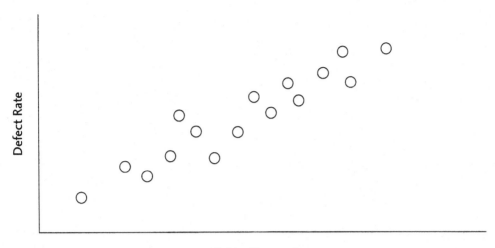

Defect Rate

Solder Temperature

However, not every item—nor even most items—fall exactly onto that center line. So most processes include an acceptable degree of random variation. In Figure 11-10, only one of the samples is far enough out of control to be considered problematic.

Figure 11-8 Scattergram showing strong correlation.

Making Data Accessible

Of course, in the real world, charts and graphs get a lot more complicated than our examples. But at least they provide a starting point for further study. And now—where to show off the metrics after they've been created?

Figure 11-9 Scattergram showing weak correlation.

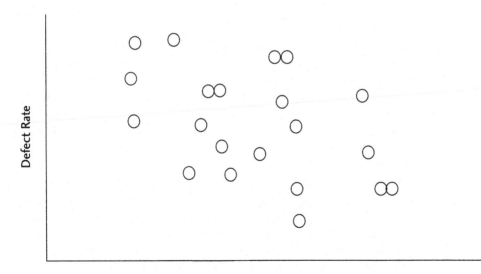

Defect Rate

Solder Temperature

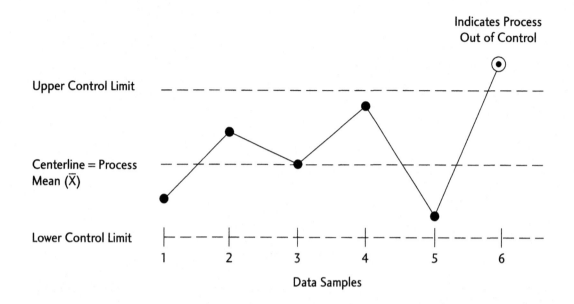

Indicates Process
Out of Control

Upper Control Limit

Centerline = Process
Mean ($\bar{X}$)

Lower Control Limit

1   2   3   4   5   6

Data Samples

Figure 11-10 Control chart.

At Kennametal's Solon plant, measures of key performance indicators are posted in highly visible areas for the people who use them. The charts are updated weekly; typically, they show a year's worth of history in monthly and weekly increments. In Chapter 9, we mentioned the "Mission Control" room of Wainwright Industries, where quality trends and performance indicators are displayed and updated continuously, available for all to see—including visiting suppliers and customers, since Wainwright holds its meetings in Mission Control to emphasize its quality commitment.

For the past decade, the Kennametal-Solon plant has been organized into four business units. At the Solon plant, supervisors work as facilitators with their business units, discussing how they can improve performance to reach the goals they have set. The KPIs help promote continuous improvement because the employee teams want to meet their goals and move the trends in the right direction.

In addition to monitoring production activities, KPIs can be used in almost every part of a business. The first step is to identify the process or procedure to be improved, then communicate the data to the people who can improve it, establish measures and goals, and empower those people to use the data to improve.

At the corporate level, a wide variety of data must be compiled and analyzed in order to draw "big picture" conclusions from it. This is one of the most difficult tasks a company faces. When the measurements have been focused on the work of individual teams or processes, it can be challenging to make sense of them as a whole, in order to assess cause-and-effect connections, as well as the resource and financial implications, and to initiate improvement. Carrier has chosen to collect measurements by product type instead of by business unit.

BENCHMARKING

When its largest market took a nosedive in the mid-1980s, Seitz Corporation lost two-thirds of its workforce and saw annual sales plummet from $12 million to $5 million. It turned to benchmarking to overhaul its business. By 1996, sales had grown to $30 million, and its benchmarking process was well entrenched. Teams of employees benchmarked everything from manufacturing automation and customer service, to safety procedures and employee cafeterias.

A **benchmark** is a point of reference. The primary definition of the word is "a surveyor's mark, made on a permanent landmark of known position and altitude; it is used as a reference point in determining other altitudes."[1] So, in the corporate world, *benchmarking* is using a company's benchmarks as points of reference for quality comparisons. Or, as the Baldrige Criteria for Performance Excellence puts it: "Benchmarking refers to identifying processes and results that represent best practices and performance for similar activities, inside or outside your organization's industry."[2]

Benchmarking itself is a process. A company does not use it to prove they are "the best" at something, but *to learn how to become the best*. Benchmarking, by itself, does not improve performance; it provides information that can be used to improve. The typical benchmarking study involves coordination and cooperation between two companies. Employees of one company go on a site visit to the other company specifically for the purpose of sharing information and gaining knowledge about a particular process or how a common problem might be solved. It is a discovery process aimed at exceeding customer expectations.

Seitz was ahead of the game when it recognized these benefits in the mid-1980s; most companies have been considering the concept only in the past few years. Many credit the Baldrige Award program with bringing benchmarking to people's attention, and early Baldrige Award winners (like Motorola, Milliken, and Xerox) showed how companies could "borrow shamelessly" from world-class benchmarks to meet ambitious "stretch" goals.

Size and type of business do not preclude successful benchmarking. The number of steps in the process varies from company to company. Xerox's process, probably the most copied in the country (no pun intended) has 10 steps. Seitz uses a flowchart consisting of 14 steps. A typical six-step process looks something like this:

1. Decide what to benchmark.
2. Plan the benchmarking project.
3. Understand your own performance.
4. Study others.
5. Learn from the data.
6. Use the findings.

Like data collection, the process is almost deceptively simple. Regardless of the number of steps, all formal benchmarking processes reflect three activities: getting ready to benchmark, conducting the site visit, and using what is learned as the basis for improvement.

It is important to note that not all benchmarking is this involved. Informal benchmarking may be done by reading about similar processes or results in trade publications, talking to competitors and peers about shared issues or problems, checking out the competition at a trade show, and asking customers and suppliers to compare companies' performance in their eyes. Naturally, these do not require the same degree of planning and execution as formal benchmarking, but they can benefit from similar background: knowing the product/service/process, finding out what other companies are doing, comparing and identifying gaps, and initiating improvements.

BENCHMARKING PREPARATION

Before a business can conduct a study, its employees must understand the value of benchmarking and feel it is worth the time and energy to undertake it. Seitz includes benchmarking in its quality training, then reviews the steps whenever a team begins a benchmarking project.

One of the biggest problems is where to begin. As with any major quality improvement initiative, the answer is, "With senior management." Executive approval is critical in order to commit employees' time, allocate resources, remove roadblocks, and reward the effort. A team that proceeds without this support exposes itself to scrutiny about how time and funds are being expended, complaints from other managers and departments impacted by the study, and if it is even completed, little or no action on the recommendations. Senior staff endorsement removes these obstructions and even ensures that the company's benchmarking efforts are coordinated, helping to prevent interdepartmental conflicts and bottlenecks.

The other difficult aspect of benchmarking is simply finding time to do the work. A formal study typically takes six months to complete, and there are no shortcuts. If the idea is to decide on and act on changes quickly, a company might be better off choosing other, speedier tools.

What, How, and Whom to Benchmark

A benchmarking study must have clear and accurate objectives based on customer requirements—so the potential study topics include any process that is critical to customer satisfaction and/or the company's success. Seitz has benchmarked tooling, customer service, accounting practices, safety, and product identification (bar coding systems), to name a few.

"Customers will tell you when you're messing up. They're a great place to start a benchmark," says Sharon LeGault, marketing manager at Seitz. "Internal and external salespeople can also see differences. Another source is people who recognize a problem: 'We're losing money because of . . .' "

Seitz does benchmarking in response to a gap, a suspected gap, or a problem. Once the need is identified, Seitz's senior staff recommends forming a team to address it, after which the team takes the leadership role.

The next step is to create a project plan, which may cover the following areas:

- Goals and objectives
- Scope and resources
- Key players, along with their roles and responsibilities
- Critical success factors
- Milestones, deadlines, and deliverables
- Performance measures
- Creation of high-level process flowcharts

Seitz asks its benchmarking teams to select a leader, process guide, scribe, and timekeeper. The leader leads. The process guide maintains the rules (e.g., no evaluating during brainstorming, and everyone is to be involved in the discussions). The scribe records everything and distributes meeting minutes. The timekeeper keeps meetings within time limits and makes sure the team is progressing as planned.

The teams use statistical problem-solving tools to develop their proposal. First, they brainstorm to make sure the perceived problem exists. If it does, the team uses a fishbone diagram to identify the reasons for the outcome, does a Pareto chart to determine the primary opportunities, and then creates a flowchart to map the process under study. Only after the charts are complete does the team leader bring the proposal to senior management with a request for the time and money to implement the study.

Once the proposal is written and approved, the next step is to identify benchmarking prospects. Teams often struggle with this step—either they do not have a clue where to find such prospects or they have one or two companies they have "heard about"—and that's their list. Other teams brainstorm until they come up with a dozen or more potential companies.

Small companies often have greater trouble finding benchmarking partners. Seitz focuses on companies of similar size, getting most of its leads from customers, newspaper and magazine articles, and conferences and trade shows. It has tried benchmarking large companies, but team members came back somewhat overwhelmed, with the news that Seitz probably could not afford to implement what the larger companies were doing, anyway.

The goal of the search is to find companies that are satisfying the same customer needs as the ongoing internal process, and are doing it with a high degree of success. The secondary goal is to find a company that will agree to be that "shining example." It is up to the team members to make the "sales calls" and ask if the target would be willing to participate. A "no" answer should not be taken personally. Some companies don't have their processes sufficiently documented for comparison purposes, or are cautious about sharing so much information. Others are deluged by benchmarking requests. Quality leaders, such as those who have won Baldrige Awards, are very visible benchmarking targets and must select projects carefully or they'd be overrun. However, many will still agree to participate—especially if they can learn something in return.

"Companies realize they have to have their processes identified and that you're going to be in their plant for three hours. That's a lot to ask for some companies," says LeGault. "Others say they're not familiar with benchmarking and don't have the resources to deal with it. Out of our short list, 50 to 75 percent will agree to participate."

Setting the Ground Rules

For companies willing to participate, an agreement should include an outline of exactly what is expected by the partner company—the time, form, and length of the site visit; an agenda; an explanation of what is being benchmarked; and a list of questions to be asked. It is important to agree first on the key elements of the process. Benchmarking teams often encounter a different set of metrics in use at the company being benchmarked. How can they compare apples to oranges? They can't—not without finding some common ground—and the time to do that is long before the site visit. Seitz faxes its questions to its partners to be reviewed before the site visit. In fact, the partner company is allowed to eliminate any topics they do not want to address.

Then, the team members decide who will go to which companies, usually in groups of two or three. Preparation for the visits includes the following:

- Team members gather information about their own processes at Seitz so they can use them for comparison and share them with the partner company if asked.
- Team members all go in with the same list of questions, since everyone picks up on different things in a discussion. All will take notes, which can be compared later.

Team members are encouraged to ask anything and everything—but only if they are questions that Seitz would be willing to answer itself. Seitz offers to share the results of its project with all partners. Most companies are willing to share their results, although some ask for confidentiality, which Seitz respects.

The issue of corporate ethics is not to be taken lightly. The act of opening up one company's facilities and processes for another company to scrutinize carries with it the potential for abuse. Many companies have adopted a benchmarking code of conduct, like the one created by the Strategic Planning Institute's Council on Benchmarking:

1. Keep it legal.
2. Be willing to provide the same information that you request.
3. Respect confidentiality.
4. Keep information internal for your use only.
5. Initiate contact through benchmarking contacts.
6. Don't refer without permission.
7. Be prepared at initial contact.
8. Have a basic knowledge of benchmarking, and follow the process.
9. Have determined what to benchmark.
10. Complete a rigorous self-assessment.[3]

The effectiveness of a site visit depends primarily on how well prepared both sides are. If both companies understand their processes and if the benchmarking team knows exactly what it wants to learn, most visits proceed fairly smoothly. During its many years of benchmarking experience, Seitz has encountered four common problems:

- **People are not prepared to actually compare gaps.** As a result, they gather information not pertinent to the project. Teams must be careful not to become "tourists" during the site visit.
- **Team members take poor notes.** "We recommend that every employee in the group has a copy of the same questionnaire. When the question is asked, everyone writes down the answer they hear," says LeGault.
- **People do not understand the purpose of the study.** LeGault talks about how one site visit backfired when a team of toolmakers returned saying they were underpaid, the target company had better equipment, and they liked their landscaping very much.
- **Senior management doesn't want to be bothered to participate on the teams.** If senior staff personnel do not show interest, people on the team don't think it's important either.

USING BENCHMARKING DATA

"Back at home," the project team analyzes the data it has collected, quantifies performance gaps, explores the implications of those gaps, and identifies which pieces of information might help improve performance. Often, the "host company" will work with them on ideas for putting the findings to work.

At Seitz, the benchmarking teams fill out comparison charts to clarify the differences on key points. Table 11-2 is an example from a team's study of plants with Kanban management systems. The study led to a new inventory system at Seitz, reduced work in progress (WIP) in the assembly area by 15 to 20 percent, and depleted 90 percent of the inventory on the floor, allowing the company to add one-third more assembly line space.

After comparison charts are completed, they pull in people from other departments to review what they learned and to develop a list of recommendations, including any savings of time and money. "If changes are in order, our employees are empowered to make the changes they think they need," says LeGault. "The only time they have to go to upper management is when they need to spend more than $500."

Companies involved in achieving ISO or QS-9001 certification, and companies that have achieved a certification, need to be careful that process changes learned through benchmarking don't conflict with their documentation—or they must change the documentation to reflect the process changes. This may impact other departments; for instance, to update training.

Interestingly, for all the work that is involved, not every benchmarking study results in change. "At times, the results are too expensive or don't work for you, so you do another type of problem-solving process," LeGault says.

Table 11-2 Sample of a Seitz Information Comparison Chart			
Question: When issuing an order, how much work is delivered to the department?			
Seitz	*Company A*	*Company B*	*Company C*
Full order amount.	1 day's work is issued.	1 week's work is issued.	2 days' work is issued.
Results			
WIP is high. Taking up large space for material storage.	No WIP. No space needed.	Lower amount of WIP. Small area for material storage.	Low WIP. Very small area for material storage.

WIP = Work in Progress

One way to improve the odds of getting usable benchmarking results is to benchmark more companies. On half a dozen site visits, the team will learn a great deal from two or three, and not much from the rest. Until the visits actually take place, there's no way to determine this.

To close the loop on the topic of benchmarking, the learning becomes part of the endless quality improvement cycle—select what should be implemented, assign resources and planning time, create goals for it, and monitor the new (or improved) process.

It is also important for organizations to share the information gained from benchmarking, both with the "host" companies and with other parts of their own company that might benefit from it.

CHAPTER SUMMARY

The new business management model promotes *systems* thinking, in terms of understanding both the internal systems around which a company is built and the external systems that affect it.

For some companies, it's not so new. Back in 1993, Carrier Corporation adopted the following "Measurement Norms." We list them here along with the pertinent points made in this chapter about measurement systems:

- **Customer-focused on our performance vs. their expectations.** Deciding what (and how much, how often, etc.) to measure can be difficult. Measuring for measurement's sake has no value. The best measures are customer-focused and goal-oriented.
- **Easy to collect, report, and understand the data.** Technology has made it easier than ever to set up computerized systems for collecting and analyzing data. Charts and graphs help people understand trends at a glance. Visibility of results, such as with Wainwright's Mission Control room, ensure access and the ability to seek further detail.
- **Managers initiate, expect, and review the data.** Those who make decisions about improvements in the system and in processes must show commitment to the idea of measuring them to help evaluate and improve them. With processes like benchmarking, senior management buy-in is critical to the success as well as the usefulness of the finished project.
- **Work groups and/or individuals develop and report the data for ownership.** The people closest to the process are in the best position to identify and gather the data. They are also in the best position to use the data to improve their process.

- **Data will be used for process improvement and not to spear the messenger.** Measure the process, not the individual.
- **Rewards by management for progress and permanent solutions.** We did not spend much time on the sheer commitment of time and brainpower that benchmarking and developing new measurements requires of individuals. Whether the rewards are monetary bonuses, team celebrations, or pats on the back, progress on key performance indicators needs to be appreciated, both by coworkers and senior management.

Benchmarking enables a company to improve its internal systems by learning from external resources. As you have seen in this chapter, it is a process of discovering exactly what is being done, compare it to "the best" (both inside and outside the company), and determine what can be done to improve. The process does not have to be incredibly formal, but some advance preparation is necessary in order to obtain useful results.

Considered a "power tool for quality," benchmarking is indispensable to a learning, growing organization. Measurement systems and benchmarking programs can guide processes and drive amazing quality improvements—all with the goal of developing loyal customers.

DISCUSSION QUESTIONS

1. Why must measurements have goals? Isn't it enough to measure accurately and keep records of important facets of an operation?
2. How does the *Balanced Scorecard* work? What makes it "balanced"?
3. If Kennametal-Solon posts its data showing "a year's worth of history in monthly and weekly increments," what types of charts or graphs do you think are being used? Explain your choice.
4. How should a manager handle employees who are clearly seeing their benchmarking project as competitive instead of instructive?
5. Would benchmarking work for the college you are attending? Who would be the "host companies"? If you were on the team, what would you ask the "competitors"?

ENDNOTES

Figures 11-2 through 11-10 are from the RAC publication *Quality Toolkit*, 2001 Edition, edited by Anthony Coppola. ©2004, Alion Science and Technology, Rome, New York. Used with permission.

1. *Webster's New World Dictionary*, Third College Edition, ©Simon & Schuster, Inc., New York, 1988.
2. *2005 Criteria for Performance Excellence*, Baldrige National Quality Program, National Institute of Standards and Technology, U.S. Department of Commerce, Gaithersburg, Maryland.
3. Strategic Planning Institute, Needham, Massachusetts.

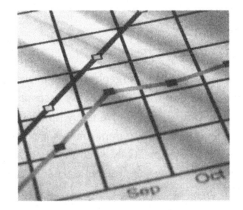

CHAPTER

12

System Assessments

In the new business management model, the role of assessments has evolved from punitive to supportive, from a hunt for problems and mistakes to a search for ways to improve, and from assigning blame to offering assistance. The change in attitude reflects the enlightened view that problems with operational performance or quality are almost always caused by problems with the system, not problems with people. To improve the system, you must first know what condition it is in and pinpoint where the improvements need to be made. That is the purpose of a system assessment. These steps require serious commitment on the part of an entire organization.

In this chapter, we look at how three companies use the Baldrige criteria to assess their business systems, using their experiences to explore these topics:

- Reasons for a formal assessment
- Methodology for conducting a system assessment
- Management responsibility in an assessment
- Evaluation of the assessment
- Using the assessment to prompt improvements

Until the Baldrige criteria came along, few organizations had ever assessed their entire business system. For one thing, no effective assessment tool existed. In addition, the search for ways to improve rarely revealed the need for a system assessment. Problems belonged to departments, work groups, and individuals, not to the system as a whole. Only when the quality movement began harping about the system being the problem did people wonder what condition their system was in.

We should note here that other types of assessments can be done; the Baldrige Award criteria certainly are not the only guidelines. But they are well known and comprehensive enough to serve as our model, and the companies that use them include the Bama Companies, Eastman Kodak Company, and Graniterock Company.

The Bama Companies. This family-owned business began with pie making in 1927 in the kitchen of Cornillia Alabama ("Bama") Marshall. It was incorporated in 1937 and has grown into a $200-million-plus company with more than 1,000 employees. Today, its CEO is the founder's granddaughter, Paula Marshall-Chapman.

Bama's production lines turn out a variety of frozen, ready-to-use food products for casual dining and quick-service restaurant chains. Specialties are biscuits, pies, and pizza crust, and one of the company's biggest customers is McDonald's, for which it makes handheld dessert pies. Based in Tulsa, Oklahoma, Bama opened a production facility in Beijing, China, in 1993, primarily to service McDonald's expansion into the Chinese market. In 2003, it launched a $20 million plant upgrade at the Tulsa facility. In 2004, Bama received numerous local awards, including "Best Company to Work For" and "Best Corporate Citizen."

Bama is especially proud of the fact that it has not raised prices for its baked goods since 1996. Marshall-Chapman has been aggressive about quality improvement, making winning a Baldrige Award a corporate goal. In addition to the Baldrige process, the company adopted Six Sigma® methodology to save more than $17 million since 2002, as well as increasing efficiency and reducing waste in the production processes. It has also used the Balanced

Scorecard system, and the teachings of author Stephen Covey's *The Seven Habits of Highly Effective People* to make progress. The company reached its Baldrige Award goal in 2004. Its current "stretch" goal is $1 billion in sales by 2010.

Eastman Kodak Company. The company that became famous as the creator of the "Brownie" camera is still the world's number one film manufacturer in a fiercely competitive industry. But in 2003, Kodak made headlines by announcing a change in focus, so to speak. It intends to make $3 billion in acquisitions by 2006—ambitious for a company with $13 billion in annual sales—and shift from traditional film to digital cameras and other types of products, including printers and monitors. The company also received FDA approval in 2004 for a new computer-automated design (CAD) mammography system. In January 2005, Bill Lloyd was promoted as the company's chief technology officer. A relative newcomer to Kodak, Lloyd spent more than 30 years at Hewlett-Packard.

The Kodak business is divided into five key segments (with their respective market segments in parentheses): Commercial Imaging (corporations); Digital & Film Imaging Systems (photographers and the film industry); Display & Components (creates the capture devices that "read" the images from digital cameras and scanners); Graphic Communications (printing and publishing); and Health Imaging (medical and diagnostic). The company has about 64,000 employees, down from a high of 132,000 in the 1990s. It maintains marketing and manufacturing operations in more than 50 countries and is headquartered in Rochester, New York.

Graniterock Company. In 2000, Graniterock turned 100—not bad for a company that began with its workers using shovels, picks, and sledgehammers to break up rocks all day in a quarry for railroad lines. Today, the company is still family-owned and produces high-quality construction materials—rock, sand, and gravel aggregates; ready-mixed concrete; and asphalt—for road and highway construction and maintenance, as well as residential and commercial building. Its sister company, Pavex Construction, is a successful heavy engineering contractor.

Graniterock's home office in Watsonville, California, oversees operations at five quarries and about a dozen plants. The company has nearly 500 employees and won a Baldrige Award in 1992. Since then, there have been ups and downs with labor unions—including four work stoppages in four years from 2000 to 2004—but the company is also routinely selected as one of the "Top 100 Companies to Work For" by *Fortune* magazine. Training averages 40 hours a year per employee, and they are paid their regular work wages to attend, whether it's on-site or at the local community college.

"Graniterock encourages and supports Graniterock people in making both incremental and sweeping changes," says its corporate Web site profile. "The company also recognizes that risk taking and honest mistakes are unavoidable parts of constantly improving our business."

WHY A SYSTEM ASSESSMENT?

If the processes are well designed and being monitored, what else is necessary? Or put more bluntly, how are we supposed to get any work done if all we ever do is observe, tinker with, and micromanage every little procedure?

It's a valid point, unless you think of a system assessment like an annual physical exam. A person may check his or her blood pressure or cholesterol level regularly and may see a doctor for an occasional illness. But a thorough, general examination—a personal "system assessment"—comes once a year. The same is true for an organization—checking corporate health seems like a reasonable annual pursuit.

The subjects of the exam may disagree. Unlike an individual physical exam, a system checkup relies on self-assessment for accuracy and completeness, and self-assessment is not a painless process. A business system is a complex set of elements. The interaction of those elements is what makes the system function, but it is also what makes any assessment so difficult. The system cannot be studied by isolating and assessing one element in it, such as one functional area or one process, and ignoring how it affects and is affected by other elements in the system. For this reason, an effective system assessment has two components:

1. A team willing to do the hard work of performing the assessment
2. A tool it can use to conduct a valid assessment

The tool must be capable of assessing the entire system as well as the key elements that make up that system. High-performance companies, including the three companies in this chapter, have chosen an assessment tool with these capabilities—the criteria for the Malcolm Baldrige National Quality Award.

Each of the companies acknowledges that applying for a national award—like doing any kind of rigorous assessment—requires quite a commitment of time and resources. However, the application process also accomplishes the following:

1. **Involves and motivates people.** To accurately assess the quality of a system requires exploration of every nook and cranny of every process, work unit, team, department, and so on. The company must rely on people to do the research, and people to provide the answers.
2. **Provides a proven quality system.** A system assessment is only as good as the assessment tool, which is why so many companies are using the Baldrige criteria.
3. **Focuses on the customer.** The goal of each company (and really, of every company's business system) is to satisfy customers. An assessment reinforces that satisfying customers must be the focus of the entire system.
4. **Assesses quality.** Not only do the criteria identify the elements in a business system, but they also provide a means of assessing the quality of effort for each element and for the system as a whole. As Joe Rocca, one of the writers of IBM Rochester's Baldrige Award-winning application, said, "We thought we had a good-quality program, and now we've got one that's 10 times better for having gone through the application process."
5. **Demands data.** Without a formal system assessment, few people are able to describe with any accuracy the quality of their system or the elements in it. Instead, they offer a nice story or a good hunch or a best guess. In a system assessment, hard data must be provided.
6. **Provides feedback.** Any company that has performed a system assessment using the Baldrige criteria will agree that the real value of the process is the feedback it provides. Graniterock's feedback reports, on its first two Baldrige applications, listed 110 areas for improvement. The company used the list to drive its quality improvement efforts, described later in this chapter.
7. **Stimulates change.** Hundreds of companies performing systems assessments understand that the goal of the assessment process is improvement. Having written criteria often speeds up the pace of improvement.
8. **Builds financial success.** Continuous assessment and improvement in quality cannot help but lead to improvement of the system's products and services. In turn, quality improvements may be linked to increases in customer satisfaction and shareholder value.[1]

Companies embrace assessment processes when they understand the benefits. At larger companies, that understanding does not often extend to the people who must perform the assessments, who may then see the assessment process as a chore they must fit in around their regular jobs. Whether companies dictate that assessments will be done or inspire business units to participate, the assessment process is always more effective if business unit leadership supports and is involved in the process.

In 2004, 60 companies submitted Baldrige applications. The Baldrige criteria have been scrutinized, debated, interpreted, and improved over the years—but they have not been replaced as the preeminent system assessment tool. As Kay Whitmore, former chairman, president, and CEO of Eastman Kodak Company, wrote in his company's self-assessment workbook: "I believe that performance against the national quality award criteria is a leading indicator of a unit's future success."

METHODOLOGY FOR SYSTEM ASSESSMENT

The Bama Companies created the Business Opportunity Management Process (BOMP), a comprehensive, company-wide system used to improve products and processes, as well as manage and measure business opportunities. BOMP is built into the company culture, so that everyone knows what it is and understands how it is used. It is this system that Bama self-assesses in its Baldrige application. Bama has entered the Baldrige Awards competition annually since 1991, not winning until 2004, but applying the lessons learned in the site visits.

Graniterock has applied for the Baldrige Award every year since 1989. Graniterock's executive committee reviews and approves the company's annual Baldrige application and uses it to gauge company-wide improvement. They say they will continue to write an application every year, solely for assessment purposes.

Kodak offers two types of assessment to its business units. First, they can do it themselves, using the Kodak Quality System Review. This is a matrix and abbreviated report processes so that the executives could assess their unit in less time than a full application requires. Second, they can submit to an assessment by an examination team. Both are based on the Baldrige criteria.

One of the first problems a company faces in a new assessment process is how to get buy-in from the business units, divisions, or departments that are the "targets" for assessment. With the trend toward decentralization and increased autonomy for business units, companies are increasingly sensitive about telling those units what to do. The benefit of relying on motivation instead of demands is that the participants recognize its value and conduct a useful assessment. The disadvantage is that units can choose not to participate, thus denying themselves and the company the benefits of the assessment.

"We've said all along that this isn't something different from your business; this is to make you more competitive, to add value, and to better serve the customers," says George Vorhauer, director of corporate quality initiatives.

Vorhauer admits that not all business units appreciate these benefits. "Early on, there was a tendency to see this as a lay-on—something you do in addition to the important job you have—rather than a way to measure and improve. We've addressed that by focusing more on the units' plans to improve rather than their score on the assessment."

What these and other companies have learned is that senior management involvement in the assessment process results in three major benefits:

1. It establishes the system assessment process as the unit for or the company's primary tool for continuous improvement.
2. It creates an annual learning and improvement cycle, beginning with feedback to the assessment, that includes planning, execution, and evaluation.
3. It improves senior executives' ability to understand and improve the system they oversee.

The degree to which these benefits are realized correlates directly to the involvement of senior executives in the assessment process. Interestingly, the organization gains most by executive involvement because executives have the greatest control over the system. Leaders who resist getting actively involved seem to believe that participating in the assessment process is not a good use of their time. The experience of our quality role models suggests they are wrong.

Any company or unit of any size can set its own deadline at any time of the year—Bama, for instance, assesses employee satisfaction every six months. A side benefit of an external program like Baldrige is that it comes with built-in, immovable deadlines (usually in May). At the same time, organizations can submit their system assessments for state quality awards— more than half the states have their own quality awards based on the Baldrige criteria.

The point is to identify a firm deadline, or the assessment will never be finished. It seems to require about three months, from start to finish. Eastman Kodak estimates that writing a full application takes around 2,500 labor-hours, which seems like a good average. Companies such as Xerox have reported spending much more time, because of the size of the organization represented in their application and because they were simultaneously working on improvement. At the other extreme, a Globe Metallurgical executive claims to have written his company's award-winning application in one long weekend!

How long it will take depends on the size of the company or unit, the availability of system data and information, and the maturity of the quality improvement process. Size determines complexity, data availability determines research time, and maturity determines how easily each topic is matched with what the criteria measure.

The process of creating an assessment document can be divided into fourteen major steps:

1. **Involve senior management.**
2. **Establish application team(s).** Teams share the work, bring different perspectives to the task, and spread the learning experience to more people.
3. **Train team members.** The first exposure to the Baldrige criteria can be more confusing that enlightening, unless people receive some training in how to understand the criteria and apply them to their organization.
4. **Assign responsibilities.** The assessment process is most effective when there is clear accountability for gathering data and information, writing responses, and producing the report.
5. **Collect data and information.** The quality of the assessment depends on the quality of the data and information it presents. A system assessment that is vague or anecdotal, or that reports glowingly on what the organization hopes to achieve, is worthless.
6. **Identify areas for improvement.** Areas for improvement materialize in the course of conducting the assessment. Wise companies understand that these areas are the primary goal of the process, the gold nuggets that make the assessments worthwhile.
7. **Communicate needs, ideas, and information.** As the assessment process proceeds, individuals and teams tend to focus on a particular category, work process, or functional area, thus losing sight of the system in which they exist. Constant communication helps to maintain a systems perspective.
8. **Edit the first draft.** Editing the responses to the criteria is an exercise in interpretation and communication that requires diligence and clarity. It is also very hard work, but the payoff—learning to think about what your organization does as a system—is worth it.
9. **Begin the layout, including graphics.** An essential part of clear communication is the presentation of information. Charts and graphs can help explain processes, information, and results.
10. **Evaluate the first draft.** Reviewers usually include the authors of the assessment document and the organization's senior people (if they did not write it). Internal and external quality experts and consultants may also be included.
11. **Write subsequent drafts.** The first draft evaluation always identifies sections that are inappropriate, weak, inaccurate, and wrongly placed. Subsequent drafts can only make the assessment stronger.
12. **Coordinate writing and graphics.** As the deadline approaches, an individual or team must coordinate all the pieces that will make up the document.
13. **Produce the final draft, either as a paper document or on CD.**
14. **Deliver the assessment.**[2]

Almost every organization that creates a system assessment document follows a similar process. Major variations occur when companies assign responsibility for the document to an individual or a very small team, but even then, data must be gathered, areas for improvement identified, drafts written, and the document assembled. Set a deadline, or the assessment will not get done. Expect resistance, no matter what deadline you establish; the people who will be involved in the assessment process are already busy. This is when senior executive leadership becomes critical.

Leadership is also needed when the assessment is used to drive improvement. People involved in the assessment are usually worn out from the process, but they are also aware of the weaknesses it has revealed. Because the assessment has little value unless it is used to improve, leadership must make it possible for employees to integrate the findings with their ongoing improvement efforts.

Some Kodak units choose to conduct the self-assessment using Kodak's own matrix. Shown in Table 12-1, it is organized into categories by Baldrige criteria: Leadership, Strategic Planning, Customer and Market Focus, and so on. In each category, the person performing the assessment ranks each statement in each row of the table on a scale of 1 to 10. A score of 1 means the department or unit is "just beginning" in that area, 6 indicates it is "growing," and 10 indicates it is "mature."

"The matrix allows you to arrive at a Baldrige-like score in eight hours," George Vorhauer explains. "If you multiply that by the number of executives who perform the assessment, you've got 80 to 100 hours for an assessment—significantly less than a full application—and you also get a way to improve."

As it developed the matrix, Kodak checked its process against business units that wrote both—applications and self-assessment charts—then compared the scores. It found a strong correlation between the matrix and application scores, suggesting that the scoring aspect of the self-assessment matrix would give units an accurate picture of their systems and of the areas that needed to be improved.

The matrix describes 10 "rankings" for each of the seven Baldrige categories. Each member of the assessment team, which is usually a unit's management team, scores every cell in the matrix, using the following codes:

Deployed (D)	The unit has fully applied the characteristics described in the cell.
Partially deployed (P)	The characteristics have been applied only to major areas within the unit.
Not deployed (N)	Application of the characteristics is minimal or anecdotal.

Table 12-1 A Quality Matrix or Table (to streamline the assessment process while using the same values as a full-fledged written assessment).

Rank	Leadership 120 points	Strategic Planning 85 points	Human Resource Focus 85 points	Customer and Market Focus 85 points
10 Maturing	Quality is placed equal to profits, market share, and stock price.	Quality improvement plans are totally integrated into long-term and short-term plans.	Measures and trends of employee well-being and morale show "Best-in-Class" when benchmarked against peer companies and units.	"Best-in-Class" in customer satisfaction for products and services (include surveys, competitive awards, ratings by independent organizations, trends in market share, trends in gaining customers).
9	Unit managers demonstrate Kodak's five Quality Principles outside the company and encourage/positively reinforce employees for doing the same.	KRA improvement plans in place at all organizational levels.	QLP usage is an essential element of reward and promotion systems.	Evidence that improvement results are caused by Quality Leadership Process approach.
8	Reward and consequence processes reinforce QLP involvement.	Rewards/consequences are based on both behaviors and results.	Training is evaluated for improvement at four levels: (1) attitude about course (content, instructor), (2) immediate knowledge gained from course, (3) application to job and performance, (4) impact on business results.	Customers actively involved in problem solving/improvement effort.
7	All teams have completed at least one full QLP cycle; management performance measures based on progress in meeting KRAs; decisions based on vision.	Planning processes are reviewed and improved at least annually.	All employees are trained in QLP, additional education and career development opportunities to support continuous improvement efforts widely available.	Positive trends evident in all customer satisfaction indicators.

6 *Growing*	At least 75% of teams have completed at least one full QLP cycle.	A documented process for employee, supplier, and customer contribution to the planning process is used.	At least 75% of all employees have some QLP training and are involved in continuous improvement.	Process for communicating customer information to appropriate units exists and is used.
5	At least top half of interlocking teams use QLP to guide all meetings.	Resource allocation is consistent with corporate/unit KRAs.	Resources are allocated for development and implementation of educational plans to support growth in core competencies.	Process exists and is in use for integrating customer satisfaction data into the continuous improvement cycle of the company.
4	Management teaches QLP to their direct reports and serves as role model.	QLP used for short-term and long-term planning; every unit has a written plan.	Education and career development plans exist and are linked to business unit goals, tactics, and strategies.	Processes exist for identifying and using: (1) market segments and customers, (2) product/service features and their importance to customers.
3	Have unitwide plan for implementation of QLP, including necessary resources.	AOP addresses: technology, human resources, suppliers, environmental issues, and competitive actions/reactions.	QLP training scheduled for all employees.	Proactive processes exist for determining and improving customer satisfaction (beyond measurement of complaints, returns, and warranty rate).
2	Mission and vision defined, published, and understood by all stakeholders.	Process in place for linking customer/market needs with the strategic planning process.	Recognition/rewards (beyond performance appraisal) occur in specific, sincere, immediate, and personal ways.	Processes exist to promptly resolve customer complaints.
1 *Beginning*	Direct interaction of management with employees, customers, suppliers, and other stakeholders regarding Kodak Quality Principles.	A documented long-term (2–5 years) and short-term (1–2 years) planning process is used.	Measures and trends of employee well-being and morale exist.	Contract/guarantee/warranty policy adhered to for product/service performance.

Key: QLP = Quality Leadership Process, Kodak's process for improving quality; AOP = Annual Operating Plan; KRA = Key result area, a broad area of performance.
Source: Adapted from Eastman Kodak Company, using 2005 Baldrige criteria.

The ratings should be verifiable through available data. After each assessment team member has scored all 70 cells, the team meets to arrive at a consensus score for each cell and for the unit as a whole.

Graniterock takes an interesting approach by gearing one of its annual assessments strictly toward an individual. In lieu of the traditional employee review process, Graniterock created the Individual Professional Development Plan (IPDP), in which employees set their own annual goals for themselves. The assessment form is filled out independently, by the employee and his or her supervisor, and it includes four sections:

- An outline of the person's major job responsibilities
- Identification of exceptional strengths on the job
- A review of the previous IPDP form
- An outline of the next 12 months' development plan

The supervisor and worker sit down together, compare results, and discuss on each area. Their new, combined document becomes the employee's action plan for the next 12 months. About two-thirds of the Graniterock workforce is union members, so the plan is voluntary, but 85 percent of employees participate. The company also gears its training programs to the needs pinpointed in the IPDP assessments.[3]

So, there are obviously shortcuts and abbreviated versions of the assessment process. Overall, our experience has shown that the more time people invest in the assessment process, the more value it has for them and for their companies. People who must wrestle with the criteria to understand what they are asking, then assemble a response that meets the criteria, become "systems thinkers" during that process. They begin to assimilate the Baldrige Core Values—customer and market focus, management by fact, process management, and so on—and apply them to their daily tasks. They think more critically, ask better questions, look for root causes of problems, and strive to improve.

EVALUATING ASSESSMENTS

Evaluating a Baldrige application, whether internally or externally, also involves arriving at consensus scores; the difference is that someone outside the unit does the assessing and scoring. Many large companies have patterned their assessment process after the Baldrige process. For example, Kodak trains about 50 people a year for its internal Board of Examiners. Graniterock hires former Baldrige examiners to score its applications and conduct site visits.

Table 12-2 Sample Achievement Awards		
Award	*Point Score*	*Description*
Gold	876–1,000	Outstanding effort and results in all categories. Effective integration and sustained results. National and world leaders.
Silver	751–875	Effective efforts in all categories, and outstanding in many. Good integration and good to excellent results in all areas. Full deployment. Many industry leaders.
Bronze	601–750	Evidence of effective efforts in most categories, and outstanding in several. Deployment and results show strength, but some efforts may lack maturity. Clear areas for further attention.
Crystal	500–600	Evidence of effective efforts in many categories and outstanding in some. A good prevention-based process. Many areas lack maturity. Further deployment and results needed to demonstrate continuity.

Like the Baldrige application process, a company's internal process may begin with examiner teams scoring the applications. Only those that meet certain thresholds proceed to the site-visit phase, where the assessment is clarified and verified. It is important, especially doing it all in-house, to reward both achievement and improvement. Samples of possible achievement awards (gold, silver, bronze, etc.) are shown in Tables 12-2 and 12-3.

The assessment process is a straightforward evaluation of how an application responds to the criteria. When the criteria request a process (i.e., How you do something?), the examiners assess the approach being taken and then determine how fully the approach has been implemented. When the criteria request results (the measures of what you are doing), the examiners study the direction and levels of trends in all key areas and compare them to the trends of competitors and world-class benchmarks. For each item, the examiners identify what the company is doing very well (strengths) and what it needs to do better (areas for improvement), and then calculates a score.

Table 12-3 Sample Improvement Awards		
Award	*Point Score*	*Description*
Gold	200 points per year	Improvement at a world-class rate
Silver	150 points per year	Improvement at an excellent rate
Bronze	100 points per year	Improvement at a very good rate

USING ASSESSMENT RESULTS

The results of a Baldrige assessment lend themselves to action. Such phrases as "process is not evident," "limited development," and "trends not given" are common in a Baldrige feedback report, and they always direct the organization's attention to specific areas for improvement. The problem many organizations face is how to tackle so many areas at once.

Graniterock organized the 110 areas for improvement listed in its first two Baldrige feedback reports into 10 categories. It formed a corporate quality team to work on each category. Each team had a senior executive as facilitator and five or six employees, usually including one middle manager and people from all levels of the company. "The executives' evaluations depend on the success of their teams," says Val Verutti, director of quality support, "while the vertical membership unified our purpose and our people to accomplish something. Each team has a definite mission, and they've all been reasonably successful at accomplishing what they set out to do."

Over time, baseline goals have replaced the work of most Corporate Quality Teams. Baseline goals are annual improvement goals that include before-and-after measurements of process or system improvement. Entire branches or departments are involved in accomplishing the goals.

Many companies lose at least some of the value of their assessments by not having a plan for acting on the feedback. Part of the problem is that the feedback is nonprescriptive; it tells you when something is missing or weak, but it does not tell you how to fix it. So at Kodak, each business unit is required to report its assessment data, whether it was obtained by self-assessment or from an independent source—with progress on anything initiated in response to the assessment, reported quarterly.

"The idea that you've signed up for a goal and you're making or not making it—and management cares—is important," adds George Vorhauer.

Assessments using the Baldrige criteria yield a detailed snapshot of the business. You cannot realize the snapshot's value by passing it around for people to admire; it must be studied for clues about key areas that need to be improved, translated into a written improvement plan, and acted upon. Only then does the system assessment make the system better.

And finally, how long does all this "improvement" take? Three years, minimum! That's the time frame most companies of any size are looking at before the transition from a traditional management model to the new "systems thinking" really becomes institutionalized. Small companies can make the change more quickly; larger companies tend to take longer. Fair warning: The transition is rarely smooth. Roles are being redefined. Responsibilities change. Routines are scrutinized. Like each person in the company, the company itself is changing jobs, *learning to take a systematic approach to satisfying customers.*

CHAPTER SUMMARY

Companies that use the Baldrige criteria to improve their business start with an assessment. They need a new understanding of the nature of their system, a baseline for gauging their improvement, and a sense for what must be worked on first. All these are available through a Baldrige assessment, whether it takes the form of a 50-page application or an improvement plan based on a more streamlined matrix or table.

It is difficult at best to get today's overworked employees to participate in what they perceive as the "extra work" of assessments. This is why senior management's role in the process is myriad: to pave the way for allocating time and resources to get it done, to recognize the hard work of those who participate, and to ensure that the mechanism is in place to use the learnings from the completed assessment to prompt improvement.

The system assessment method may also be used for personal quality improvements, as shown in the Graniterock IPDP system. A good system assessment should be expected to identify strengths and weaknesses for every area discussed in the previous chapters of this book. By using the criteria to assess a business process or system, you set in motion a process of discovery and improvement that can jump-start a failing system, or reenergize a lumbering one. Just ask the Baldrige Award winners. (Or check their results at the Baldrige program's Web site: www.quality.nist.gov)

DISCUSSION QUESTIONS

1. You are the senior manager of one division of a company that encourages but does not require an annual system assessment. Your teammates believe that the assessment is just another hassle and set of deadlines in their already-busy lives. How do you convince them otherwise—in 500 words or less?
2. Why is senior management involvement in an assessment process necessary? Briefly summarize three reasons.

3. Suggest some ways to make the application process take less time than three months.

4. Why are union employees less likely to take advantage of a "personal improvement" system assessment such as the one at Graniterock? If you were the union member, what would you choose to do?

5. Self-assessment or external team assessment—which would be more valuable, and why?

ENDNOTES

1. Adapted from *The Baldrige Quality System: The Do-It-Yourself Way to Transform Your Business,* by Stephen George, John Wiley and Sons, New York, 1992.
2. See endnote 1.
3. Dawn Anfuso, "1994 Competitive Advantage Optimas Award Profile: Graniterock Co.," *Personnel Journal*, a publication of Crain Communications, Detroit, Michigan, April 1994.

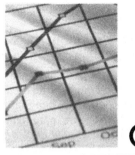

Glossary

A

acceptable quality level (AQL)   A standard that a product must meet at various stages of its production to ensure the best chance of it being defect-free when it is finished.

B

Balanced Scorecard   A management system that translates an organization's strategy into four areas of equal importance that can be measured. Some companies use different names for them, but the four basic areas are customer knowledge, financial performance, internal business processes, and learning/growth.

bar chart   A chart on which number values are represented using oblong bars on an axis. Bar charts are used to compare number values by showing them in relation to each other, side by side.

benchmarking   The process of comparing performance levels between two companies or organizations that both have high performance standards, strictly for learning and not for competition.

C

Capability Maturity Model Integration (CMMI)   A trademarked process management system that is specialized for engineering applications. CMMI can be introduced in one area of a company at a time ("staged"), or the program can be rolled out all at once ("continuous").

cause-and-effect diagram   See *Ishikawa diagram*.

concurrent engineering A product design process in which individuals with different specialties (or from different parts of a company) work together as a cross-functional team rather than completing only their portion of the work and handing it off to the next function. Sometimes called *quality by design*.

continuous quality improvement (CQI) The ongoing improvement of products, services, or processes through sustained effort and incremental enhancements over time.

control chart A chart made by plotting the measurements of a group of samples in sequence along a horizontal line that represents the mean or average measurement for that item or parameter. Measurements that fall far below or far above the mean are *out of control*, indicating a problem with the process.

corporate citizenship A company's public commitments to support causes it deems important. These may include social, charitable, artistic, environmental, educational, and other activities; involvement in industry and trade groups; and sharing quality improvement practices with others in business. Also referred to as *social responsibility*.

corporate responsibility The public's expectations of a company, such as conducting business ethically, following the laws, and protecting public health and safety and the environment.

cycle time The amount of time between the original design of a product or service and its introduction to the public.

D

DMAIC The basic Six Sigma® problem-solving framework; each letter stands for a step in the process (*Define* opportunity, *Measure* performance, etc.).

E

Earned Value Management System (EVMS, or EVM) A process management system in which a budget is established for each task in a process, and as the work progresses, that portion of the project's total budget is "earned" a step at a time. Used extensively by government agencies.

environmental stewardship See *total quality environmental management*.

F

fishbone diagram See *Ishikawa diagram*.

flowchart A chart that shows the exact steps in a process, or actions that transform an "input" to an "output." Used to identify redundancy or inefficiency in a process.

G

global sourcing A term for outsourcing jobs to workers in other countries.

H

Hawthorne effect A measurement of the impact of human personality in the workplace; that workers who feel valued perform better.

histogram   A type of *bar chart* in which the area of each bar is proportional to a number it represents.

I

inplant   Short for *inplant representative*, a person who is employed by a supplier but works onsite in a client's business (headquarters, plant, factory, etc.) to facilitate faster orders and greater cooperation between the supplier and client companies. Inplants are a critical part of the *JIT II* system.

Integrated Product and Process Development System (IPDS)   A combination of a company's processes, methods, and quality tools. In companies that use IPDS, a team is established for each process to work with other groups or teams as active and equal contributors to a product or goal. IPDS can be used for any function—manufacturing, training, customer support, and so on.

Ishikawa diagram   A method used to isolate the possible causes and effects of a problem, which looks roughly on paper like a fish skeleton. The center of the diagram (the head and backbone of the "fish") represents the problem or effect; the "fins" coming off the center represent the possible causes. The diagram is named for its creator, Dr. Kaoru Ishikawa.

J

Juran Trilogy   A management theory advocated by Joseph Juran that includes three basic requirements of any business process: planning (determining needs and resources), control (measurement of processes), and improvement (modifying processes or products to improve them).

Just-In-Time   A theory of minimizing waste by producing just enough product to fill current orders as they are due, thereby eliminating the expense of buying extra materials and storing inventory. Also refers to a manufacturing or assembly process in which materials or parts are pulled just as they are needed from the previous function.

Just-In-Time II   The added component of having sales representatives from supplier companies office on-site with a client (usually a manufacturing plant) to facilitate cooperation and immediate orders of goods as needed.

K

Kaizen   A Japanese management system based on small, incremental improvements, simplifying complex processes, involving employees as team members, and creating a culture of workers who are all striving to do better.

L

Lean enterprise   A combination of improvement-centered tools and methods used to eliminate waste (of time, effort, and materials) from a production process. Also known as *Lean manufacturing* and/or simply *Lean*.

loss function concept   A mathematical equation developed by Genichi Taguchi that quantifies the decline in a customer's perceived value of a product as its quality declines, based on a combination of cost, target, and variations in the product.

M

management system   A system designed to create products or services under certain laws or customer requirements to meet minimum health, safety, or quality standards.

mapping   The use of a *flowchart* to visualize a process.

motion economy   The theory that the way a task is performed is as important as the time it takes to do it; that jobs can be broken down into individual steps and streamlined so that each step wastes no effort.

multichannel marketing   Making goods available in a variety of ways (in retail stores, online, by mail order, and so on) to appeal to customers' needs for convenience.

N

noise (or noise factors)   A term for uncontrollable variables in a manufacturing process.

O

Out-of-control occurrences   Variations in a process. Also called *noise factors*.

P

Pareto chart   A chart used to sort problems or complaints in order to determine the ones with greatest overall impact, or to identify the cause of a problem. May be used to monitor progress or as a starting point for problem solving. Named for an Italian economist.

partnership   A long-term business relationship that signifies a commitment between two or more entities to produce a particular product or achieve a specific goal.

performance-based model   The use of a set of award criteria to measure how well a company is doing (performing) in certain predetermined areas of business.

poka-yoke   A Japanese term for "mistake-proof" that refers to taking human judgment out of some types of production, thereby minimizing human error. *Poka-yokes* are simple, low-cost, common-sense methods of eliminating defects by eliminating mistakes.

process   A group of related tasks that yields a product or service.

process improvement   Delivering a product or service more efficiently, quickly, and/or effectively by breaking it down to a series of processes and managing each one by measuring, analyzing, and making improvements in it. Also referred to as continuous improvement, Continuous Quality Improvement (CQI), Total Quality and Productivity (TQP).

process-oriented thinking   The practice of approaching business situations with teamwork, interconnectedness, and the "big picture" in mind, not just one person's individual duties as part of a larger project or goal.

Q

quality by design   A catchphrase for *concurrent engineering*.

quality circles (QC)   A team effort in which people are grouped together to solve a particular problem or improve a process. Also called *Quality Control Circles*.

R

robustness   In manufacturing or mass production, a term for the level of accuracy of the outcome.

S

scattergram   A graph that is used to show the relationship of two parameters by simply plotting each point of data on the graph. If the points are close together, the parameters are closely related.

sequential engineering   See *serial design*.

serial design   The development of a product or service in pieces or stages by people from different departments or with different experience, working separately and handing off their "portion" of the project to the next group. Also called *sequential engineering*.

silo   A commonly used nickname in business for companies that are structured in a strict hierarchy, with senior executives at the "top" of the silo, and other departments or employees in "layers" below.

Single Minute Exchange of Dies (SMED)   In a manufacturing environment, the goal of reducing all setup times to as close to one minute as possible, in order to perform a task with maximum efficiency.

Six Sigma®   A trademarked process improvement program developed by Motorola as a metric for measuring defects and improving quality. The goal is the attainment of virtually zero defects (3.4 parts per million) in a manufacturing or business process.

socially responsible investing (SRI)   The selection of investments based on the ethical, social, and environmental stands that the company has made and, conversely, refusing to invest in companies the investor perceives are not doing the "right" things.

Statistical Process Control (SPC)   The evaluation or control of a process using statistics to measure the variations over time and, if they are not stable (in control), identifying the causes and removing them. See *Statistical Quality Control*.

Statistical Quality Control (SQC)   A way to measure the quality of a process. SQC's underlying theory is that not every lot or item on a manufacturing line must be inspected for defects as long as the acceptable quality levels (AQLs) set for the manufacturing process are high enough. Used interchangeably with *Statistical Process Control*.

sustainability   The practice of considering the full life cycle implications of a product, process, or business decision, including its safety, the waste it might create, the ultimate benefits or hazards to the environment, and so on.

T

Total Quality Environmental Management (TQEM)   The application of quality management principles to a company's environmental policies, in such areas as waste reduction, recycling, conservation of natural resources, and so on.

Total Quality Management (TQM)   An active, company-wide quality improvement system that focuses on careful, team-oriented planning, design, and control of processes during the creation of a product, instead of simply inspecting finished products or analyzing complaints after a sale.

Toyota Production System (TPS)   The management system of the Japanese automaker, which revolutionized automotive production in the 1980s with a broad range of techniques to eliminate waste in production, thereby reducing costs. TPS is an example of *Lean manufacturing*.

V

virtuality   The term for using computers or other technology to communicate or share work when a person is physically removed from coworkers or a meeting site by time or distance.

Visual Control Systems (VCS)   The practice (in manufacturing settings) of showing progress on video screens as work is accomplished to increase productivity.

W

waste identification   Taichi Ohno's theory (and part of the Toyota Production System) that learning to identify the wasted time and materials in any production process is necessary in order to improve the process.

Index